Bilingual Learners and the Mainstream Curriculum

Integrated Approaches to Learning
and the Teaching and Learning
of English as a Second Language
in Mainstream Classrooms

Edited by
Josie Levine

 The Falmer Press
(A member of the Taylor & Francis Group)
London • New York • Philadelphia

UK   The Falmer Press, Rankine Road, Basingstoke, Hants RG24 0PR

USA   The Falmer Press, Taylor & Francis Inc., 1900 Frost Road,
            Suite 101, Bristol, PA 19007

First published 1990

British Library Cataloguing in Publication Data
Bilingual learners and the mainstream curriculum:
  integrated approaches to learning and the teaching and
  learning of English as a second language in mainstream
  classrooms.
  1. Non-English speaking students. Curriculum subjects:
  English language
  I. Levine, Josie   II. Bleach, Jean
  428.2407

ISBN 1–85000–494–3
ISBN 1–85000–495–1   Pbk

Library of Congress Cataloging-in-Publication Data is available on request.

Jacket design by Caroline Archer

Typeset in 10½/12 Garamond by
Chapterhouse, The Cloisters, Formby L37 3PX

Printed in Great Britain by Burgess Science Press, Basingstoke
on paper which has a specified pH value on final paper
manufacture of not less than 7.5 and is therefore 'acid free'.

Contents

Writing History and Acknowledgments

This book originated in the reflexive study of the curriculum practice of its contributors. *En route* to its final drafted form various sections of it, either in whole or part, have appeared elsewhere in shorter or earlier draft versions. Spode's 'Social and Antiracist Reasons for On-site Provision for Developing Bilingual Students', Burgess and Gore's 'The Move from Withdrawal ESL Teaching to Mainstream Activities is Necessary, Possible and Worthwhile', and Brightmore and Ross' 'Bilingual Children and their Infant Schooling' were originally drafted for the Schools Council Programme Three Activity (Education for a Changing World) Language for Learning Project: Second Language Learners and Mainstream Curriculum Group's submission of evidence to the (Swann) Committee of Enquiry into the Education of Children from Ethnic Minority Groups, whose report, *Education for All*, was published by HMSO for the Department of Education and Science in 1985. Sections from Spode, Burgess and Gore, Bleach's 'Finding a Voice and Conversational Competence: Mixed Ability English, a Social Base for Negotiated Learning', and Levine's 'Student Cooperation and Support in Mainstream English' formed sections of Levine (1982) 'Second Language Learning and Mainstream Curriculum: Learning as We Go', a paper given at a conference, *The Practice of Intercultural Education*, November 1982, Nijenrode, Breukelen, The Netherlands. 'The Move from Withdrawal ESL Teaching to Mainstream Activities is Necessary, Possible and Worthwhile' and 'Yogesh and Kantilal: A Case Study of Early Progress in a Mixed Ability English Class' by Burgess and Gore are the basis of their article 'Developing bilinguals in a secondary school' published by the National Association for the Teaching of English (NATE) in *English in Education*, **19**, 3, Autumn 1985. We are grateful to the editors of *English in Education* for their kind collaboration.

Introduction

Josie Levine

The concerns of this book are:

— to demonstrate the need for and to establish and maintain the place of developing bilingual students as learners within the mainstream curriculum in schools;
— to argue this as a necessary requirement for gaining more equitable access to the curriculum for bilingual learners.
— to demonstrate some of the ways in which, to the benefit of all, a mixed ability, equal opportunities (race, class, gender) educational environment can be, and needs to continue to be, promoted and developed;
— to show how teachers as researchers can contribute to and help to develop curriculum and pedagogic theory via the day-to-day learning they do about their own teaching and their students' learning;
— to focus on a 'language for learning' pedagogy as a significantly productive element of such educational enquiries;
— to make available accounts of practice that are accessible, well-grounded in theory, and which contribute to the continuing development of educational theory.

While few, I think would want to argue that the central concern of this book, learning to use English both for its own sake and for the sake of educational achievement in a society whose schools' medium of instruction is English, is not a proper one, it is absolutely necessary to position ourselves in opposition to the assumption that so often accompanies statements about the importance of learning English, namely, that other languages and cultures negatively interfere with successful learning of it and with achievement in the curriculum. We recognize a dialectical relationship between the languages that the students already know and their becoming adept in the new one, just as we recognize the relationship between successful progress in a new language and having motivating reasons for using it. Our overall practice is based on these intersecting relationships. It is our hope, and what we work for, that English will become an *additional*, not a displacing, language in our pupils' lives.

The book itself is a product of a teacher action-research group which I was able to convene under the aegis of one of the last initiatives of the Schools Council. We came together informally, on the invitation of Jean Bleach, the coordinator of the Schools Council Programme Three Activity (Education for a Changing World) Language for Learning Project: Investigating Talk — or through hearing about the possible formation of a group by word of mouth among teachers within the then small mainstreaming network. That we would be unfunded we knew would be the case since we had opted into the project on an individual basis and not in accordance with the funding structure available to the Schools Council at that time, i.e., through a local education authority. The conditions of our starting point did not allow for the creation of a group which covered all the age phases or all the constituencies of teachers who might have a concern for the education of bilingual pupils. Furthermore, our enterprise could, at that point, command only a minority interest. Apart from already having some commitment to mainstreaming, those of us who came to form the core of our network had varying experience and expertise. We came from different institutions (schools and teacher-training) in inner and outer London boroughs; from infant and secondary schools, but in secondary schools mainly from the departmental areas of mainstream English, Humanities, and English as a second language. As a teacher-trainer having had the longest experience in the issues of mainstreaming, I convened the group. Our commitment was to share our ideas and evidence, to learn as we went along. We met (on Saturdays about once a term, from March 1981, over a period of about eighteen months) as one of a number of groups within the Schools Council Language for Learning Project. We called ourselves 'The Second Language Learners and Mainstream Curriculum Group', and set about gathering documentation that would support the case — on social, educational and language-learning grounds — for full access to mainstream education for all students needing to learn to use English as an additional language. It is this documentation which is reflected upon and analyzed in the central chapters of this book.

It is part of recent history now that some of this documentation was part of evidence influential in persuading the Department of Education's Committee of Enquiry into the Education of Children from Ethnic Minority Groups (The Swann Committee) to recommend 'in favour of a move away from E2L provision being made on a withdrawal basis, whether in language centres or separate units within schools' (DES, 1985, p. 392). This was one of those (rare) occurrences in education when a policy shift and an innovation can truly be said to have derived from the ground work of teachers themselves. Satisfaction, however, is circumscribed by two connected problems which the move into the mainstream has uncovered.

Firstly, even though the call for mainstreaming began with teachers, and is for many of us a personal commitment, it is not so for everyone who is now being called upon to implement it. For almost all those teachers new to it, 'mainstreaming' is just another government or local education authority plan they are being asked to take on, on the cheap, in addition to everything else. Furthermore, the term itself seems to have become sloganized. It is often used, both for bilingual learners and pupils with other special needs, to indicate only a superficial readiness to support the 'forms' of equal opportunities, without necessarily providing or managing the 'means'; for example, in terms of the number of bilingual, 'special' English and special needs support teachers needed, and in terms of the inservice training needs of mainstream classroom teachers. This focus on mainstreaming too often as slogan rather than substance, also causes the pedagogic imperatives related to *learning through interaction* that lie behind our call for the mainstreaming of bilingual students to be little attended to. Unless that vital element of the 'mainstreaming' equation is also there, the strategy of mainstreaming must fall short of what it is intended to achieve: pupils' achievement in schools.

However, there is a second reason to stress the pedagogic aspects of mainstreaming. The statutory provision for the National Curriculum, particularly its requirements for testing at key age phases, is guaranteed to leave many developing bilingual students with little prospect of fulfilling the key stage criteria within their age group. Combine this with the possibility of teaching procedures being dominated by targets and tests at the expense of a focus on the interactive, communicative pedagogy necessary to language learning, language development — indeed to all learning development that purports to encourage autonomy and self-confidence in children — and we could have our society in extreme danger of closing down even further the life chances of bilingual learners along with the chances of other pupils at risk, that is, working-class pupils and pupils with special educational needs.

Teachers interested in developing interactive, communicative practice need access not only to educational learning theory but also to other teachers' experience in this field. The project network teachers were, therefore, invited to present their experience in organizing, developing and learning from their work in setting up interactive, communicative environments for their pupils. They have written descriptively, setting their analyses within descriptive contexts, to be accessible and to show how being inside the investigation offers illumination about what might follow as further, developed practice.

The first part of the book offers a personal perspective on the history of a relatively recent addition to the school curriculum, the teaching of English as a second language to bilingual learners in the UK. The second section offers the experiences and classroom case studies of teachers, both in mainstream classes and with groups of bilingual learners in support lessons. The final section addresses some connected questions affecting bilingual students, English in the National Curriculum, and the achievement of good educational practices in equality of opportunity in education.

* * *

To move from collecting and analyzing data for purposes of improving one's own practice, even in the company of like-minded, supportive colleagues, to a commitment to write up one's findings for public scrutiny is not a simple undertaking for anyone. For teachers it is doubly difficult, the teaching profession, as we know, not being one which is granted time to write. Everyone in this collective has had to carve this time out of their busy schedules, including the editor. I am, therefore, more than usually grateful for my colleagues' efforts, and for the tolerance shown to me by them in the face of the slow preparation of this manuscript.

However, and jointly, our greatest debt is to our students who taught us so well to hear their meanings. In the deepest sense possible, they have been our teachers, enabling us first to imagine and then to begin to create the means to become better teachers ourselves.

A Note about the Term 'Bilingual Learners'

The term 'bilingual learners' presently carries a number of connotations. It can be used to mean all those pupils who use one or more languages other than English in their ordinary lives in and outside school. This usage sits alongside a broad working definition of 'bilingualism' which 'is not intended to suggest equal proficiency ("balanced bilingualism") nor any judgements about range or quality of linguistic skills' (Bourne, 1989). Many of the school students who come into this category are multilingual with English being one of their languages, even the dominant one. Our use of the term in this book is with these inclusive intentions.

However, we have a further reason for wanting to use it. Too frequently the term 'bilingual learners' gets used to refer only to those pupils who, however many other languages they know, are in the *process* of developing a use of English. Such children, and their first languages and cultures, have suffered successive negative classification related to their developing knowledge of English. They have been classified as 'non-English speakers', 'children with no language', 'beginner learners', 'English as a second language children' — all indicative of prevailing prejudiced attitudes towards them. We want to move away from this terminology which so diminishes their status, abilities, and talents, which has so directly affected the educational provision that has been made for them, and hence, has so negatively affected their chances of achievement. Even though we are aware, the past being ever with us, that the term 'bilingual learners' can just as well stand as a euphemism for all the earlier longstanding, detrimental attitudes, it need not. Meanings are not permanently ascribed to terms; they come to mean different things as attitudes change. Thus we have chosen to use the term 'bilingual learners' to denote the students' strong other linguistic resources, the desire for the maintenance of these other linguistic resources, and the constructive reality that the pupils themselves are normal learners who are bi- or multi-lingual.

A Note about the Term 'Mainstreaming'

As a concept, the application of the term 'mainstreaming' extends well beyond any desired provision for pupils whose need it is to learn to use English as an additional language to all those who have traditionally been excluded from the benefits and advantages of participation in 'normal' schooling. For example, Warnock (DES, 1978) made the public case for the liberalizing of Special Educational Needs through the means of mainstreaming well before it made its first formal appearance as recommended provision for learners of English as a second language (DES, 1985). The two constituencies share much common ground in their advocacy of mainstreaming, particularly their genuinely humanistic concern for the deconstruction of structures in educational provision that maintain false and harmful distinctions between children as learners. Both constituencies are also concerned about the promotion and development of the strategies of partnership teaching.

On the other hand, it also needs to be pointed out that the early history of classing bilingual pupils who needed to learn English as 'remedial' has only been to the detriment of the educational achievement of pupils in the process of learning a use of English. It is to the good that the so-called category of 'remedial' has been broadened to include the special educational needs that almost *all* pupils are likely to have in one way or another during their school careers. The fact is, however, that the call for mainstreaming is an outcome of a complex set of discourses in equality of opportunity education which have created its necessary implementation but not yet a full understanding of the concept itself.

We must be concerned with the administrative and structural facets of putting mainstreaming and partnership teaching into place in schools, yet, without an equivalent appreciation of its pedagogic and curriculum principles and practices, it will not be able to serve its intended purpose of being a means of improving educational attainment for all pupils and especially bilingual learners. Alongside the necessary structural and administrative changes must be the means of developing practice for teaching in mixed ability, mixed experience classrooms.

This indispensible aspect of mainstreaming expertise applies across the curriculum and equally to primary and secondary schools. It is grounded in understandings about the role of language in learning, and therefore, in the importance of a strong social base for successful learning. School learning can then act as an important contextual base both for new language learning and development and the interactive and communicative teaching and learning of English as a second language. It is these pedagogic aspects of mainstreaming on which this book concentrates.

Part One
An Historical Perspective
1960s–1980s

1
Responding to Linguistic and Cultural Diversity in the Teaching of English as a Second Language

Josie Levine

Preamble

Bilingual learners are normal school students. They can engage, disengage, be committed to, and become alienated from school learning. They can acquire knowledge, reject it, take risks or refuse to do so. Each of them will acquire a use of the languages and language varieties around them to the degree it makes educational, political, social and psychological sense to do so. Consciously and unconsciously, the extent to which the positive options are taken up — again, like all students — depends as much on the social and learning environments each is in as it does on what each of the individuals brings to the situation. The purpose of mainstreaming is to offer more positive options than earlier arrangements for supporting bilingual learners in their school learning and their learning of English.

The purpose of this chapter is to sketch, in relation to the teaching of English to bilingual learners, a history of the emergence of that educational concept which today we refer to, in convenient shorthand, as 'mainstreaming'. It is not intended as a comprehensive mapping of two vitally important and connected issues:

— policy and provision for teaching English as a second language in schools in the UK (see Derrick, 1977; Ellis, 1985; Bourne, 1989, for example), and
— bilingualism and mother tongue maintenance (see Tosi, 1984; Robinson, 1985; Linguistic Minorities Project, 1985, for example).

Rather it is more a personal construing of educational events in the teaching of bilingual learners in the UK over the last thirty years.

These educational events reflect two very different perceptions of how a new language is best taught and learned when it is also the language of the wider community. And these two perceptions reflect two very different attitudes, the one hostile and the other welcoming, to cultural and linguistic diversity. To understand how and why positions on language teaching and learning and on diversity have altered, and at the same time, to realize how despite this improving change, the past is still ever with us, is to be better positioned for establishing one's own personal practice for supporting bilingual students' learning within the mainstreaming movement.

We have to recognize that antipathy to diversity has so governed educational provision, not only for bilingual learners, that every aspect of the equal opportunities movement for mainstreaming has had to be developed by teachers in resistance to received educational opinion and practice. For example:

— mixed ability in resistance to the social evils of streaming;
— multicultural curriculum in resistance to ethnocentricity;
— antiracist education in resistance to racism;
— antisexist education in resistance to sexism;
— integrated approaches to learning as opposed to learning segmented chunks;
— learning through interaction in resistance to a dominant transmission mode;
— teaching for critical analysis as well as for skills and knowledge;
— functional-communicative approaches to additional language learning in resistance to language teaching based on grammatical syllabuses;
— the recognition of pupils' own linguistic resources, rather than their eradication, as genuine bases for further language development and the development of language-linked skills.

And, further, we have to recognize that despite the considerable headway made, despite these resistances and the teaching practices developed recognizably offering alternate modes of thinking through which to develop practice for supporting and facilitating students' school learning, the legacy of this society's deep-rooted, comprehensive hostility to diversity (and, therefore, to change) means that teachers are still forced to fight, often other teachers, for space against the old paradigms of separatist organization of schooling, and against teaching content, methods and attitudes to pupils' learning which put the majority of children in opposition (one might say understandably) to the 'education' on offer to them.

Response to Diversity: Hostility

In the 1960s, while the population of the inner cities in the great urban centres of the country was changing through immigration, the prevailing attitude was one of preservation: how to keep everything the same. The children who came,

Responding to Linguistic and Cultural Diversity

whether of West Indian origin or from backgrounds where English was not a first language, entered urban primary and secondary modern schools to the teachers' growing sense of unease about their own ability to cope. The children also entered a context of school and community prejudice about their presence being a threat to the quality of education for indigenous children. Diversity was seen as a threat; not speaking English perceived as having no starting point for learning. The great dispersal debate, one of the period's most public responses to diversity, was about nothing else but a drive to maintain the status quo.

Nationally, the preservation of 'normality' centred on the issue of numbers. Apparently sane people debated (without any seeming conscience about the consequences to the newcomers) what percentage of immigrant children could be 'tolerated' in a school before it ceased to function in its usual way. In a parliamentary speech made on 27 November 1963 by Sir Edward Boyle, the then Secretary of State for Education and Science, the figure was set at 30 per cent (Hansard, vol. 1685, cols. 433–44). Above that figure, it was recommended that children should not be admitted to their neighbourhood schools, but dispersed to others further afield (Rose *et al.*, 1969, p. 268).

The educational status quo, the preservation of which was so desperately being pursued, was, in origin, itself a response to diversity — another divisive response. The English educational system has historically made separate provision for its school age populations: on basis of class (private and state schooling); on basis of 'perceived' intelligence and achievement (grammar, technical and secondary moderns), with streaming and resultant remedial classes as common features. An ostensible purpose of streaming was to create groups of pupils of the same standard — as a strategy for effective teaching. Thus, paradoxically, the overall structures of separatism produced the illusion of homogeneity. It was this 'homogeneity' and the narrow teaching techniques it nourished which the newcomers so threatened.

Looking back, it is painful to note both how easy it was to 'dispose' of children who did not fit the 'normal' categories just by using the category system itself, and how damaging a legacy categorization of children bequeaths to us. Separatisms permeate the socio-economic structure of this society and result in the social, economic and cultural positioning of children and adults as inferior or superior to each other. When these separatisms are encultured in schools themselves, the consequences of the damage to pupils' individual self esteem, achievement and regard for each other is thoroughly compounded. Moreover, these separatisms, inferiorities and superiorities remain in the collective unconscious as 'natural' and not constructed phenomena, hidden from inspection by their very taken-for-grantedness. The educational system continues to be alarmingly capable of 'disposal' on grounds of spurious, constructed differences.

However, there are teachers and educationalists who work hard to intervene in whatever ways they can to oppose these divisions in schools. Through their educational practice, e.g. of mixed ability, equal opportunities education (undertaken as a means of enabling pupils to achieve their real potential, to be confident, and to understand and support each other) they find that it is also a teaching mode that exposes how these divisions, both in society and in schools, are constructed and become so dangerously naturalized.

English Language Teaching: the First Moves

Naturally enough, from within this status quo culture of educational categorizing, a first response to providing for the needs of immigrant pupils who spoke first languages other than English was to remove them to remedial classes. Where else? Labelled as non-English speakers unable to cope in normal classrooms, they quickly came, in that climate, to be seen as having *no* language. Even so, while most teachers could not see what else to do, there were some teachers who recognized that the newcomers were not remedial in the sense for which the remedial classes has been established. These teachers were not questioning the validity of remedial classes themselves, only whether they were the right places for the newcomers to learn English. Correctly judging that they were not, the next move saw the initiation of what was to prove to be a major local education authority innovation: Special English Lessons. Of course, the new provision was not extensive enough (nor could it ever be), so its introduction by no means saw the end of the newcomers finding themselves inappropriately placed in remedial classes for slow learners.

The 'special' English service began as a peripatetic one, mainly, but not exclusively, staffed by women, mostly returners from overseas. Some of them had perhaps worked there in the helping professions or accompanied their husbands on missionary, diplomatic or overseas teaching missions. Others who 'joined up' had experience of teaching English as a *foreign* language overseas. Inevitably, it was the language teaching methods in which these teachers had themselves been trained which formed the basis of the methodology of the Special English Lessons. This methodology, based on a structural analysis of the English language and a behavioural psychology that called for learning sentence patterns through drilling, clearly so different from the methodology of 'normal' lessons, fitted in well with the separatist organizational structures of schools. If it was 'special' English, it clearly did not belong in 'ordinary' classrooms, nor did the children who needed it. They were to be someone else's responsibility, to return to the 'normal' classroom when they knew English. That is, when they became 'normal' children.

Thus, questioning the received opinion of how schools should be organized was avoided, and thus was the threat to classroom and subject teachers' competences temporarily removed, and thus was a token of security in an otherwise unwelcoming educational environment offered to bilingual learners. Certainly, the notion of the special English classes being a haven for the pupils was not misplaced, for when the children were not in their special English lessons, in addition to the overt racism they experienced, they spent an inordinate amount of time sitting on the edge of classroom activity being given 'busy' but unrelated things to do. However, it was not only time spent in this way in 'ordinary' classes which conspired to construct the newcomers as both 'different' and 'unable'. The establishment of the special classes, haven or not, also served to intensify the negative perceptions of pupils' ability and contributed to sharpening racist attitudes among the dominant group.

As for the peripatetic nature of the service, that was an inevitable consequence of having too few teachers to provide for perceived needs and of seeing those needs as short term. We have already seen that the best intention was that pupils would return to 'normal' classes when they knew enough English. Yet, this situation, as well as contributing to the negative attitudes towards the pupils, also positioned the special language teachers as doing a different job from other teachers; in addition, their small special English classes were seen by quite a few class and subject teachers as a 'cushy' number — despite the fact that they themselves did not want 'these children' in their classes.

At the beginning, teachers visited as many as three or four schools in a week, with students going to special English lessons in accordance with the teacher's time in the school. For specialist language teachers the question of how best to organize their time with 'their' students has always been a perennial one. How could they 'cover' all the children in need? Which students were to be withdrawn? And from which 'normal' lessons? (Not practical subjects, if it could possibly be helped.) How often should pupils come to special English classes? Should they let pupils come when they did not want to go to their 'ordinary' lessons? The answers to these questions, unsurprisingly, were almost as numerous as the situations in which they were asked, although one principle which governed the answer to some of them was not generally perceived as problematic: teaching groups were selected according to pupils' level of English (to be as homogeneous as possible), not according to age, mother tongue, friendship groups, or mainstream curriculum need.

It is interesting to note that these early provisions were almost always on a partial withdrawal basis from 'normal' lessons. 'Special' English lessons were rarely intended to be full-time for students. Yet such was the climate of the times that the existence of these part-time withdrawal classes unwittingly contributed to the construction of an attitude which, henceforward, was going to 'allow' people to think about and behave towards bilingual learners as if they did not exist in so-called 'normal' classrooms. The fact is that the pupils, right from the start, have never not been in the mainstream. It is only *as if* that had been the case (Levine, 1983).

It is necessary to emphasize that the Special English provision was a virtuous response at a time when the analyses we have available to us today about equality of opportunity, institutionalized racism, how languages are best learned by interaction and participation in the events in which they are to be used, were not in evidence. The effects of the marginalization that the special English teachers and 'their' pupils were exposed to by the arrangements that were begun in the early 60s, based as they were in historically divisive structures for handling diversity and on the notion that learning English was a *prior* requirement for education, were felt by the special language teachers, but stoically put to one side. Instead, it was the rescue aspect of the operation which was the focus of the English language teachers' attention. With lessons, in those days, often taking place on corridors and in cloakrooms, it was a step forward, within this structure, when teachers got their own classrooms and a base to house their equipment!

By the late 60s there were large numbers of beginner learners of English in the inner city schools as well as those beginning to reach a second stage. The special language service itself, though, was mainly seen as committed to work with beginners. As the numbers of beginners increased so did the role of the service, and one response made by some authorities to try to maintain, with not enough teachers to do it, an active contact with as many beginners as possible, was the establishment of off-site language centres. Some authorities had pupils attending full-time for a period, and some organized for them to attend part-time, e.g. for half a day every day. This move to off-site language centres was rationalized as giving children a better chance than they would otherwise have had in unhelpful school situations (and in too many cases this was literally true) — just as other withdrawal classes in schools had often become a haven from unsupported mainstream learning and from racism. Some specialist language teachers would remain in schools and withdraw second stage learners for language support, and, in those authorities where language centres were not established or were established on a half-day basis, would continue work with beginners.

Some features of the legacy of separatism have now been established:

— the newcomers as 'inferior' students;
— 'lack of English' being equated with 'having no language';
— 'special' English as a dumping ground;
— 'special' English as a haven;
— virtually no structural opportunities for pupils to get to know each other on equal terms;
— virtually no structural opportunities for teachers from mainstream and withdrawal constituencies to interact, and hence, suspicion of each others' roles;
— special language teachers outside the school structure left to fend for themselves, organize their own use of time.

A Second Move: the Need for Materials

As the 'special' English provision grew, it became increasingly clear that there was a need for materials. At first, people had used the books published internationally for the teaching of English as a foreign language (EFL), some of which, although books for second language beginners, were intended for adult learners. Others, often more attractively produced and quite recently published, were for students of school age, and encouraged the linguistic structural-situational approach to language teaching then enjoying its heyday. The structural syllabus to be taught was contextualized within situations that could be depicted on the pages of the book through illustrations and by building on the language structures and vocabulary previously presented. The chosen structural syllabus itself was constructed round a standardized notion of structural complexity: what was deemed structurally simple always being selected for teaching before what was deemed structurally complex (e.g., a present tense form before a past tense form). Also 'direct method' (i.e., an immediate focus on speech, with translation between mother-tongue and target language heavily frowned upon) was recommended both because there was a new and a welcome emphasis on EFL on speaking as prior to reading and writing, and because it was thought that to use the target language exclusively would help to avoid what was then thought to be a singular barrier to new language learning: mother tongue interference. Practice was provided by drills, which teachers' ingenuity often made good fun by turning them into games and other kinds of 'doing' activities. Another orthodoxy of the 'direct method' approach was that one did not move on until what was presently being taught was well learned.

The clear call for new materials was not, however, based on a critique of the structural-situation approach itself, but on the inappropriacy of the chosen situations of the internationally published materials for English language learners in schools in this country. If the children were going to learn English more quickly, then school and local neighbourhood events would surely better provide situations for teaching structures, sentence patterns and vocabulary — which is, of course, true, insofar as it goes.

Individual teachers, and the special language teaching services in which they worked, began to develop their own materials, but importantly, a national materials project was established, the Schools Council Project in Teaching English to Immigrant Children, the first outcome of which were the *Scope, Stage 1* materials (Schools Council, 1969). All these materials were based on the structural-situational approach to language teaching that has just been outlined. The *Scope* materials were, however, innovative as published materials for they included follow up suggestions of a school curricular kind so that learners could practise using the English they were learning doing the same kinds of activities as were ordinarily pursued in 'normal' classrooms. Significantly so, in that these activities were grounded in the good primary school practice of active learning, the writers of the materials realizing that *an active learning approach* would both be good for learning the new language and might also achieve the desirable objective of showing how it might be possible, especially in junior schools, for the newcomers to do some of their learning *alongside their peers in the 'normal' classroom* — where they were, many of them, for most of the time, anyway. Reading, writing, craft work and storytelling were incorporated into the project materials, although the language of the reading materials, while not being of the Janet and John kind, was so based in the taught language of the materials, that the reading books had their own form of restricted language.

'Special' English: Myths and Mystique

It is probably true to say that this early curriculum development work by teachers, along with the publication of *Scope, Stage 1*, played a large part in enabling authorities to establish their specialist services — at the time much needed, as I have tried to indicate, for little else was being done for the children. The publication of the *Scope, Stage 1* materials also helped to legitimate the special English teachers' linguistic curriculum work, and the two together enabled teachers within the service to see themselves as having both special expertise and a role to play in 'their' children's welfare. This was good for their morale but, to return again to my main theme, changed nothing structurally. The children continued to be seen as different (not 'normal') and had little access to school curriculum work; the service was still peripheral to the mainstream, functioning to 'help' it by withdrawing 'difficulties' from it. Furthermore, with hindsight, we know that its language teaching methodology, although increasingly professional, was based too much in a language-structure approach for it to be able to achieve what everyone wished of it: the fast and efficient learning of English so pupils could 'take their rightful places in the normal classroom' — a phase much spoken and written in the late 60s and early 70s.

I am convinced that whenever people used that phrase, it reflected their genuine concern for their pupils' school curriculum achievements. It was just that these were to be brought about by learning English first, in special circumstances away from the mainstream. It was a wish that gave rise to the cherished myth of its possibility. That, in turn, helped to confirm mainstream teachers as people who had no part to play in the English language development of children for whom English was not a first language, and specialist language teachers as having all the parts to play. If this had been a consciously thought through position at the time, it might have been expressed like this: the children don't know English well enough; we must make provision for them to learn it; when they have learned it well enough their schooling can properly begin; until that time they are clearly the responsibility of the special English teacher; if they are the responsibility of the special English teacher, they are not a mainstream teacher's responsibility *even when they are in the mainstream class*.

A contributing factor to this positioning was the mystique that had begun to surround the specialist language teachers' expertise; it being a different methodology, logic seemed to suggest, but erroneously, that students' language learning processes must also be different from other learning processses. Even among mainstream teachers who were well-motivated towards the newcomers were those who thought they ought not to intervene for fear of slowing down or spoiling these mysterious second language learning processes. With this notion added to the naturalized, long-standing practice of removing all who did not fit from 'normal' classes, it was but a small step in wishful thinking to a perception of the classes for teaching English as a second language as catering for the children's entire education needs. This is the way divisive structures work to mythologize untenable positions. People's common human sense gets defeated. They accept the overall position, and *then* use their wit, intelligence and creativity to try to save people from the worst effects of the structure. This human pattern of response was what was being reproduced here.

Many caring specialist teachers accepted this mythical role. Whether or not they questioned the possibility of achieving the education of bilingual pupils within language classes — and quite a few did — it was inevitable that they should want to do things to improve their pupils' situation. As they saw it, few people wanted beginners in their ordinary classes, and it was also proving difficult to get pupils who had progressed a little *back* into the classes full-time. Despite all the English language learning they were achieving, the children were still seen as not knowing 'enough English' to take their rightful places in the 'normal' classroom. They were still seen as having nothing to offer the schools they inhabited — certainly not the languages they already spoke. The idea that their first languages might, could or should play any part in their school learning lives was not yet on agendas for professional consideration by established teachers and educators. It was an assimilationist ideology which demanded one type of linguistic 'competence' from bilingual learners while ignoring both those pupils' actual linguistic competences and their real educational needs. It certainly did not recognize that there might be a fruitful connection between the two. The opposite, in fact.

Diversity of Approach in the Specialist Language Teaching Service: Some Counter Moves

I have attempted to outline some of the dominant discourses in which the provision for teaching English as a second language (ESL) in the schools of this country were grounded, and to show how these discourses facilitated the creation of practices and affected outcomes. It is not my purpose to belittle the steps taken by teachers and organizers of the service. We need to remember that everyone involved in establishing the services was doing so in an atmosphere of resistance to their efforts, that however tokenistic, or racist (see Chatwin, 1985; Commission for Racial Equality, 1986), the 'special' English provision may now be perceived, within that provision these were people's best responses and represented extremely hard-won achievements in the context of that separatist situation. Furthermore, this work positions the teachers within the same tradition in which innovative teachers see themselves today: responding to changing circumstances by initiating new practices.

Now, however, it is time to stop writing about teachers, whether specialist or mainstream, as though they all accepted the structures in which they worked, as though none could see their damaging nature, as though no one was constructing theories from which more wholesome responses to diversity might be developed both structurally and methodologically. In the same period of time in which the materials and specialist provision that I have just been referring to were being established, the mid to late 60s, innovative teachers in the mainstream were fighting the battle for comprehensivization, and had begun to state the case for mixed ability teaching, for interactive practices based on an appreciation of the role of language in learning, for holistic approaches to learning to read and write, for seeing pupils as active learners, for taking a developmental view of learning, for making process as well as product important in learning. Specialist language provision today is in a position to benefit from so much of this space having been won by others, as it benefits from the fact that activity to combat racism in education is undertaken on a broader front than when specialist language teachers first saw and tried to counter the effects on their pupils of institutionalized racism. In the same way, mainstream teachers are in a position to benefit from the fact that not all specialist language teachers were wedded to a separated service nor to one language teaching mode. Just as the dispersal policy was not acceptable to all teachers, so the language centre solution was not an acceptable one to all the teachers within the specialist service — though their arguments against them on what are now recognized as anti-racist grounds (not a term that had yet been coined) proved to be unavailing. As for English as a second language teaching itself, it was an ill wind that blew the responsibility for the pupils' education, misplacedly, into the 'special' English teachers' laps. In the paradoxical way in which these things work, it created the conditions for some teachers from within the specialist service to experiment in curriculum based language teaching.

Pupils need food for their minds if they are to learn — language or anything else. Would it not be more productive, therefore, for both language and other learning to derive the language syllabus from the content and activities of mainstream curriculum lessons, rather than look for content and activities with which to clothe any preconstructed language syllabus? The development of language-based skills (like reading and writing across the curriculum and, for example, learning to use reference material) could then be integrated into general learning following a more natural acquisition path than, as we saw it, even the best structural-situation approach could achieve. As can be seen from the list below, direct language teaching is not abandoned, it simply falls into a different place in the lesson plan. Significantly so, in that it is *a possible* end activity should it be required. The authors of *Scope, Stage 2* (Schools Council, 1972–4), which exemplifies this different methodology and in language teaching terms is classified as *functional-communicative*, used this approach in planning lessons. Simply to set their workplan down is to reflect a broader view of what language is, what is entailed in learning it, and also what learners' needs in schools might be.

— choose the topic
— gather the subject matter
— decide appropriate activities and organizations for the learning to take place
— allow to emerge, from the subject matter and the activities, the language functions necessary for understanding and exploring of the topic
— choose for the benefit of any second-language learners who may need such support, structures and vocabulary which would enable them to perform the functions
— find or create material which is core and other which has the possibility of providing extensive practice of language in use
— undertake specialist language practice if needed
— across a series of lessons check that a range of styles, registers and language-linked skills have been called for to make sure that the learners have access to acquisition of a wide language repertoire
— make sure that they get regular opportunity to work interactively and have regular access to consultation with their teacher(s).

(adapted from Levine, 1981)

We saw from our attempts and from our pupils' responses that when they had food for their minds and access to process oriented activities for doing their learning, almost naturally their use of English increased in power. What we learned to do was 'offer' pupils new language *as they needed it* in comprehensive contexts. Our notions of complexity were based in *meaning* rather than on a graded set of structures. We tried not to distort the language of our materials and our teaching. Although we might simplify the language we used, there remained, nevertheless, a wide range of language available. Thus students had access to natural language.

As far as I am concerned, having worked as a specialist language teacher throughout these times and having had an instrumental role in developing this curriculum-based, communicative approach to second language acquisition and development, the point (in my case *c.* 1964) when some of us began to work in this way, is the origin, in the specialist service, of the call for the mainstreaming of bilingual pupils developing a use of English. It would, however, misrepresent the case to claim that this was our immediate perception. In the first instance, we were simply, but creatively, and against the thinking of the time about what language teaching was, trying to create, in our withdrawal situations, a rich language learning environment — one in which our pupils could learn to use English for educational purposes by *using* English for educational purposes. It was through trying to make our special language classrooms as 'normal' as possible that we slowly began to perceive the potential of the mainstream for our students' development of a use of English. In mainstream lessons, *if they were of the 'right' kind*, 'our' students might have even wider, more productive access to a range of language and a range of opportunity to develop a repertoire of skills than we were able to construct in the 'special' language situation where everyone was in the process of learning to use English. Meanwhile, we first had need to argue the case not for mainstreaming but for this functional-communicative style of teaching.

'Special' English: Functional-communicative vs. Structure–situational Teaching

If one or two 'special' English language teachers had begun to try out bits of teaching which were to become an interactive pedagogy, mutually beneficial to learning *and* language development, it was not the development of this functional-communicative approach to language teaching which was principally promoted during the late 60s and early 70s. Rather, this period, and into the mid 70s, was characterized by the acceptance and embedding of withdrawal provision and the development of a growing expertise in the more dominant structural-situational approach. Of course, the newer approach was increasingly attempted and developed as some teachers in the 'special' English service at off-site language centres and on attachment to schools (still generally in withdrawal situations, though) began to work in more school-content oriented ways. However, these people were a minority within a minority and, because of separate provision, had not yet made practical contact with a then other minority of teachers in the mainstream, those who were developing practices based in ideas about the role of language in learning (see Barnes *et al.*, 1986; Britton, 1970; Barnes, 1976; Barnes and Todd, 1977, for example). Nor had ideas about multicultural curriculum or commitment to antiracist teaching yet gained much purchase.

The functional-communicative approach threatened the previously hard won 'special' English teaching expertise in ways not dissimilar to those that the coming of the children had done the expertise of the classroom teachers ten years before — although for different reasons. Internationally, too, the early and mid-70s saw the beginning of the communicative approach to language teaching with the same arguments being enacted there — arguments which set narrow *accuracy* in learning a language in incompatible contrast to *fluency* in using it. Particularly, the dominant structuralist group in 'special' English teaching were concerned that it would not be possible to be systematic about language teaching, nor to know what structures had been taught. There was, too, a fear that if pupils were left to do so much language-learning independently, not only would that learning be haphazard, leaving enormous gaps in their linguistic knowledge, but also we were likely to take them back to the days when they were left to cope with lessons and pick up English as best they might.

Nor were the structural-situationalists comfortable with our responses to their concerns. We told them that a *communicative* approach necessarily means giving up some of the control over the pupils' linguistic output, but it would still be possible to describe both what was being taught and what the students had learned to do: now, however, in terms of *functions* not grammatical structures — for example, express obligation, describe, argue, give directions, tell a story, etc. We told them accuracy would be gained over time, through the confidence and experience gained in interactions where attempts at expression were valued for their meaning content. We said that the pupils would progressively gain facility in spoken and written expression and develop reading skills through the practice they got by handling the content of lessons — many school activities have systematic features, and their recurrences would provide the regularity of practice in sentence and discourse patterning that our colleagues feared would disappear. We claimed that they need not be concerned about returning to the bad old days when children were left to sink or swim, because those days were characterized by their being unsupported in their learning. (Besides, what did they mean by 'return to'? For too many children, despite all the language teachers' considerable efforts, 'sink or swim' — with the emphasis on the 'sink' — was all they knew). We told them that we were not here talking about unsupported learning, since we were using what we knew about the ways language and texts were structured to help plan lessons and design accessible materials to act as good models for our pupils' production of spoken and written language.

It is worth noting that *Scope, Stage 2* (Schools Council, 1972–74), the only published example of a functional-communicative approach written specifically for use in this country, came out during this period of relative hostility to the approach. It is also worth noting that the materials were conceived as a language *development* programme, and that they flag at least a conceptual shift, at the time hopefully idealistic in terms of accepted practice, towards the mainstream as the true base for bilingual learners to develop a use of English. The authors of *Scope, Stage 2* expressed it thus:

> When we started this work, we were looking for a context, for an approach to learning and teaching, and for teaching techniques which would facilitate productive language learning and help to bring the educational performance of second-language learners closer to their real potential. To meet these demands, for the context and approach we used the subject matter of school itself and a thematic style of teaching. Into them we incorporated as a natural extension of our earlier work with non-English speaking children, many of the techniques and practices of second-language teaching. Happily, the children we were aiming at were not generally segregated in special language classes but were in normal classes along with native

speakers, a situation of which we wished to take advantage since we believe that the interests of children at a second stage of learning English as a second language are best served by following the curriculum of and being a part of a normal class (Schools Council, 1972–74, 'Teacher's Book', pp. 3–4).

Ahead lay both the task of developing the practice itself and the further difficult task of persuading other 'special' English teachers, administrators and 'ordinary' subject teachers, that joining in the mainstream was best. Of course, also ahead of us lay the task of working through the ways in which such a shift might be organized.

Response to Diversity:
Mainstream Reality and the Construction of A New Paradigm

No amount of arguing the case by just one branch of the special English teaching service — and a minority one at that — for what it believed to be best for the educational chances *and* the English language learning of bilingual learners would have been successful on its own. Despite the fact that by the late 1970s there were special English teachers developing the practice of a functional-communicative, education-based English language teaching who were also anxious to get into the mainstream, it was to take a conjunction of a complex set of relevant issues, circumstances and developing practices, across the whole of schooling, and wider, to begin to effect that. A brief summary of the features that would provide the necessary starting climate for maintaining must suffice:

1. The pragmatic recognition of the reality of diversity in schools; most bilingual learners were in the mainstream for some, most, or all of the time.
2. A dawning awareness of racism and the ways in which schools were institutionally racist in their organization, curricula and practices was starting to have effect; few teachers, once they had such perception, remained convinced that their practices were adequate either to the needs of the bilingual learners in their classes in the process of developing a use of English or to the whole membership of the class in terms of promoting good attitudes towards each other.
3. Parents were beginning, forcefully, to argue the case — against heavy odds of embedded institutional racism — for the same basic rights for their children as those which ostensibly were available for the dominant groups *vis-à-vis* a full curriculum.
4. There had been a noticeable organizational move to mixed ability teaching; and within that, a shift to the promotion of group activities and talk as a means of learning, with an ensuing, but as yet incipient,

recognition of pupils' vernaculars as a base for developing their spoken and written repertoires; mixed ability practices, taking account of mixed experience and taken together with the concept of developing repertoires, meant there was now a real possibility of bilingual learners inexperienced in using English having an active place in mainstream classrooms.

5. The cumulative effect of a significant minority of mainstream teachers developing mixed ability, equal opportunities practices, and first, multicultural, and then antiracist curricula; these teachers were no longer prepared to see bilingual learners marginalized on the edges of those classrooms.

6. Classroom and subject teachers, wanting to know better how to teach in their multilingual, multicultural, mixed experienced classrooms, were beginning to look to language teaching strategies as a possible answer.

The equal opportunities policies of many authorities were yet to come, but by the end of the 1970s, most authorities in inner cities had well developed special English services funded, in the main, by monies obtained under Home Office Section 11 provision. There was off-site and on-site provision, and one or two schools had begun to appoint special English teachers to their own staff. The educational world may not yet have noticed it in a big way, but it was changing from one in which diversity was seen as unusual and unwelcome to one in which diversity was becoming the norm (even if not always welcomed) and in which, by some, it was greeted as desirable.

Going into the Mainstream: Transition Difficulties

An alignment between mainstream and special English teachers is no simple matter to achieve. Clearly, it has been hugely complicated by the piecemeal nature of the response to it, and by varying perceptions of what it might be; not to mention that such a shift in provision was not universally welcomed by teachers on either side. The envisioned new provision was going to need partnerships between the two constituencies of an as yet undelineated kind, not a mere continuation of the passing of pupils from one to another. What roles would the teachers have *vis-à-vis* each other and the different constituencies of pupils in a class? Who was responsible for the bilingual learners? What changes in teaching would it require? The way had not been prepared by any kind of systematic LEA training provision for either set of teachers. Furthermore, the only certification that was available at this time, through the Royal Society of Arts Certificate in the Teaching of English as a Second Language in Multicultural Schools, was still training people for the specialism of teaching English as a linguistic enterprise. It was not until 1981 that this syllabus was revised to cater both for those specialist language teachers who saw their work as language development *through* learning rather than simply as language learning, and for the increasing number among subject and class teachers who were wanting to know more about this kind of second language teaching and learning *in order to do their normal teaching better*; and only relatively recently did the Institute of Education, University of London, extend its specialist Diploma in the Role of Language in Education so that teachers following it could gain a formal qualification in this educationally based ESL.

The situation, as we entered the 1980s, then, was one in which the theories about language and learning which underpinned good mixed ability practice in the mainstream were not yet well understood, as was similarly the case with the educational approach to English as a second language, and being newly come upon the scene, the teaching practices based upon them were clearly viewed as radical from within both their constituencies. Furthermore, although the two modes proved, over time, to have much in common, another legacy of the separatist provision was that the two sets of practitioners did not know this of each other. There was, therefore, much suspicion of each other from both sides, since it was only by chance, and rarely when taken within the whole context, that like-minded teachers from each constituency found themselves working together. And even then, it took time and much negotiation to recognize each other. Yet it is these relatively few people, amongst whom are numbered the contributors to this book, who have laid the foundations of and continue to explore the possibilities of the integrated approaches to learning and the teaching and learning of English as a second language which we advocate as desirable mainstreaming practice — but now with a much broader consensus.

Part Two
Mainstreaming, Why?
Evidence of the 80s

The evidence offered in this second section stems from teachers recognizing the needs of bilingual learners in the mainstream, and the potential of the mainstream for fulfilling those needs. At the time when the work was undertaken, Special English teachers and the LEA support services were beginning to see themselves as having a role, not just in withdrawal lessons, but in supporting bilingual learners in the mainstream. Also, an increasing number of mainstream teachers were beginning to want to know how to teach better in their multicultural, multilingual classroom contexts. Importantly, the practice of separating bilingual learners from the mainstream curriculum was beginning to be clearly perceived as having racist implications both in terms of bilingual learners' equal rights to the mainstream curriculum and in terms of the inculcation of implicit and explicit attitudes of personal and institutional racism in both mainstream teachers and mainstream pupils.

If, however, these matters were becoming clearer, how to build a new provision, new mainstream and ESL teacher partnerships and new pedagogy was yet to be revealed. The roles and practices of all teachers supporting bilingual learners in the mainstream were going to have to be worked out in the on-going day-to-day reality of schools and classrooms. The teachers would be learning how to develop their practices to meet all their pupils' needs as they went along. They would, if they chose to see it that way, be engaged in very productive, innovative work in whole school curriculum development.

In the case of the contributors to this book, that innovative work focused on talk or, more theoretically, on the development of interactive, communicative classrooms based on the theory of the relationship between language and learning. In the project network group, talk, especially recorded and transcribed talk, was seen as a 'window' capable of revealing learners' needs, and thereby helping teachers to arrive at better ways of meeting these needs. The chapters of this second section reflect that concentration on talk and demonstrate ways in which it can offer illumination. In terms of teacher action research, the teachers offer analyses of the contexts in which they work as well as of their work. These analyses show how traditional perceptions and practices can be transformed not only for the equal educational opportunities of bilingual learners but for the equal educational opportunities of all *children and, indeed, to the advantage of teachers themselves. The section starts, however, with a chapter offering specific suggestions for classroom practice and on how to begin some teacher action research.*

2
Mainstreaming, Partnership Teaching, Teachers' Action Research

Josie Levine

In recent years, mainstreaming, partnership teaching and teachers' action research have been emerging as new professional teaching practices. Geared initially to trying to meet the mainstream classroom needs of bilingual pupils and pupils with special educational needs, they also have much to tell us about how to meet the needs of *all* pupils.

Mainstreaming

Mainstreaming is a move away from the established practice of withdrawing bilingual pupils from the mainstream curriculum — a practice which negatively affected their status and achievement in schools. Institutionally, mainstreaming is a move away from bilingual pupils being seen chiefly as the responsibility of specialist language teachers, to the view of all teachers having responsibility for them. In language learning terms, mainstreaming for bilingual learners is a move away from disabling monolingual notions which held that:

1. a person must have considerable facility in an additional language before it is possible to undertake school learning in it;
2. that new language learning is hindered by continued use and development alongside it of one's first, more familiar, language.

Mainstreaming recognizes the beneficial relationship that exists between additional language learning, and learning and continuing language development in the first (or more) languages. In terms of resourcing for learning support, mainstreaming increases the possibility of ending the isolation of specialist language teachers and makes way for the productive integration and sharing of their expertise in the mainstream. Further, from the point of view of bilingual learners 'taking their rightful places in "normal" classes', mainstreaming fits the principles of an entitlement curriculum, along with mixed ability grouping and with interactive teaching practices.

Mixed ability, multilingual, multicultural classes are not a new phenomenon. What is relatively new are the perceptions and attitudes which consider diversity as normal. The growing numbers of teachers who have as their goal the provision of equal opportunities education for all pupils recognize that the achievement of it depends essentially on the degree to which teachers are able to institute classroom management techniques, curriculum development and pedagogic practices which respond systematically to the diversity represented in their classrooms. Teachers' success here, in providing equal access and improved achievement, is dependent upon supportive school management practices, LEA policies and government attitudes.

However, all those teachers interested in the improved achievement and learning confidence of their pupils — an interest which, in effect, is coexistent with the further development of learning theory and teaching practice — are not likely to wait around for the 'right' political moment. They are usually anxious to get started whenever and at what points in their teaching they can devise. It is from the collective experience of such teachers that further knowledge about educational theory and practice evolves.

Partnership Teaching

Partnership teaching is a term which implies attempts to construct specific conditions for more than one teacher to support pupils' learning. In reality, it often includes that 'team' teaching which, despite the best of intentions, gets little beyond a recognition that more classroom support is needed, and school management logistics of filling up teachers' 'spare' timetable space with 'support' periods for already-set classroom agendas. Not included in this kind of 'team' teaching is the necessary liaison and planning time to make truly productive curriculum development use of a real partnership teaching arrangement.

In such an arrangement, teachers attempt to shape a partnership which includes a shared understanding of joint aims and objectives, agreement about respective responsibilities, and the working out of a kind of 'contract' for partnership, which includes sharing of expertise, agreement about work load, about classroom management and about curriculum development. These professional agreements between partnered teachers need the support of school management, with recognition of the necessity of providing adequate liaison time, if the partnership is to be productive for not only the pupils and teachers concerned but for the school-wide promotion of curriculum and pedagogies developed.

Despite what may have been negative 'team' teaching experiences in the past, teachers should not back off from trying to establish more developed teaching partnerships. Through doing so, they may be able to influence the shift away from the old type of 'team' teaching to this new professional mode. Worked at, teaching partnerships are one of the best ways of developing the expertise needed in multilingual classrooms for improving prospects of achievement for *all* the pupils. Developed partnership teaching is far better than having teacher expertise fragmented, unshared between teachers, and so leaving pupils, bilingual learners in particular, to try to bring the bits together for themselves. Of course, good partnerships don't just happen. In any arrangement between a mainstream teacher and specialist language teachers (of English and/or Community Languages) or special educational needs teachers, or 'float' teachers in a curriculum area, prior consideration of roles needs to be undertaken.

Teachers need to ask themselves what kind of partnership they want for the perceived needs of any particular class, as well as what is feasible in the circumstances. For example:

— Is the partnership to be for a short or long time?
— Is the expertise of the specialist language teacher better used as support *in* lessons or *between* lessons (i.e., on teacher consultation, analysis of, suggestions for and/or production of materials, activities, etc.)?
— Is it to focus on certain pupils or on the whole class?
— Is it to focus on whole or selected parts of the learning unit?
— Is it to focus primarily on developing new or supplementary content, or on new teaching strategies, or is it to focus on analyzing and supporting various learning processes?

Such suggestions open up the possibilities within partnership teaching, but do not mean that the decisions of teachers should be sacrosanct. Roles and activities will be adjusted in the process of the partnership. Success comes not just from discussing the work *vis-à-vis* the pupils but from discussion and analyses of the nature of the partnership process itself. It is also important for teachers to bear in mind, as they reflect on the progress of their partnership, how their particular classroom situation can develop into one which confers status on *both* specialist language teachers *and* bilingual learners. If the language teacher and the bilingual learners are marginalized in terms of focus and status, the negative messages that arise from that have an effect on all concerned, most importantly on already marginalized bilingual learners.

The fact is that there are likely to be a variety of class arrangements and teacher functions found across the range of multilingual classrooms. However, teachers should be warned against thinking of all the possible arrangements as being of equal weight in effecting equal opportunities education. Some classroom arrangements, when they are the *dominant* strategies, are antipathetic to creating an overall good environment for supporting the learning of bilingual students in the mainstream. To take an extreme example as illustration, it would be foolish to suggest that bilingual learners in the process of developing their use of English should *never*, under any circumstances, be withdrawn (either from or within the classroom), either individually or in small groups, to work on materials and tasks specially prepared for them; or that the specially prepared materials should *never* offer alternative work to that being done by the rest of the class. That would be to eliminate useful strategies. But when such strategies become dominant ones (in combination with the specialist language teacher being the only one of the teaching partners who ever works with bilingual learners), then a useful strategy — when sparingly and appropriately used in the context of other kinds of *integrated* group and whole class activities — is transformed into a negative and separatist device.

The most fruitful partnerships will facilitate appropriate and easeful moves between different combinations of:

— both teachers working with whole class, groups, or individuals;
— teachers changing role, e.g., as lead or support teacher;
— consultation over the choice of materials, tasks and processes to be employed.

In consultations over materials, tasks and processes a variety of approaches may be agreed, for example:

— using the same materials and tasks with the whole class (i.e., students all do the same work and tasks and the teachers facilitate access to materials and tasks through supporting students according to their needs;
— adjusting and mediating materials, tasks and processes in such a way as to assist bilingual pupils in the progressive development of listening and speaking and reading and writing skills in English (i.e., the students are doing the same kind of work as that being done by the whole class, but the work is more clearly staged for them);
— supplementary materials and tasks to reinforce the main ideas of the overall lesson (i.e., based on those initially used by everyone);
— alternative materials and tasks to those in general use in the class (i.e., not the same subject matter or range of activities).

Working out partnerships is not simply a matter of attending to the issues already indicated. There is also the all important matter of the *process* of partnership teaching development itself to be considered. Even the best intentioned partners throw up problems and difficulties for each other. Teachers consciously engaged in creating pedagogy and curriculum development for a particular classroom need also to have a conscious interest in considering the appropriate means of developing their professional working relationship. *Discussion* and *negotiation*, on a basis of trust, are the ways out of any difficulties they may be creating for each other, perhaps by virtue of their different starting points and orientations, or, yet again, by possible different interpretations of classroom events. *Discussion* and *sharing* of ideas, observations and expertise are the ways into the joint creation of a pedagogy for a particular classroom at a particular time. *Discussion* and *reflecting* on what is happening in the partnership (to pupils, their engagement with the work, the preparation of materials, the sharing of planning, teaching and marking, the growth of trust between the teaching partners, etc.) are the ways in which teachers monitor their own progress in developing partnership teaching. Discussion is as central to the growth of teachers' personal and professional understandings for successful partnership teaching as discussion and collaborative learning are for the learning achievements teachers are attempting to promote in their pupils.

Extending the Notion of Partnership Teaching to Pupils: Co-management[1]

Ideally, mainstreaming promotes partnership teaching between teachers. It advocates the development of professional modes designed to improve teaching and learning situations for pupils in our care. But we can usefully take the notion of partnership one stage further, extending it to the idea of *co-management* with pupils. To do so makes use not only of the notion of partnership teaching but also of the techniques and pedagogies of good mixed ability teaching, e.g., collaborative learning, pupils working together in pairs, threes, and groups, with teachers organizing the class and various groups according to learning needs and working in turn with different groupings to optimum levels at particular points in time.

The teacher is usually regarded as the *sole* classroom manager. But we know that pupils already assist each other with their work, both implicitly and explicitly. For example, bilingual learners with the facility to do so informally translate for others, and in most classrooms pupils do a variety of co-management tasks on an occasional basis. We also know that in most classrooms there are pupils who are skilled organizers.

The likelihood is that explicit acknowledgment and careful development of such skills and learning attitudes would help pupils considerably. Yet, for a variety of reasons, there is often reluctance to offer explicit and consistent roles and responsibilities of co-involvement in management tasks:

— There is the notion that asking pupils to assist (e.g., by translating for others) is to 'use', or 'overuse' them in some sense that can be counted as 'immoral'.
— There is the fear that in making co-management explicit it would increase the dominance of some pupils and the passiveness of others.

— There is the fear that involving pupils in class management will make the management process even more complex than it already is.
— Perhaps the greatest fear is that more regular involvement of pupils will change the role of teachers so that teachers become rather more first among equals than classroom managers in *sole* authority.

However, involving pupils more in co-management is *inclusive* of making them *aware* of problems which may be encountered — such as those listed above — and when we do that, the opposite of what we fear is likely to come to be the case. Rather than pupils being 'used' they get the opportunity to develop a wider range of skills. Instead of dominance and passiveness being left un-inspected, that becomes part of the agenda and so may be addressed, under-stood, and a process of change set in motion. Instead of being overburdened by the complexities of management, sharing the load gives teachers more time to teach. And, though it is true that a teacher's role changes and with it the basis of authority, it is just that, a *change* in the basis and not a *loss* of authority.

By making the co-management role explicit to all pupils, and inviting involvement, they get more opportunity than before to develop their interactive organizational skills, and their confidence, sense of purpose and sense of responsibility. It should also begin to mean that the aims and objectives of the work in hand are made explicit by the pupils themselves, rather than the teacher always 'telling' the pupils and the pupils 'forgetting' about the organization of the work.

Because of the way in which it brings pupils together in focusing and cooperating on learning tasks, collaborative learning has become a well recognized feature of equal opportunities education. It is a learning mode that relates to co-management. But collaborative learning is work which is planned, managed and delivered by teachers. Co-management means inviting pupils to take part in the actual planning of the best ways for *all* pupils, including themselves, to achieve their learning goals and, indeed, to help them set those goals. Here are some suggestions for putting co-management into practice:

— Involve pupils in thinking how best to arrange the classroom to facilitate group work and pair learning.
— From time to time, classroom arrangements — whether for a few or the whole class — need to be changed; discuss reasons with the pupils concerned, and involve them in managing the new arrangements.
— Make opportunities for pupils to engage with and assist others who are learning English (or who have other special educational needs), e.g., by working with them, helping them with tasks, listening carefully to what they say; involve all pupils in this, not only out of responsibility as colleagues towards each other, but also on the basis that a productive way of learning is having to teach and extend what you yourself are learning; some pupils sharing a language with them, can translate and interpret, and help to prepare bilingual texts; it is easier

to encourage such interaction specifically if your classroom is a place where bilingual learners' languages are welcomed and encouraged through displaying them in their written forms and through opportunities for pupils to read and write in their other languages.

— Involve pupils in developing materials for classroom use, e.g., worksheets, game-like activities for concept development and language practice.
— Involve pupils in the devising of appropriate homework assignments, including pair and group homework tasks.
— Devise together a system that enables pupils to record their co-management achievements.
— Provide opportunities for reflection and evaluation of the co-management processes in the class.
— Involve pupils in selecting work, emanating from co-management tasks, for display and presentation, etc.

Interestingly, although the development of co-management practice between and with pupils is not dependent on partnership teaching, its establishment will undoubtedly benefit any teaching partnership in which you are involved — not least, because it will provide a much more enabling environment for you and your 'support' teacher to work in a consultative mode with specific groups and individuals and to evaluate better their learning needs. For bilingual learners, you will be particularly concerned to check:

— that they have the regular opportunity to use all four language modes in lessons (listening, speaking, reading and writing);
— that the work that they do gives a good enough opportunity, over time, to learn grammatical structures of English;
— that they have the chance, when they choose, to speak, read and write in their own languages within the lesson;
— that they get equal opportunity with others to have a voice in co-management decisions.

Interactive Environments

For all pupils we emphasize the centrality of talk for working towards understandings of new concepts and as a basis for learning through the other language modes of reading and writing. Through talking and listening to each other (not only the teacher) and working on activities involving reading and writing (not only on their own), they are able both to develop increasing facility in all modes and increasing control over their use for social interaction, learning, thinking and analysis. An interactive environment is importantly so by virtue of providing opportunities to interact in whatever means supports learning. But it is also important to ensure the interaction of all four language models (listening, speaking, reading and writing) and to conceive of them as interdependent. This is not to say that the *weight* given to each of the modes will not differ according to learning stages and needs. For bilingual learners, an interactive environment should acknowledge the value of conference between speakers in their own languages, and also acknowledge the value of pupils' literacy in their own languages. It is often only such acknowledgment and conference that frees pupils to activate innate learning and language acquisition devices right from the start, and helps them to construe meanings — even when, as is only to be expected, they do not immediately express that learning in English.

For these reasons, it is important to recognize that while devising individual strategies for learning support is important, such narrowly individualized support work, often devised by the support teacher on her own, is not really sufficient to facilitate wider learning, nor will such strategies on their own assist bilingual learners in valuing themselves as active participants in classroom life and learning. Individual strategies work best when they are complementary to interactive learning, the integrated use of all the language modes, and the encouragement of bilingual pupils in the use of *all* their language knowledge and abilities, inclusive of their own first language and learning abilities. The simplest arrangement for inexperienced users of English to enter into is with a partner in *pair work*. This can be followed up through a carefully built structure for *reporting* (one pair to another, then the quartet to the class). We should not expect bilingual learners to offer themselves as reporters to the class at first, but this strategy will enable them to learn what is expected, make a contribution to what gets reported and, as confidence grows, thereafter to take part in reporting.

Classrooms are language loaded places, but meaning is not conveyed only through language. Bilingual learners will be helped in their understanding if what is being taught is supported *visually*. Charts, maps, illustrations, diagrams can be used as appropriate, both in presentation and for pupils to use themselves later in follow up work. Film and video programmes are especially helpful as a means of enabling pupils to get a general, overall grasp of what is being taught. It is also very worthwhile building up a bank of supplementary materials relating to the subject in hand, of picture books, bilingual texts and texts in pupils' languages.

Pupils will be helped if what is being taught is done through *active learning* methods, e.g., handling materials in a concrete assignment, participation in dramatic activities. It will also help them if follow-up work includes opportunities *to go back over* the material presented in some way, with a teacher or peer. This recognition of the recursive nature of learning also allows our pupils to be given the chance to initiate questions and make comments about what they have so far understood — or not understood.

Pupils learning to use English will need work to do that allows them to make meaning, and to that extent is demanding and satisfying — but work that at the same time is not so complex, either in concept or amount, that response is stifled. Choosing which strategies to employ at any one time, so that materials and activities are well enough staged to act as a base for further progression in understanding and skill development, must necessarily be down to the teachers even in co-management situations. They are the people who know pupils, what is being taught, and by what intended means. However, there are some clear principles to go by in making the choices, and some useful strategies to choose from to help pupils do specific curriculum area work and get the supportive language experience they need to build speaking, listening, reading and writing skills in English.

Expectation of Response from Beginner Learners of English

Bilingual pupils' oral and written responses will increase in frequency and accuracy both as they become more familiar with the requirements of school procedures and as their confidence and knowledge of English grows. But it is essential to realize in the case of beginner learners of English that such things as hesitation in responding to direct questioning, little or no initiation of conversation, marked silence, even, do not of themselves imply lack of interest, understanding or progress. A more or less silent period in a new language is a natural and very necessary feature of learning it. In this period, pupils spend a lot of time listening actively, attending, concentrating on what is going on, gleaning useful information. You will be able to discern this from pupils' body language, eye contact, and the attention they give to the activities and assignments they do. However, the fact that they are not yet speaking in the new language does not mean that they do not want or need to communicate with English speaking people. It should also be remembered that they are already competent speakers in their first languages, and more likely than not to be literate in their first languages also. Where pupils are not literate in their first language, teachers will need to take into account whether reading and writing are in fact part of their experience. Whatever the case, make sure that bilingual pupils are not left in isolation either from other children or from teachers. Set up situations, consistently but not relentlessly so, that make collaboration, cooperation and interaction necessary, constructed and paced in such a way as to allow learning and confidence to develop.

Consider the bare bones of an intended learning activity: pupils work with a problem-solving activity in a new area of knowledge, in a collaborative setting, where a teacher is available for consultation but not lead teaching. Included in the activity is the collection of observations. The tangible outcome is to have a record of observations (results) and of related ideas (speculations) which have sprung from doing the activity. This fairly complex task is not of itself inherently difficult. What makes it, or any single other task, more or less difficult to respond to is the degree to which the different features that comprise it are familiar to pupils. It will be an accessible and challenging assignment if, for example, most, if not all, of the ways of working are familiar to pupils, and only one feature, the area of study, is new. As the number of features which are unfamiliar to pupils increases so does inaccessibility. Difficulties can be intensified even further if, as the unfamiliarity increases, the support offered at various points in the activity does not also increase. Such support, as well as comprising specific strategies for supporting pupils' development of linguistic and other skills, includes looking overall at assignments to assess their incremental levels of difficulty *vis-à-vis* what you as teacher will also know about pupils' familiarity with the range of features in any given assignment.

The interrelated factors within such task analysis might include:

— whether or not the subject matter is familiar;
— what kind of activity is to be undertaken, and whether or not the activity is familiar;
— how much of the vocabulary and grammatical structure is familiar;
— how complex the task is in terms of written and spoken language;
— how complex the presentation is to be in terms of written and spoken language;
— how much help and of what kind is built into the task and/or pedagogy.

Such analyses provide pointers as to what might form useful adjustments of the task, to the lesson plan, to the materials, to the pedagogies used in order to help pupils gain productive access to and learning and language development from the task. Sometimes all that is needed to make an assignment more accessible is to alter appropriately one or some of the variables so that more of the activity is familiar to pupils.

A further overall analysis which will help to position teachers better for choosing strategies for the support of curriculum learning *and* development of language skills is a task analysis from the point of view of the language-linked demands of the task. The following example is adapted from 'Developing pedagogies for multilingual classes' (Levine, 1981). It 'unpacks' a specific LESSON from the point of view of the STAGES of a lesson and then of the smaller units which they comprise, LESSON ACTIVITIES

LESSON AIM: Reading and discussion of a text leading to making a report

LESSON STAGES	LESSON ACTIVITIES
Getting started	— organizing the group
	— reading the text (shared reading)
	— reading comprehension

Collecting information	— picking out ideas from text
	— selecting appropriate bits as examples
	— note taking
	— matching ideas from text with own thoughts and experiences
	— stating these, and
	— stating the relationships made between them
Conducting discussion	— listening comprehension
	— expressing own ideas
	— agreeing with others' opinions
	— disagreeing
	— questioning
	— responding to questions
	— interpreting
	— interrupting
Collecting opinions together	— listening comprehension
	— note taking
	— organizing strategies
	— etc.
Reporting (orally)	— organizing strategies
	— using notes
	— speaking extended logical text.
Reporting (written)	— organizing strategies
	— using notes
	— incorporating new ideas that come by virtue of doing own writing
	— writing extended logical text in an appropriate style

'Lesson Stages' describe units of the general language-linked tasks. 'Lesson Activities' describe the specific units of language linked tasks. Sorting out the latter tells you what language-linked *skills* are required. Thus, from the lists which you create by doing this kind of analysis, and comparing them with the language experiences specific to members of your class, you will be able to see at what point in the stage of a lesson you may need to offer support, what skills need supporting, and therefore what kinds of strategy you might need to employ to support specific aspects of learning so as to encourage meaningful response.

Before moving on to list some support strategies for helping with listening, speaking, reading and writing, it is worth considering the use of questions in learning support. Taking the complexity of required response as the yardstick, the simplest questions are those which require a Yes/No, tick/cross answer, e.g., *Will you be my partner?*; *Is it safe to drink unfiltered water?* Remember, though, that there is often the need to express uncertainty, lack of knowledge, or incompleteness in response to these so-called Yes/No questions, as, for instance, with questions like these: *Did you enjoy the 'Theatre in Education' programme?*; *Is ice heavier than water?* These kinds of questions (or statements derived from them for purposes of creating tick charts) allow students the freedom to demonstrate the state of their knowledge or express their wishes without the additional burden of having to think how to frame an extended response. They can also be used as follow-up, focusing questions to help pupils respond to open-ended questions or general instructions, such as *Find the marshland* or *Where's the marshland?* when pupils are doing map work. If there is no immediate response or pupils are bemused then almost inevitably those working with them will point to an appropriate section of the map, asking a question like *Is this marshland?*

A second level of questions is characterized by the use of the word 'or', e.g., *Is this area here marshland, or can it be used for growing food?* This kind of question is in everyday use in classrooms as a cue question to narrow the focus for those uncertain of a fact. Importantly, for pupils at an early stage of using English, such question forms can be used to help them to express their knowledge, since in the question form they can hear and pick out the form their answer may take. However, in order to use the question forms as a means of enabling responses and knowledge development, you need first to ensure that pupils have had, or that you have provided, prior experience in using question formats.

The third level of questions contains those often referred to as 'open-ended', although they are not always as open-ended as they might appear at first sight. These are the ones which begin *What . . . ?*, *Who . . . ?*, *When . . . ?*, *How . . . ?*, *Why . . . ?* For bilingual learners, they also fall into several categories relating to the increasing complexity of the responses they demand:

— Those which are targetted at facts (observable either at first hand or verifiable from visual or written materials or from memory, e.g., *What's this?*; *Who went to rescue the trawlermen?*; *Why was [x] so angry?*; *Where did they go?*).
— Those which demand description (e.g., *What did they do?*; *What happened on the journey?*; *How did you make that?*).
— Those which demand reasoning or marshalling of facts (e.g., *Why do you think it is dangerous to swim in polluted water?*; *What would you do if . . . ?*).

It makes no sense not to require pupils to express reasoning until they can respond descriptively; nor that demands for either reasoning or description should be delayed until pupils can express facts. Listing questions in this increasing order of complexity is not to suggest an order for introducing or teaching them. Neither is the order of listing to be read as a suggestion that the use of open-ended questions should be deferred until pupils have mastered response to Yes/No and Or questions. Rather, the nature of questions is being highlighted so that you can use your heightened awareness of the variable complexity of demands they make on pupils' written and oral powers to better facilitate response. What you need to bear in mind is:

— that a response to an open-ended question can be prompted by cue questions;
— that the Yes/No type of cue question (or statements derived from them) are good to use when response is all that is needed;
— that the Or type of cue question is good to use when it is helpful to offer pupils a linguistic form for more extended response.

Note, however, that none of the open-ended questions offer a form for response, although there is frequently a typical framing, especially with those directed at facts (e.g., *What's this?/It's (a)* . . . ; *Why* . . . *?/Because* . . .). Furthermore, as well as open-ended questions frequently leaving response free in terms of form and content (and so a good thing in relation to encouraging independent thinking and freedom to initiate or contribute one's own ideas), their form can be misleading to new users of English since response may require a different grammatical form from that used in the question. For example, *How did you make that?/I made it by* . . . ; *Why did he swim the channel?/He swam the channel because* . . .

Because bilingual learners are able to interact with native speakers of English, and so hear in natural circumstances how various grammatical forms, e.g., the irregular verbs noted above, enter into English language usage, and because their teachers and other pupils can offer them instruction in how to say things, they will quite quickly move from getting the forms 'wrong' to getting them right. However, when pupils are still uncertain, it helps them to overcome initial difficulties with English verb forms to rephrase such questions as statements. For example, instead of *How did you make that?* you can say *Tell me how you made that*, thus offering the correct form for the response.

A Schedule of Useful Strategies

The strategies listed in Figure 2.2 are not an exhaustive list, but examples of possible types of strategies which teachers can employ to support *both* learning *and* the development of skills in English language usage. However, they take their meaning as learning activities from their use in the context of interactive curriculum learning (represented in the first half of the schedule in Figure 2.1). Isolated from this context, they are just exercises hardly likely to promote sustained interest in school learning or confident development of a use of English. Teachers will not be dependent on such lists for the strategies they devise, but will bring to bear knowledge of their pupils and of the learning task to create the necessary supportive tasks and pedagogy for their situation. It is not possible here to give detailed examples of individual strategies as devised and used by teachers in interactive curriculum contexts, but examples of strategies and descriptions of use can be found in the articles, journals and books listed at the end of this chapter.

Figure 2.1: A Schedule of Useful Language Linked Strategies to Support Curriculum Learning

(part 1)

strategies begin in
APPROPRIATE CURRICULUM CONTENT
APPROPRIATE FORMS OF INTERACTIVE PEDAGOGY

are chosen in relation to
KNOWLEDGE ABOUT PUPILS
AWARENESS OF PUPILS' LINGUISTIC NEEDS
AWARENESS OF OVERALL CONCEPTUAL AND LINGUISTIC DEMANDS OF LEARNING
TASK

and from within a context of using OVERALL STRATEGIES for learning support that

SUPPORT INTERACTION	SUPPORT UNDERSTANDING	FACILITATE RESPONSES
via	via	via
partnership teaching	use of visuals	unpacking tasks
pupil co-management	media	focused use of questions
pupil partnerships	active learning	'going back over' work
strategies	materials in pupils' languages	strategies supporting
supporting understanding	strategies supporting	interaction + understanding
+ facilitating responses	interaction + facilitating responses	

AT THIS POINT IT IS USEFUL TO SELECT PARTICULAR STRATEGIES TO

Focus on	Help with	Promote	Promote
LISTENING	SPEAKING	READING	WRITING

remember to
give pupils plenty of time for listening, observing and quiet joining in
+
plenty of working with more experienced others in mixed experience groups
+
plenty of time to go back over work

Figure 2.2: A Schedule of Useful Language Linked Strategies to Support Curriculum Learning

(part 2)

LISTENING*   SPEAKING △   READING†   WRITING°

working in pairs in collaborative learning tasks

being involved in work which actively encourages talk, e.g., questionnaires, surveys

teachers' planning of collaborative assignments ensures that everyone must contribute

* listening to stories
* carrying out instructions
* joint activities with a partner which require active listening, e.g.,
  - reading together selecting, e.g., key passages to show understanding or to require explanation
  - extracting information from charts or entering information onto charts or grids or by selecting correct sentences

△† adaptation of board games to reinforce content and concept learning involving reading (e.g., instruction cards) and discussion on order for 'moves' to be made

△ joint composing of stories or preparation of answers to questions

° using tape recorder
  - to record results, results of work
  - to prepare retellings of stories or other oral presentations
  - to compose stories and answers to questions set

†° being read to (fact and fiction) and hearing and telling stories, narratives or giving information

* drawing/diagramming, talking about them to teacher or other pupil who write down the story

†° labelling drawings/diagrams from given words or sentences

† matching words and sentences to pictures

† joining correctly key sentences that have been cut in half

† reading own composed text

† sequencing text

† predicting

† reading + selecting information by underlining

° copying text previously matched to pictures or transcribed by others

° guided writing (see list below)

NB *This is not an exhaustive list but a list of examples of possible strategies*

Figure 2.3: A Schedule of Useful Language Linked Strategies to Support Curriculum Learning
(part 2, continued)

GUIDED WRITING STRATEGIES

e.g. 'SELECT AND COPY'
(very useful when pupils are just beginning to write in English: they help pupils to record work done)
— filling in blanks (best if the blanks are key words, and for beginners, if the words that go in the gaps are chosen from a seen set of words)
— completing sentences
— selection from sets of whole sentences
— selection from sets of 'Or'-type questions
— sequencing given sentences

e.g. PLANNED SETS OF QUESTIONS
— sets of questions are devised, the answers to which, when written out, will provide pupils with a sequenced paragraph

e.g. MODELLING
— writing another piece of one's own like something just read or offered for study (pupils stay as near to or move as far from the original as their confidence allows: this is a very useful strategy for personal and autobiographical writing)

e.g. GROUP WRITING
— this is written work arrived at by discussion and decision making: make sure all pupils in a working group contribute

Teacher Action Research

Until recently, it has hardly been expected of a teacher that she or he should contribute directly to educational theory-making or to be an initiator of new curriculum developments. It has been a traditionally held view that the role of a teacher is as practitioner, one who puts into practice what has already been defined elsewhere — by edict and/or as a curriculum development package — by the people, sometimes seconded teachers, whose role it is to think about and research into education. Where classroom teachers have been connected with educational research, it has commonly been as the subjects of someone else's research rather than as initiators of it.

For any learning, thinking person embarking on the profession of teaching, becoming the object of someone else's research can be something of a culture shock. The subject/object orientation of much educational research minimizes the opportunities for, indeed the inclinations of, teachers to 'own' the research or its outcomes. Hardly surprising, therefore, that large numbers of teachers frequently reject research and innovation as being useful to them in their daily work. Yet the fact is that teachers themselves have a unique role to play in educational research. And it is gradually being recognized that teachers, when they take on the concept of *teachers' action research*, have significant contributions to make to educational theory and practice; that they have significant contributions to make to pedagogic curriculum development, indeed, to institutional development; and by no means least that, as self selected participants in action research, they develop their own individual practice and contribute to the professionalism of education in general.

Action research is a significant form of research for teachers because it involves theory-making grounded in practice, and perceives the subjectivity of the researcher as illuminating on-going reflection and assessment of the progress of the research. This also means that teachers are 'freed' to investigate their practice without stopping the doing of it.

Where teachers share and discuss their work and findings, the involvement can be translated into equally constructive forms of group, or even institutional, in-service training. Through the development and acquisition of greater knowledge about what constitutes effective educational theory and practice, teachers are also more able, by involving pupils in the research processes and sharing the outcomes of work with them, to improve the partnerships between themselves and pupils, parents and community. A teacher action research perspective also means that teachers are better equipped to evaluate curriculum content and pedagogy.

Action research is a means by which teachers' theoretical understandings, actual experience and professionalism develop. It is also the means by which it becomes acknowledged that teachers have a central role in educational research and innovation.

Leaving aside the simplistic notion that all research, in the sense that it is done, is action research, teacher action research involves the following components:

— 'action' as in taking an initiative and planning the progress of an enquiry;
— 'action' as in participation in an enquiry;
— 'action' as in construing the events and progress of the enquiry, and in making analyses and drawing conclusions, both individually and with teacher colleagues;
— 'action' as in taking action to effect the changes called for by the implications of the findings of the research.

It is the last of these forms of action which, when combined with the other three, gives teacher action research its specific meaning as a research mode.

Teacher action research sets out to effect change, not just to understand the causes and effects of present circumstances. In other words, the power and usefulness of action research is best appreciated when it is seen as critical enquiry into past and present circumstances which is directed at future action for change, the implementation of which can itself then become a focus for action research. Such changes, when called for, or when the attempt to implement them is made, will have implications at a variety of levels and be more or less controversial depending on the circumstances in which they have arisen, whether or not they 'simply' affect an individual teacher-researcher's own practice or have wider potential application. As Carr and Kemmis (1986) put it:

> Individual thought and action have their meaning and significance in a social historical context, yet, at the same time, themselves contribute to the formation of social and historic contexts. This *double dialectic* of theory and practice, on the one hand, and individual and society, on the other, is at the heart of action research as a participatory and collaborative process of self-reflection. Action research recognizes that thought and action arise from practices in particular situations, and that situations themselves can be transformed by transforming the practices that constitute them and the understandings that make them meaningful. This involves transformations in *individual* practices, understandings and situations, and transformations in the practices, understandings and situations which *groups* of people constitute through their interaction. The double dialectic of thought and action and individual and society is resolved, for action research, in the notion of a *self-critical community* of action researchers who are committed to the improvement of education, who are researchers *for* education (p. 184)

When viewed from the point of view of this 'community of action researchers', it can be further appreciated that another virtue of action research is that *individual* starting points and perspectives can lend breadth to, or usefully challenge, traditional orientations and practice.

What we must not do, however, is allow the evident worth of teacher action research for the development of more appropriate curriculum, pedagogic and organizational practices to minimize or ignore the problematics inherent in the relationship between individual or small group starting points, and the challenge their investigations may bring to traditional orientations and practice. These problematics are themselves part of the context of action research — as much a part of teacher action research as is the excitement teacher researchers experience in the learning inherent in it — and govern its success, however relative.

By taking place *in* the world, and not apart from it, and being about teachers themselves *and* their professional communities, teacher action research is set in a cultural context of constraints and oppositions as well as permissions and mutuality. Because it is the nature of the construction of each individual's experience that this experience will membership them differently to the prevailing consensus, they will have different perspectives on particular issues.

Inevitably, because of their commitment to more effective education and, therefore, to change, much of what teacher action researchers do positions them on the margins or outside the prevailing consensus. Not everyone in a teacher's working community will welcome the critical inspection, or agree with the analyses made, or welcome the implications for innovation and change so evident to the action researcher. In trying honestly to understand and *state* the social, cultural and historic discourses that together have constructed the very curriculum and pedagogic practices they wish to transform, many teacher researchers are likely to find themselves in confrontation with colleagues who, seeing things differently from them — albeit, mostly, from an uninspected or merely pragmatic standpoint — may find the analyses and proposals for change difficult to accept. Their position as teacher researchers, as opposed to 'outside' research tradition, is ironically used against them as well as for them.

A teacher action research group (Teachers Research Group, 1989)[2] sums it up:

> An action research enquiry is a long term, reflective process which, for its outcomes to be valid, depends on rigorous attention not only to the ostensible focus of the enquiry but also to the various kinds of cultural, political and linguistic contexts in which it is embedded. To understand the nature of these contexts, and the way in which they govern the events of a particular enquiry focus is crucial both to the emerging analysis of what you are studying and to being in a position to act upon your newly realised knowledge. It is a sure way of revealing hidden currcicula which, unless we do, it is unlikely that there will be any fundamental going forward in our enterprise of refining practices . . . .

Because embedded practices and the move for change in education both exist in the same socio-economic and politico-cultural contexts, we need to recognize not only that tension between them is unavoidable but also that our own premises for wishing to develop educational theory and practice need constant examination. Develop from where to what? 'From underachievement to achievement' is a common response. However, while that transformation is one which we all wish to achieve that still leaves the fundamental issue of equality of opportunity, and indeed, equality of outcome in education, unstated. The fact is teachers' action research is *likely* to take place in an ethos of promoting the equal rights of all children. It is not, however, inevitable that this will always be the case.

How can we ensure that this issue is always part of the analysis we bring to bear in examination of our action researches? The answer must be in making clear our premises — something we can do quite simply by stating them as the aims of our research undertakings. For example, the Teachers Research Group (TRG) includes the following among the major orientations of its work:

TRG locates its work within the institutional and other constraints under which teachers work. It recognises the broad spectrum of educational politics. Nevertheless, TRG's research is directed towards outcomes which can help facilitate children's learning and teachers' understanding within an anti-racist, anti-sexist, egalitarian and collective framework (Teachers Research Group, 1989).

By making such aims an essential component of the dialectic, a community of teacher action researchers improves its chances of resolving the tensions they experience — in such a way as to promote independence from, rather than symbiosis with, the pressures to conform to the dominating voices within the contexts of their work.

Some of the procedures of teacher action research are embedded within our professionalism. By that I mean that the deep competence of our professional lives provides us with a template for action research, in that to be effective as professionals in almost all the areas in which we are called upon to act, we have to:

— consider the nature of the 'problem';
— consider aims and objectives;
— think about the actions that need to be taken;
— think about the processes involved in teaching and learning in particular contexts;
— gather together the means for taking the action;
— monitor the procedings and reflect upon outcomes.

At its best, our professionalism also gives us other kinds of knowledge and perspectives that we need for teacher action research:

— our everyday work requires attention to process;
— we expect — even as the work proceeds — to reorganize our thinking about it because new 'evidence' comes along all the time;
— we know that discussion with others frequently takes us further than we can go on our own.

Furthermore, when we undertake an enquiry as action research we do not need to be trapped into thinking that we have to 'get it right' from the outset. Rather, we already 'know', from within our professionalism, that we will be involved in an unfolding both of knowledge and procedure, and that each will be facilitated by on-going discussion with colleagues in an enquiry-like stance towards each other. For action research, we will bring all this into our conscious control, while also choosing specific strategies for collecting documentation for the research enquiry.

Action Research: Some Particicular Methodologies

Taping and transcribing. If you are interested in talk and interaction in classrooms, and what they can tell about pupils' ways of construing and learning, then you will need to make recordings. These can be audio and/or video. The question of what effect the presence of tape recorders and videos have is also one the researchers will want to consider. However, it is also the experience of teacher researchers that once pupils get used to the idea of recordings, they are able either to ignore them, or turn them into a tool for their own learning and reflections.

It is not difficult to get individual recordings. When pupils work in small groups, a tape recorder at their place of work will pick up their talk efficiently enough for you to be able to transcribe, even though there will be background noise from other groups. A video recording used in these circumstances will provide added information about interaction; a linked microphone needs only to be placed close to the group. The camera itself can be focused on them and left fixed in position. If you want data of the whole class at work, you will probably find it easier if you brief someone else to act as camera person while you work with the class normally. A tape recorder can also be used for collecting data about children's oral composition, and video-ing is an excellent way of collecting data about children's written composing. Comparisons between the recordings and the pupils' actual written work will illuminate their composing processes and help you both to construct lessons and to make interventions based upon those illuminations.

Whether you have taken the recordings for the purposes mentioned above or for others, the next step will be to review the data and to transcribe some of the evidence it provides. There are several stages of these procedures, and you can expect each succeeding stage to provide you with further insights.

1. Review each recording you make as a whole, using a machine with a counter on it so that you can note where in the recording are the sections of particular interest to you at the first stage of analysis. Keep a note of the nature of each of the salient points.
2. Decide what you want to transcribe. This may be only those sections which have already been highlighted for you, or it may be the whole event — which you do depends on what you want to find out, either from the initial making of the transcript, or from the next stage of more detailed study of it. Many people do transcribe all the recording, going on after that to study sections of the transcript in greater detail than others. This two-stage procedure allows them to learn a greater variety of things from making the transcript than they do if they go straight to excerpts.
3. In making the transcript most people, as a first level of transcription, set out their transcripts as if they were writing a play. Count each speech act as one utterance, and number all utterances consecutively in

order to facilitate reference to parts of the transcript later, as has been done with the transcripts quoted by contributors to this book. Count hesitations (like pauses and 'er's) and conversation noises (like 'uh uh' and 'mm') as part of an utterance — or when they stand alone, as utterances in themselves. These will be of interest when considering processes in oral or written composition. Keep notes of what you notice about what is happening in the dialogue as you make the transcript as these will help to form the second stage analysis of your data. It is also often useful to make a second version of the transcript, this time set out in columns, one for each speaker (still numbering the utterances consecutively). This enables you, amongst other things, to go on to study each individual, plus the turn-taking within the group, more easily, thus bringing further useful information to your analysis.

Finally, transcribing is a lengthy and laborious business. However, the outcomes reward the labour. Transcripts are important not only to the teacher researcher, but to pupils and colleagues, as important evidence for theoretical pedagogical and curriculum developments. They also function as a celebration and acknowledgment of pupils' work.

Interviewing. Interviewing ranges from informal chat to an interaction formally structured to a pre-arranged schedule of questions. Somewhere in between is a 'focused' conversation conducted relatively informally in which the interviewer, through open ended questions, invites opinion and comment. This method allows the interviewee some relative status in the conversation and some room to share in its shaping. The virtue of this method is that relevant areas of interest and ideas can emerge, which interviewers on their own have not thought of in their pre-planning of the interview.

A tape recorder — if the interviewee is happy to allow it — can again be used in collecting this kind of data, but it will be important to make notes, too. Some notes can be taken during the interview. Notes can also be written up afterwards. In certain circumstances it would also be appropriate to invite interviewees to reflect on the interview in writing.

Triangulation. This is a technique for reflecting back to participants in a teaching situation alternative readings they may have had of it for the purpose of improving practice. One example of its usefulness is when teachers are in teaching partnership in some way in a classroom, since, from time to time, they can take it in turns to act as facilitator on reflecting to their colleague:

— the success of materials pupils are being asked to use;
— the teaching situation as the other teacher perceives it;
— the pupils' responses and processes in learning.

The facilitator may also interpret to the pupils the teacher's intentions, and can refer the pupils' comments back to the teacher. Negotiating triangulation techniques in teaching partnerships is not a simple matter however, and needs to be based on considerable professional trust. Nevertheless, within a partnership, through triangulation, there is the possibility, not otherwise available, for both teachers to reflect their readings of classroom events to each other in such a way as to bring both the teacher partnerships and the pupil/teacher understanding closer together.

Another example of a situation in which triangulation may be useful to furthering teachers' understandings might be of a designated teacher in the school — perhaps the teacher in charge of teaching English as a second language, or the special educational needs teacher — 'following' the lessons of one or a group of learners in order to uncover the cognitive, linguistic and social demands mainstream lessons make on pupils, and to reflect back to colleagues the nature of the difficulties encountered. The exercise is illuminating for all concerned, providing insights into general teaching practices — not only as they relate to the individual pupils being observed. If insights from triangulation are to be reflected on in the long term, a record of events would need to be kept. However, such a record would also need to maintain a productive balance between observation and sensitivity in reporting style.

Document collection. For almost all investigations it will be necessary to make some kind of document collection, whether this is to form part of the contextualization for other data, or is to be the main focus of study. Documents include teaching materials, pupils' work, policy documents, minutes of meetings — indeed anything you might consider to be relevant. And, of course, a relevant document would be notes on your own perceptions of the starting point of your investigation and of the historical context (as it relates to your particular circumstances, your school, as well as nationally) in which it is embedded.

Keeping a log book. Taping and transcribing, interviewing, triangulation, and document collection will form, as appropriate, only part of the methodology of creating data. A log can also become the raw material of research just as much as any other evidence you may collect and create. It is a handy thing to keep both as a running record of what happens and of reflections on those events. Some people divide the pages of the log into two, even three, columns so as to be able to separate, for ease of reference, their running record of events from any reflective thoughts they may have at different times about those events. This is a simple device which accommodates well to one of the most significant features of action research enquiry, namely, that before you reach an end point for your enquiry, you can expect to experience some uncertainty. This is because, as you reflect on what you have been doing, or on the evidence you have been collecting, your findings may confound your original expectations. Thus, you may wish to alter not only how and what you collect, but even your original questions. It is worth remembering, though, that this is an expectation of any enquiry based in practice: ensuing stages of the enquiry emerge in the process of action and investigation.

Some people also like to record in their log any comments, complaints, 'moans', or expressions of pleasure that reflect a mood or attitude, or any questioning or bewilderment, that they or others experienced at the time of any of the events they record. This is because they have realized that they could forget (and come to regret the loss of) small, but nonetheless, telling, details that might later, on reflection, inform their enquiry.

Finally, teachers' action research, while likely be carried out by an individual teacher, benefits from discussion with teacher colleagues. Such discussion may take place in your own institution or through a teachers' network at a teachers' centre, college of education, etc. Such discussion can benefit the actual research, but also, the sharing of teacher action research is important for both the insights it can offer to other colleagues and for the support that colleagues can give to the teacher researcher.

Notes

1. This section 'Extending the notion of partnership teaching to pupils: co-management' was conceived and written by Helen Davitt, initially as an in-service document on bilingual learners.
2. Teachers Research Group (1989) *TRG Directory 2*, Joint Department of English and Media Studies, Institute of Education, University of London, for Teachers Research Group (limited circulation).

Further Reading

(See bibliography for complete source listings).
Suggestions for the Organization and Practice of Teaching in Multilingual Classrooms

BLEACH, J. and RILEY, S. (1985) 'Developing and extending the literacy of bilingual pupils through the secondary years'.
CHATWIN, R. (1985) 'Can ESL teaching be racist?'
DAVIES, A. M. and STURMAN, E. (Eds) (1989) *Bilingual Learners in Secondary Schools*.
EDWARDS, C., MOORHOUSE, J. and WIDLAKE, S. (1988) 'Language or English?'.
EMBLEN, V. (1988) 'Other mathematical puzzles: entering the discourse'.
HESTER, H. (1983) *Stories in the Multilingual Primary Classroom*.
HESTER, H. (1985) 'Learning from children learning'.
HOULTON, D. and WILLEY, R. (1982) *Supporting Children's Bilingualism*.
LEVINE, J. (1981) 'Developing pedagogies for multilingual classes'.
MARLAND, M. (1987) *Multilingual Britain: The Educational Challenge*.
RILEY, S. and BLEACH, J. (1983) 'Three moves in the Initiating of Mainstreaming at Secondary Level'.

SCHOOLS COUNCIL (1972–74) *Scope Stage 2: a Language Development Course.*
SUTTON, C. (1981) *Communicating in the Classroom.*
WALLACE, C. (1986) *Learning to Read in a Multicultural Society.*

Journals
The English Magazine.
Issues in Race and Education.
Language Matters.

Video materials
BLEACH, J. and RILEY, S. *Learning in a Second Language in the Secondary Curriculum.*
Second Language Learners in Primary Classrooms Project (SLIPP).
Language in the Multi-ethnic Primary Classroom.
WALIA, S. and WALIA, Y. (1988) *Language is the Key.*

Action Research

CARR, W. and KEMMIS, S. (1986) *Becoming Critical: Educational Knowledge and Action Research.*
CROLL, P. (1986) *Systematic Classroom Observation.*
EDWARDS, D. and MERCER, N. (1987) *Common Knowledge: The Development of Understanding in the Classroom.*
HAMMERSLEY, M. (Ed.) (1986) *Controversies in Classroom Research.*
HITCHCOCK, G. and HUGHES, D. (1989) *Research and the Teacher: A Qualitative Introduction to School Based Research.*
HOPKINS, D. (1985) *A Teacher's Guide to Action Research.*
LOMAX, P. (Ed.) 1989 *The Management of Change.*
STENHOUSE, L. (1975) *An Introduction to Curriculum Research and Development.*

3
Social and Antiracist Reasons for On-site Provision for Developing Bilingual Students

Catherine Spode

Spode, as a teacher in charge of ESL in a secondary school, in 'Social and Antiracist Reasons for On-site Provision for Developing Bilingual Students', *describes graphically the searing disjunctions experienced by students caught up in the structures of off-site provision. She shows how being away from mainstream activities, albeit with the intention of providing a form of support, in effect contributes to marginalization and neglect, onsite, of bilingual pupils' curriculum learning and social needs. She offers some ideas for supporting language, learning and social needs in the mainstream. She recommends the use of 'form' time as an opportunity to introduce structured activities, some of them enjoyable as games, as a way of bringing together on an equal basis bilingual learners and the other constituencies of pupils in the social grouping of their 'form'. She also signals the need for ESL teachers and subject teachers across the curriculum to work together to deepen their respective under-standing of the cognitive and linguistic demands of learning tasks through the joint creation and teaching of learning materials.*

Background

I started work at Shoreditch School in January 1979 as a .8 teacher of English as a Second Language, following in the footsteps of a well established colleague in a school which had decided, by virtue of an NUT resolution of the staff, to appoint its own ESL teacher rather than send students off-site. I had had previous experience of working with students developing English as a second language both in school and at a language centre in East London. I was, therefore, well aware of the problems faced by students sent out to language centres on the half-day basis established within the LEA, and also of the need to support staff in the main school in their own learning how to cope with students learning to use English as a second language in their classrooms.

Problems of Sending Students to Language Centres

The problems of sending students to language centres, to my mind, hinge round the questions of peer group relationships and of continuity of timetabling. Children make and consolidate relationships begun in the classroom in the playground, in registration time, and at lunchtimes. That whole social life is as important a part of their view of the school as are the role, presence and interventions of teachers. That is to say, there is a dialectical relationship between the way in which students conduct themselves in the playground and performance in the classroom; if students miss half the school day (which includes the morning or afternoon breaks and a large part of the lunch hour), then this will have a major effect on their school life. The feelings of marginality and exhaustion engendered by this kind of language teaching provision can easily be appreciated by teachers who themselves have worked on a peripatetic basis or in a split site school. Yet we impose this experience not on to the most able, adjusted and secure students, but on to those who have just undergone the traumatic experience of coming to this country, leaving friends and familiar faces, and often, also, have undergone excruciating experiences of bloodshed and war.

A Bengali girl came to the East London school I was then working in and hated going to the language centre. As one of the remedial teachers in the school, I had the task of dragging her, weeping, down the street every morning to put her on the bus to the language centre. A year later, after being on an ESL course, I went to work at the same language centre where she was by now a happy, relaxed and very able student. She was then pronounced fit to go back to school full-time. It was my unhappy task again to support her through floods of tears at leaving a place and friends and, even possibly, teachers she had grown close to.

As you will appreciate, my argument is not that language centres cannot be happy havens for the children nor that they do not learn in them — although I do think better learning environments will be achieved on-site, as I say below. Rather it is, simply and very powerfully, that we deal cruelly by not attending to children's emotional and social needs; and that we do so by virtue of the structures and provision that are intended to help them should not be overlooked. Nor should it be overlooked that such arrangements 'shelter' even caring pastoral teams in a school from the traumas experienced by this group of students. Neither pastoral teams nor the staff as a whole are 'under pressure' to take notice of the newcomers. The children remain marginal and outside the mainstream of events and yet are often treated as if this were not the case both inside the classroom and, no less importantly, as far as playground incidents are concerned. Is this racist in intent? Surely not. But the message to the pupils may be that of hostility and indifference.

The same argument works in relation to those students not on-site full time, and their access to a full curriculum. What is a teacher in the main school to do when a child or children appear for one lesson and not the next because that is their time to go to the language centre? You do not have to be an ill intentioned teacher to send them to a remedial teacher to ask for them to be taught for that period, or failing that, to send word to the language centre asking them to provide work for the children to do in their lessons. Bright, intelligent children can thus each day be spending half of it in a language centre and the other half in a remedial department or at the edge of the class doing 'busy' work, or even nothing at all.

Again, my argument is not that teachers don't care, nor that they are deliberately acting against children's rights in education. Rather, that an off-site withdrawal system takes the whole question out of their hands. Further, it leads to a lack of teacher experience of the processes of second-language learning and teaching, so that through their innocence they remain unaware of strategies and techniques which could help them in the teaching of multicultural, multilingual classes. Instead, such work is seen to be outside their realm. Structurally removed from pupils' needs, teachers remain unaware of them.

On-site Support for Learners of English as a Second Language

I started work at the school absolutely determined to look at the situation of all developing bilingual students in the school as a whole, in terms of their social interaction, their participation in lessons, and the development of their abilities in spoken and written English. The rest of this section looks briefly at some meaningful first steps taken in relation to social interaction and participation in lessons — clearly necessary precursors for being able to assess development in learning to use English.

Social Interaction

As far as social interaction is concerned, we looked very carefully at what kinds of activities could be participated in by *all* pupils in the school during form time. We needed to engender a participating atmosphere which could create *natural* interaction among ethnic and cultural groups, and which would not leave the relative newcomers always playing a minor social or linguistic role.

The playing of games in language teaching is a well known strategy. Here we took it a considerable and meaningful step forward by setting it in a social context. This is true despite the problems noted below. The reversal of the usual expert-to-lay role meant that the games-playing expert (the English language learner) would have a genuine context for the use of English to explain and encourage, but equally important, the people who wanted to know (the more experienced English language users) would be learning to give more space to people they had not before necessarily treated with much regard. Strategies of this kind cannot but change the social and racial expectations of relations in a school. Newcomers can be regarded as beings who 'have' something rather than merely people who lack something. Of course, teachers need to provide the means, the opportunity, and often that means the equipment — if it is indeed through games that they are going to try to achieve such form-time interaction — and they will, too, need to set the tone by demonstrating through their actions and attitudes that they regard all the people in the class as beings who 'have'.

We suggested to pastoral staff that they make use of a number of games which we had available in the ESL department. Snakes and Ladders, 'Guess Who?' (a commercially produced game in which quite simple language structures are employed as the basis for questioning in a detective game), and *Qerem* (an oriental board game requiring the combined skills of shove ha'penny, draughts and snooker to play it). By having the opportunity to be experts, the Bengali boys, newly come to our school, could move from muteness into interacting. Other pupils (mostly boys) asked how to play and intermingling was established at this level — no mean feat. But what about the girls? The question remains. What can be done to draw the girls in, and not only into the social interaction? It would be wrong to think that the Asian girls are at one end of the spectrum from the majority of the rest of the girls. The issues they contend with are part of the continuum with which all girls contend. What, indeed, has school to offer girls? It is a complex business to put alongside our striving for an anti-sexist as well as an anti-racist education.

Participation in Lessons

Inevitably, withdrawal teaching continued, but a second intervention on behalf of the learners of English as a second language was to establish working relationships with some of the subject teachers in the school, and particularly with the Biology department. Because of my need to understand the Biology course for the Third Year as a whole before we could begin to devise individual worksheets for it, we negotiated timetabled time to work together. But it was necessary to develop understandings from the 'other side', too, for if I needed to know some Biology than my colleagues also needed to understand that the answer to a question like 'What will they be doing in the lesson tomorrow?' is not simply to name the topic of the lesson. It is also to be aware of and able to state the tasks that will be set, what the tasks require of the students linguistically and cognitively, exactly how much we are asking of them, and whether the assumptions we make about what they may know before we start are accurate. A deeper understanding of task demands is needed by all teachers so that lessons can both start where the students are and also stretch them cognitively and linguistically.

Learning from our Discussions

One of the ways through which my understanding of these matters began to develop was through discussion with my teaching colleagues and by analyzing what happened when we and our students used the materials we had prepared. Another route for my learning was discussion with colleagues in the Schools Council Programme Three Activity (Education for a Changing World) Language for Learning Project: Second Language Learners and Mainstream Curriculum Group.

Colleagues' Responses to Materials

Lest I give an impression of us moving easily into the creation of rigorous but apt learning materials, I need to say that our early attempts were far from perfect, as can be inferred from the response made by my project colleagues and reported below. The report is from notes[1] compiled after a project discussion of some of the early materials prepared for Biology at the school. It is included here because the particular questions raised by my project colleagues are also questions which are always worth asking when we inspect or reflect upon the learning support materials we make and use. Certainly, they refer to changes that we found we needed to make and to issues we needed to attend to. The discussion took place some time after the work in school had got under way.

> We looked at worksheets prepared by Biology teachers in conjunction with Cath Spode which dealt with the classification of animals and were intended for use with Third Year students. The course itself is topic based and involved initially a full examination of resources. Teaching notes were produced collaboratively. Several points were raised quite early on in the discussion. For example:
>
> — was the material provided too thin?
> — was it appropriate to face the students with a sheet listing the categories under their latinised names?
> — was the material too far from the students' city experience?
> — is the notion of classification too structured a starting point in Biology?
> — was there real learning, or mere labelling required?
>
> Cath Spode spoke about her own position as an ESL specialist in the Biology lessons. Initially, she was seen as someone providing simpler worksheets for the students learning English, a position which had comparatively low status. This gradually changed as the whole matter of syllabus content and learning strategies inevitably came under consideration. Small steps at first, for example, changing instruction

sheets which were proving difficult to follow (and therefore contributing to discipline problems) to providing instructions through flow charts; asking students to bring in their own collections of materials for Biology so that they could compile their own classification categories, justify them within small groups which later reported back to the whole class. These steps prompted a rethink of classroom practices, particularly a consideration of the tactics by which teachers can get students discussing. Thirdly, they came to the identification of what tasks the students could be expected to perform, what kinds of talk they would need to use, how any writing could come about, what concepts were assumed and what stages of understanding were to be met in what sequence so that the comprehension of specific items of course content actually take place.

Cath Spode made clear that while the ESL teacher is there in an advisory capacity there is the potential for being very fully involved in the classroom, especially as being an assistant can be frustrating on a permanent basis. But even this role requires the ESL teacher to be willing to adjust to the rules of the laboratory and to be conversant, at the very least, with the aims of the lessons. Perhaps the most important point to be raised during the morning's discussion was that it seemed likely that an emphasis on the needs of the student for whom English is not a first language, or, indeed, third language, leads to the production of a more acceptable Language for Learning policy within the subject for all students ...

Had mainstream support not been embarked upon for its most immediate reasons, to counter the institutional racism suffered by bilingual pupils, then how much longer would it have taken for us to look at and raise questions about the quality of our mainstream work as it affects *all* pupils?

Notes

1. The notes of the discussion reported here were compiled by Betty Rosen, then Head of the Communications Faculty, Somerset School, Haringey.

4
Finding a Voice and Conversational Competence: Mixed Ability English, a Social Base for Negotiated Learning

Jean Bleach

Bleach in 'Finding a Voice and Conversational Competence: Mixed Ability English, a Social Base for Negotiated Learning', *from the perspective of a developed practice in mixed ability English teaching, shows some ways in which this practice is positioned to help bilingual learners — by giving learners opportunities to use English for mainstream curriculum learning, for organizing and exploring thought and experience and for construing the world. Bleach also indicates how this mixed ability practice could develop for teachers through their understanding better how to support pupils' efforts as they attempt the mixed ability, mainstream English work. One way is to build on bilingual students' propensity to get the whole shape of a narrative 'right' before they are able to get sentences correct, rather than force them to concentrate principally on the latter. She then shows how the concept of 'modelling' is useful to teachers in the enterprise of helping students to get the two aspects of narrative, the whole shape and the sentence particulars, closer together. Modelling appears to be a process by which pupils internalize what to do, and which, at the same time, offers teachers clues to developing teaching practice. She looks at the structured help ESL teachers offer pupils within the theory of modelling, at how reading aloud to pupils helps them to internalize the 'voice on the page', and at how experience of oral and written fiction and non-fiction, by the same process of internalization, fosters pupils' ability to use these oral and written genres within their own writing.*

Background

At the time I am thinking of, 1979, beginner learners of English as a second language attended the divisional language centre for half a day each day of the week and returned to school full-time after about four terms. Some students who went to language centres, through the exigencies of their timetables, were, from the beginning, fortunate enough to go to mixed ability mainstream English lessons which were — also by chance — well-motivated towards language development. Others, on their return to full-time, might, again fortuitously, be a part of such a class. Their good fortune lay in the fact that to be a member of such a class is, potentially, to be part of a developing social and academic network from and in which one can, over time, learn, contribute, make friends and help others. English teachers who have recognized the power of language as a tool for ordering experience of the world and who have a tradition of encouraging English speaking students to say what they want to say in the language that is closest to them are, in my view, in a position to benefit developing bilingual students in their classes. That is to say, on the one hand, we recognize that the students will have a need to use their new language to construe the new experiences coming to them (not necessarily translatable into the languages or cultural experiences of their homes), and to reflect on the past (for example, where social trauma has preceded and accompanied a family move to a different country and is often possible of expression only in a language other than the one in which they have experienced the trauma). In addition, in our response to diversity in the classroom, we are always looking for ways of structuring tasks and/or working with other teachers and/or students in the class so that everyone in the mixed ability class can take part. On the other hand, what we have not been so good at doing — unless we have been very unusual — has been to recognize the ways in which learners of English as a second language could not follow the (unconscious) developmental patterns for the production of English that native speakers, no matter what their dialect, can and do. The major consequence of our failure to recognize this has been that children full-time in English classes have not, as a matter of course, got any systematic help in developing particular structural aspects of their competence in the production of English. Lexis and semantics were, of course, better catered for in the typically open system of a mixed ability English class than was syntax. Again and again it was possible to see what has come to be known as 'frozen competence' (Derrick, 1977) in, for example, children's writing. Why weren't they developing? What were we not doing? Furthermore, it was hard to believe that formal language/grammar lessons would solve the problem when, in those students who had received them, they patently had not prevented it.

There are not many ESL teachers now who hold to the most rigid notions of teaching structures through repetition and through 'modelling' of a foreign language learning kind and who won't allow learners to move beyond the structures taught, or to 'find their own voice' (Levine, 1981), though there are a few. From within the specialist English as a second language field in this country, the work of June Derrick (Derrick, 1977) and Josie Levine and Hilary Hester (e.g., Schools Council, 1972–74), amongst others, helped broaden the thinking and practice of teachers of English as a second language. More recently, foreign language teachers in English schools have begun to move towards communicative competence as an objective of their pedagogy. In my experience, English as mother tongue teachers were frequently very slow to make the same kinds of move in the opposite direction.

Theories of Modelling

Modelling in ESL Teaching: What does this Mean to English Mother Tongue Teachers?

I want now to look at the ideas of models and 'modelling' that ESL teachers have brought to the awareness of English teachers. If very inexperienced users of English are to be enabled to show what they know and can do in the classroom they will need help to find a way to say what they know and to understand what needs to be done. In, for example, certain kinds of class teaching, students are asked to be receivers of knowledge given by the teachers, and producers or written confirmations of their 'learning'. Josie Levine *et al.* (Schools Council, 1972–74; Levine and McLeod, 1975) have suggested ways in which, in classrooms like this, students with limited ability to produce written English may still show what they know if tasks are presented in ways that allow them to fill in blanks, complete sentences, choose from sentences, or answer questions that provide models of the structures they will need to use in their responses. Just this short list are examples of the sorts of awareness most of us mainstream English teachers have lacked in the questions we have asked and the tasks we have set for learners of English as a second language in ordinary classrooms.

It seems to me that Asha, who produced the following in answer to test questions on a series of lessons in her Child Care option, might have been better able to show to her teacher her knowledge, and also the places where she had distorted or misunderstood the learning inputs, had she had the support of some of the strategies I have just mentioned — had she had models of the structures she needed to 'do' these questions. In the process, she would have been improving her competence in the use of English orthography and would have been able to see how to use the structures she already had in her head from listening to her teacher.

> Some mothers bune [burn?] thir Child because Thay donat whant and they purr [prefer?] to be with their friends other then looking their Child Thay wish Thay did not have the Child so they bune them and put them in a hot. bath head first and schar them . . .

> The creket word for a miscarig [miscarriage] is a vasen [abortion] (The lost of a pregnancey befer the baby is abell to siave [survive] on it's own that is before the 28 week . . .

It is clear that the writer has understood the lesson very well in some respects, but with distortion and probable change of emphasis from her teacher's intentions in others — a manifestation of all students' learning.

In English lessons, when students are working on the comprehension of texts, we already know that sensitive questioning can lead them to the heart of the text. It is clear that we could learn to write questions in such a way that our students would be given the necessary support to code their answers to the questions. Within this sort of task, too, we should be able to ensure that some systematic work on new structures was being done in the mainstream English lesson.

For all these cases, though, Levine and McLeod (1975) writing for audiences of mainstream English teachers in secondary schools, remind us of the power of talking before they write for developing and structuring the writing of students for whom English is not a first language. This is just as well for subject English teachers who work in the developmental frame since it does not take long, without it, for demands to structure everything to seem very restricting. I suppose that talking with other children in linguistically mixed groups in mixed ability classes might also be something to which we could stretch the meaning of the word 'modelling', but, as an English teacher, I would prefer to see it in terms of individuals within the group exploring and sharing their personal construing of the task. Very often, this sort of talk work tells the inexperienced users of English what it is that represents the performance of the task. Perhaps that is a model, after all; whatever it is called, though, it provides necessary support for learners who are needing to take on new knowledge, through the medium of a language in which they have as yet little experience, and in ways with which they are unfamiliar.

Voice and Text: Students and their Teachers

I want now to look at the work of a particular boy and how a chance event led to an eventual shift, both in his competence and our understanding, and thereby to the development of a strategy for helping other students in similar situations make the move into writing using the cadences of English.

Kwok Ken was shy, reliable and persevering, a Ha'ka speaker — at the time the only one in school — able, however, to communicate with Cantonese speakers. (Does he say he is a Cantonese speaker in the first line of the piece quoted below in deference to the ignorance of teachers about Chinese dialects, or does his first sentence mean that he regards himself as bidialectal in Chinese; the word 'Chinese' standing for Ha'ka, the word 'Cantonese' referring to his second dialect?)

This piece of work from the beginning of his Sixth Form year is painstakingly written, and exhibits the hallmarks of Kwok's writing till then: the lack of flow, and an apparent lack of much ability to hear the rhythms of English in his head.

> My languages is Chinese or Cantonese. When I met a English Friend,
> I had to spoke some English to him or her. I feel that I was someone
> else because I had to keep thinking of words to speak to him or her.
> When I was at home or meeting some Chinese Friends, I felt
> that I was myself once again because I didn't need to think the things
> I said, they seem just came to my mouth when I was speaking. When
> I speak English in the telephone I just didn't know what to said say to
> the other person and I have *to thinks and spoke* very carefully,
> otherwise *he or she wouldn't just didn't know* what was I saying.
> When I was speaking Cantonese someone in the telephone, I was felt
> free that I didn't have any problem of speaking it. I thought because
> I was brought up that way and Chinese was my Language [my italics].

When Kwok writes it feels to me as though he is continuously building up each structure from the few rules that he knows, but is often elaborating, almost at will, upon those rules because he knows English is often complex. He can even often identify where a puzzlingly difficult structure should come (especially one attached to a verb: look at the double infinitive 'to thinks and spoke' or the negative subjunctive 'he or she wouldn't just didn't know'[1], but he has no way of coping with the difficulty because he does not yet seem to hear alternative voices.

His teacher decided to do some work with her Sixth Form group who were retaking CSE that was closely parallel to her work with the First Year. She was retelling and reading stories from mythology, especially Greek mythology, to her First Years, and had seen how the younger children seemed to be able to express the explanatory power of the myths in symbolic terms but be unable to do the same in words. She wondered what would happen if the Sixth Form were to 'look back' on the kind of work they may have done in their First Year (although many of them, like Kwok, would not have done it since, at that age, they were still in their countries of origin). She told myths to her Sixth Form group and was excited by the reponse she got when she and the students talked about the structure of myth on a comparative basis. Then she showed me work by Kwok of which this is the first page.

English   K. Ken

Daedalus

Daedalus was a clever magician and
a clever inventer of things that
nobody had seen before.
He lived in Athens, Daedalus had a
nephew called Talus, his nephew
Talus was a very clever man and
skillful at making things with his
hand. Daedalus knew Talus had great

ability, so he told him to be
his apprentice.

When he was Daedalus apprentience, he
soon showed his ability and cleverness
and had overtaken Daedalus in
inventing new kinds of things, Daedalus
was jealous of this, he thought to
himself that he was the most clevererent
inventer, and the cleverness inventer only
needed one and no second one, so he
plan to get rid of his nephew Talus.
It was a day of sightseeing in
Athens. Daedalus took Talus to see
the great sights of Athens, he took
him to the stop of the highest
temple and pointed to Talus from . . .

This piece of writing was done a few months after the last. It is the beginning of a recounting of the myth that lasts for five sides, and while there are errors, some very similar to those in the first piece, there has been a dramatic transformation in Kwok's writing. How? It seems obvious now that his teacher's voice, her intonation patterns, rhythms and phrasings has got into his head and stayed there. There seems also a sudden awareness of the shape of a story in English. Most astonishing of all, it seems, once he has got the music of English inside his head a lot of other knots in his writing are released.

There really do seen to be some clues here about how, as English teachers, we can tackle 'frozen competence'. Surely, we need to read and tell stories more to our older pupils inexperienced in using written, 'book' English. How, indeed, other than that we can expect them to internalize the tunes of English prose, and if that can play a part, too, in releasing the grammar, then we should need to think twice about it. Kwok has been able to use his teacher's voice as she tells stories as a model for his writing in ways in which he could not use written prose. But to be able to make use of this new power, it needed to come to him in conjunction with work that dealt at a wholly conscious surface level with the tangled verbs that Kwok knew were wrong, but had no means of his own to put right.

When his English teacher talked to Kwok about the improvement in his narrative writing (not so obvious in his answers to comprehension questions yet) and analyzed what she thought had happened, he agreed, saying, 'It's been in my head a long time but nobody gave me what to do to let it out'. He followed this up by pointing out that his History teacher had done a lot of work with him over time in helping him to form verbs in English correctly. Finally, I believe that in telling Kwok stories which profoundly symbolize human experience but entirely at the level of story, his teacher had enabled him, perhaps for the first time, to see how English story writing/telling works. There is narrative strength, shape and feeling in his writing here that his work had never shown before.

Writing and 'the Theory of the Practice of Reading'

Nancy Martin (Martin, 1976) went some ways towards exploring the power the theory of modelling might have in explaining the processes by which native speakers of a language come to differentiate writing into many kinds of verbal structures, in both 'poetic' and 'transanctional' modes. But for hints of the real power of this process, at least at the 'poetic' end of the writing spectrum, we need to go to the literary critics (e.g., Iser, 1974; Josipovici, 1976; Barthes, 1976) who base their work in 'the theory of the practice of reading'. We have, so far as I know, no elaborated exploration of the ways in which reading shapes and transforms experience and of how the two together fuse into a newly created 'hypothetical verbal structure'. Such knowledge is vitally needed. However, we do know that students express their knowledge and understanding of the genre and conventions of the stories they know through their own fictions. In the business of helping students learning to use English as a second language, in asking them to construct their own fictions, greater knowledge about how this modelling occurs would help us to be much more conscious of the gaps that we teachers have to fill in.

It seems to me that 'modelling' of this kind works at many different levels from surface to deep, and with various kinds of models. For example, another way to help students learning English as a second language take on some of the patterns of English is to use the repetition and rhythm of certain kinds of verse. Such imitative writing is recommended and examples offered in *Scope, Stage 2* (Schools Council, 1972–74, *Teachers' Book*, p. 27). Maurice Oliphant (Oliphant, 1979) has written a collection of pieces for this purpose, many of which have feeling and awareness that tug down to levels beneath the verbal surface, but that can still perform the same structural functions.

Polite request

I've been in London
since last May.
But today I think I've
lost my way.

Excuse me, could you
tell me where
I catch the bus for
Euston Square?
I'm very sorry my
little mate
I'm in a hurry and
terribly late

Excuse me could you
tell me where . . .

Prakash Hindocha, a secondary school student, wrote an (unpublished) collection of poems with a very gifted Special Needs teacher in a small group situation. I do not know what his model was for this poem, nor even whether he consciously had one.

Hate

They slammed the
door in my face
They hate me.
Do I care?
What shall I do?
Their hate stings
Like nails in my skin

There are many examples. At the time of writing, in the ILEA Language Centre in Hackney a boy, newly arrived from Morocco, had found in Mohammed Elbaja's story *My life* (Elbaja, 1979), a model on which he could graft his own tale. Both boys had had the experience of being left behind when their parents came to this country to explore the possibility of getting work here. They write about this pain, and then of the pain of being torn from their known world when their parents return to bring them to London. In Majoub Laamine's (unpublished) story, he stays in many ways so close to the original that it is hard to tell whether he is using it to tell his own story, or to take into himself an idea of what a story is in English, or, of course, both. They are both, however, potent tales in which the potential of the creative possibilities of autobiography are movingly demonstrated.

A great many English teachers could give testimony to the power of this sort of modelling from their work with native speakers of English; my point is that we do not yet fully understand how powerful it may be in helping learners of English as a second language take on reading and writing in English. Nor do we know just how important hearing as well as seeing stories is for these students, but it looks to be vital.

One last example, Jilu Miah chose a story starter 'When I looked down the well . . . ' to tell a story whose origin may belong directly, but certainly belongs indirectly, to a story telling tradition of his community's culture, and perhaps a little to English story telling traditions, too.

One upon a time there was a boy called Mustafa he lived in a village
he had little brother and sister. He used to look after cows and sheep.
He goes out with cows and sheep every day on the fields near the field
there was a Jungle the Robber used to hid in the Jungle.

> When his birth day came his father asked their friends to come . . . [because his daughter couldn't come] the father put sweets into a silver box for the children he gave it to his son Mustafa. His daughter's house was on the other side of the Jungle . . .

In the course of his journey, Mustafa is, of course, attacked by robbers, but drops the silver box into the well, and, sending the robber down after it, succeeds in trapping him.

Voice and Text: Work and Social Life

Nothing I have said so far would suggest any reason why a mixed ability setting should be better for their language development of school students like Kwok than any other. However, there are some profound reasons: a range of work takes place in mixed ability classes; students learning to use English as a second language are not isolated with their writing problems, but can ask for help from their neighbours at any time. For me, though, one of the most important things about people working together in linguistically mixed small group situations is that language learning for the as yet inexperienced user of English is going on all the time in a whole range of conversations about work, but in many social conversations, too. Here is a fragment for a video I have of a Fifth Year class.

Two girls at the table where Serpil is sitting — they are working separately from the main group — call me over to ask a question that arose from the poem they are reading together, 'she being brand new' by e.e. cummings. The question they ask is about orgasm. I prevaricate, and then explain. As I move away from the group, the girls I had talked to laughingly threaten me with blackmail. The rest of the group, of whom Serpil was one, and who had, of course, been listening, too, joined in the 'threats'. Serpil, prevented by experience and cultural taboo, rather than language itself, from active participation in this kind of conversation, found the relevance of what was being said in the context, and then joined in the laughter and picked up the cry of 'Blackmail!'.

Later, it became obvious that Serpil's written work was 'stuck'. She had, by then, been in England (from Turkey) about three and a half years. After a conversation with the very supportive group of girls she sat with — ('You mean if we were having to do this work in Turkish, we'd be having the same trouble? Say no more, miss, we understand') — they talked through with her the demands of work in English as it was set. They also undertook systematically to talk through Serpil's work before she started and to read it in progress and afterwards. Her work made distinct and recognizable progress. She began to talk to me, too, in more specific ways about her work. It was as if she could now see the wood for the trees.

Endword

Not all students, for reasons of their own temperament and that of others around them, or because of the structure of the class they are assigned to when they arrive in the school, find their way so easily into groups that aid their language learning. It is one of the demanding tasks of mixed ability teaching to try to ensure that they do find support groups. Most children will aid the learning process of those learning English as a second language much more adequately if they are taken into the teacher's confidence about the need for their help and about what forms it might take.

Clearly, mixed ability English teachers have already set up learning situations that can work extraordinarily well for people learning English as a second language. It works because some of the work they do gives these learners vital opportunities to use English for learning, for organizing and exploring their experience, and for construing the world. But we still have much to learn about the ways in which we can support learners, both inexperienced and advanced, within this developmental environment, in their progress towards equal facility bilingualism.

Notes

1. [*Editor's note*] An alternative reading is also possible. Kwok might have smoothed over in the writing, or his teacher smoothed over in the reading of his work, what might in fact be two (but unedited) attempts at expressing his meaning. That is, he could have been going for 'otherwise he or she wouldn't know what I was saying', got as far as 'wouldn't', and then had an idea about expressing it differently, perhaps more emphatically. 'Just didn't' might serve nicely for that and result, after editing, in 'otherwise he or she just didn't know what I was saying'. However, without the editing, we are left with ther original complex sentence ' . . . wouldn't just didn't know . . . ' and an interesting insight into process.

5
The Move from Withdrawal ESL Teaching to Mainstream Activities is Necessary, Possible and Worthwhile

Ann Burgess and Leon Gore

In 'The Move from Withdrawal ESL Teaching to Mainstream Activities is Necessary, Possible and Worthwhile', Burgess and Gore describe the withdrawal conditions that existed and created their decision, as ESL teacher and mainstream, mixed ability English teacher, to team teach, or partnership teach, in the mainstream. In this case study, they set out the stages they moved through to arrive both at their equal responsibility partnership teaching and also their well planned working groups for the students. Their purpose was to give all students access, in varied settings, to pupil-pupil talk, to pupil-teacher talk, and to the learning processes they wished all the students in the mainstream class to experience. Through joint reflection and discussion of their evolving practice they arrive at an antiracist, collaborative teaching and learning pedagogy in which the skills of the ESL teacher and the mainstream teacher are marshalled to enable all students to be supported through doing the same work, i.e., the same work in terms of content and in terms of the opportunity such work provides for interactive classroom communication, but supported appropriately for their differing needs. In this sense, the concept of 'mixed ability' is inherent to successful mainstreaming.

Background

We have consistently argued in the past (e.g. in DES, 1985, pp. 434–5; and Burgess and Gore, 1985) that students learning English as a second language should be in mainstream classes rather than the situation we have more commonly encountered where they are withdrawn to be taught away from the general run of mainstream activities. This more common situation has not only institutionalized them into failure but has also compounded any differences between them and other members of the school community. Divisions within our multicultural society are thus hardened. Furthermore, on educational grounds, separation of developing bilingual students from the curriculum followed by all the other students cannot be theoretically justified since, in practice, it leads to both their curriculum and social learning being impoverished and, thus, both linguistic and intellectual development is hindered. It also means that the burden of joining in is always placed on the newcomers and never on those already established in the mainstream. It is not enough, however, to put students developing a use of English as a second language into mainstream classes in the hope that they will 'swim'. They will need support, and that support must be of the right kind — otherwise, even in the mainstream classes, the worst features of their previous separation can be exacerbated. For example, though they may be in the mainstream classroom they could still remain a very separate group. Their sense of failure could increase with incomprehension of work set, and their inability to cope with the tasks set can feed other students' views of them as being of low status within the group. In consequence, though we are advocating that they should be in mainstream groups, it can only be a successful move if strategies to counteract these problems are developed.

The arguments we make here are based on personal experience, first as a specialist ESL teacher and a mainstream English teacher, and then in joint teaching of mainstream English lessons where students developing a use of English as a second language are included in the mixed ability English class. We look at bilingual students' own strategies for English language learning elsewhere in this volume (see pp. 104–20).

Here we concentrate on why we engaged in this particular action research in curriculum development, and describe the steps we took to implement antiracist teaching strategies.

The Development of ESL Work in a Boys' Secondary School[1]

Before February 1980, the ESL teaching practice in the school was typical of standard practice: withdrawal for English language lessons where the focus was on the teaching of structures. Bilingual students inexperienced in the use of English were considered the responsibility of the ESL Department, and their admission to mainstream subjects was held back until such a time as they were judged to have attained a 'satisfactory' level of English. Assessment in the first place was made by the ESL teachers, but because 'satisfactory' is a shifting, relative description of achievement, this initial assessment was often overruled by subject teachers. No matter how 'successful' a student had been in the withdrawal class, he could be judged never to have reached a satsifactory level merely by upward changing of the criteria. The effect of this worrying situation was that boys could leave school with an inadequate educational experience and attainment, a low level of language achievement in English, and, furthermore, without the experience of positive interaction with their peers from other groups.

In January 1976, when I first began teaching English as a second language at the school, there were already present a large number of older students from language backgrounds other than English and who had little spoken English. As I have previously said, any boy with little or no spoken English accepted by the school was considered the responsibility of the ESL department which, at that time, consisted of a head of department, a teacher from the remedial department, and myself who was attached to the school from what was then the borough Language Centre. Except where we could make arrangements with PE and Craft teachers, 'our' students remained full-time with ESL teachers. At that time, teachers in the school, both ESL and subject teachers, felt that such students could not usefully participate in the ordinary classroom until they had sufficient knowledge of English.

Many of the students were 15 or 16 years of age and had little chance of learning English quickly enough or to a sufficiently high standard to participate in CSE and O level classes. We, the ESL teachers, had, therefore, to provide them with classes which not only developed their use of English but also attempted to provide them with some kind of general education. So it was that teachers and pupils laboured at basic Geography, Maths, Science, Careers and Social Studies.

Their lack of participation in the full academic life of the school was reflected in social groupings. Our students did not mix with other groups in the school — neither peer group nor ethnic group. They were isolated from normal school life. Such worrying problems, we realized, would have to be overcome, especially when, at that time, even new arrivals into the Third Year could not automatically expect to reach full integration into class by the time they left school.

The first step we took to enable newly arrived students to have some experience of mainstream classes was to 'feed' them into PE, Craft and Maths lessons. Another move was to set up Craft and Science groups, taught by mainstream teachers, but for ESL pupils only and accompanied by their ESL teacher. Specific topics, vocabulary and structure were prepared with the pupils beforehand and the content was 'reinforced' afterwards. None of us felt this to be a particularly successful experiment: the pace of the lesson was extremely slow, a great deal of time was taken up in withdrawal classes either preparing pupils for a topic or going over it afterwards, and both conceptually and linguistically nothing much seemed to happen.

In the meantime, the ESL teachers took up subject syllabi and text books in order to teach pupils the language structures and specialized vocabulary of particular subjects in the hope that this would prepare students better for admission to these classes. We had set ourselves an impossible task: teaching the language and concepts of several subjects, when we, the teachers, had not always enough knowledge of the subjects or experience of how they were taught or what was expected of the pupils. Furthermore, and quite naturally, what teachers said they would do in lessons was not necessarily what did happen in any particular lesson. In reality, all that was achieved was that we allayed some of our students' fears about going into mainstream classes by putting in their way a little bit of English and a little bit of school knowledge.

When students went into subject classes, left to sink or swim, unfortunately many of them seemed to sink: teachers complained that they were extremely withdrawn, did not seem to understand what was expected of them, and could not cope with the work. It has to be said that at this time subject teachers were reluctant to have learners of English as a second language in their classes. How could students possibly learn Science and Maths, etc. before they had learned English? It didn't seem to make sense, and they appeared confirmed in this view when the students they received, so unfamiliar with ordinary classrooms, silent, awed, were so obviously at a loss. Such students were obviously the ESL teachers' responsibility until such a time as they knew English well enough to take part in subject lessons. What other view could there be?

It was a puzzling business, for it seemed that there was no way in which the students could be prepared. ESL teachers were seeing them in withdrawal classes, were using these lessons for support work for subjects, and the students could understand the work, it seemed, in the small group situation. Yet in the large mainstream class they seemed to lose all confidence in their own abilities. We had to ask ourselves if we had been over-protecting them from the 'rough and tumble' of school life, and importantly, too, from the language of the classroom.

When we looked at what we had been doing, we saw that we had been trying to 'feed' pupils into subjects which had a well defined content — Geography or Science, for example — because as teachers untrained in these subjects we could grasp a topic or analyze the vocabulary and language structures involved. It was easier for us to deal with photosynthesis or glaciation. We avoided sending students into mainstream English for two reasons. We didn't really know what went on in the classes, and on the basis of this lack of information, we reasoned that the language demands of a CSE/O level Mother Tongue English course must of necessity be beyond the English language capabilities of our students, and that being the case, we didn't want them further demoralized. When pupils reached the Fourth Year, therefore, and had to choose four options, students who had not yet developed a satis-factory use of English as a second language were directed to chose an Extra English option, basically a language/study skills course.

To provide some objective for the boys in this withdrawal group and also to try to make sure they had some examination qualification in English at the end of their school careers, we entered them for the Royal Society of Arts Stage 1 Examination in EFL (an exam oriented towards European teenagers). Then, becoming dissatisfied with low-level demands of the RSA exam, we attempted to run a CSE English course for the 'ESL' students, running parallel to, but not with, the mainstream English classes. Even with an inexperienced, nonspecialist teacher, the first group of boys passed the CSE, Mode 1 exam with Grades 4 and 5. Not brilliant, but at least a qualification.

I was finally convinced to take the step into the mainstream proper, when I looked at the work of some of my students who had joined the mainstream class from this CSE withdrawal class. More able and confident than the rest, they had been frustrated in the small withdrawal group and become troublesome. I had transferred them to mainstream English more to 'teach them a lesson' than in the expectation that they would cope. They did in fact do more than survive, and their use of English developed far beyond that of the boys who remained in the protection of the withdrawal groups. They were more confident, more articulate and were undoubtedly using structures and vocabulary which had not been formally taught to them by their teachers. I talked with their mainstream English teacher about these phenomena, differences in quality which could not be put down to ability alone, and we made the decision to team-teach one of the mainstream English classes and to include in it students still inexperienced in using English as a second language. We argued that the greater range of language that they would be exposed to would enable them to bring their natural learning abilities to bear on the situation, and that this — combined with the fact that the tasks set would present a greater intellectual challenge than the pre-selected language structures (hard to internalize because not learned in use) — would, through the struggle for language, create a dynamic learning environment. In addition, we hoped for greater social integration, for an increase in confidence in the bilingual students' approach to school work, and that they would come to view themselves generally in a better light.

We began our experiment in March 1980, and it was with some trepidation that I brought 'my' group of pupils into that class. Although I had been in the school for four years by now, I had always taught small withdrawal groups and had never taught a full mixed ability class — somewhat ironic as this was the situation I was working to push the 'ESL' students into, and yet I had no experience of it myself!

Initially, I felt I could only accept responsibility for 'my' pupils, sitting with them separately and letting the English teacher carry on as before, initiating the work and taking responsibility for the day-to-day assessment of all the pupils. Although this was quite literally the simplest way for us to begin — simplest, that is, for both teacher and pupils unfamiliar with the mixed ability, mainstream class — it certainly wasn't simple or fair to the mainstream teacher who now had to organize the work of another teacher as well as all the pupils in the class. However, this was not the only reason we needed to move away from this organization. I was obviously in a subordinate role, one which signalled very clearly to all the members of the class that I was the lesser of the two teachers. That, combined with the fact that the 'weaker' of the two teachers looked after the children most at risk, the 'weaker' children in the class, simply served to underline the separateness of the bilingual students. That kind of joint teaching went against everything we were hoping to achieve in that it reinforced differences and hardened attitudes towards students for whom English is not a first language. The specialist language teacher had to be seen as equal to the mainstream teacher by the pupils within the classroom.

Talk, Collaboration, Interaction and Mixed Ability Grouping[1]

Working from the hypotheses put forward, we concluded that we should attempt to integrate ESL pupils into mainstream English classes, and bring about a situation where the pupils

1. would have to cope with the language demands of a mixed ability classroom;
2. would be exposed to a range of experienced English speakers; and
3. would not be so obviously apart from the rest of the school.

We decided to begin by integrating Fourth Year 'ESL' students into the mixed ability English class. The ESL teacher would be in the classroom supporting the pupils yet still maintain support lessons as one of their options (two double lessons weekly).

The ESL teacher brought three students into my class in March 1980. There were already within this class at least three boys who were also experiencing a range of difficulties which overlapped considerably with those experienced by the three newer entrants to the class — an indication of the arbitrary way students have been selected as being in particular need of withdrawal for English.

Though we teachers spent time together planning lessons before beginning the experiment we did not realize how many were the implications for practice of our hypotheses; nor did we foresee various problem areas which were present, themselves problems which pushed us immediately into taking our thinking further, recasting our ideas more clearly. These problem areas emerged in the form of the following linked questions:

1. What are the respective roles and responsibilities of subject teacher and ESL teacher in the classroom?
2. How do we ensure that a range of language experience is made available within the classroom to students developing a use of English as a second language?
3. How do we avoid segregation of students within the classroom?
4. What are the best means of providing support for them in this new, socially and academically threatening situation?

Consider the first of these: there is the obvious temptation for the subject teachers to continue practically as before, initiating work, taking responsibility for day-to-day progress and assessment of the students and leaving the ESL teacher to follow the subject teacher's lead somehow, or sit separately in one corner of the room with 'her' students, helping them to cope with the tasks set. This was our temptation at first, and not only on the ESL teacher's part. It was mine, too. Teaching styles of some classroom teachers have tended to be so insular that the incursion into the classroom of even a trusted colleague can be very intimidating. There are natural anxieties for teachers in allowing their pedagogy to come under constant scrutiny. The move to integrate students learning English as a second language into the mainstream is threatening, and not only to them and the ESL teacher. However, a serious consequence of these differing role relationships was that of undermining the ESL teacher's credibility in the eyes of the pupils. In addition, the isolation of ESL students in relation to mainstream pupils was further underlined by being made more visible.

We felt it important, therefore, to work towards establishing a way of collaborating successful enough to act as an example to all the pupils and which would be one that helped the integration of the newcomers within the class. It was our view that the best arrangement would be one of equality of status between us in the classroom. We attempted, therefore, to make our roles, in relation to *all* the pupils, interchangeable. Thus, while one of us had to assume the new and, hence, daunting role of mixed ability English teacher, I — through paying particular attention to the demands of the bilingual learners — was soon made painfully aware of how inadequately I had been presenting materials to many pupils for whom English was *the mother tongue*.

Significant in enabling us to function as equals was joint planning of lessons. Indeed, once there was equal responsibility for preparation, presentation of lessons *and* marking, we welcomed criticisms and evaluations of our individual professionalism. We were benefiting from the other's strengths.

The concern we had for each other to feel comfortable in the classroom was significant, too, for this led us to paying attention to the development of strategies which maximize the use of the two teachers — good enough reason in itself for giving an appreciable amount of time in class to various kinds of group work and collaborative learning. The bonus was that we found that group work facilitated the interchanging of roles between the two of us.

The topic of group work leads me to the second of our questions. Having argued that learners of English as a second language needed exposure to a greater, richer variety of the English language if they were to learn to use it effectively, it was necessary to organize the class so that this wealth of language experience was available to them to hear, and then to use. Learning through talk had, therefore, an obvious and significant part to play in class activities if ESL students were going to be able to interact in the learning process with native and other more experienced users of English. So we had further argument for the frequent use of group work. We worked with the group sometimes as teachers, sometimes as consultants, sometimes as questioning audience. In this way we were able to give all pupils access to both pupil–teacher talk, in varied settings, and pupil–pupil talk.

Even so, the use of group work did not of itself lead to satisfactory integration. When we came to evaluate the first term of our team-teaching in relation to our third question, we found ourselves pleased with the way the students developing a use of English had adjusted to new academic demands, but felt ambivalent about the nature of the integration that had occurred. It would be true to say that integration had been made more difficult than it might have been by virtue of the fact that the decision to mainstream was made in the middle of the academic year. It would be equally true to say that both of us in this early phase of the experiment had too easily accepted the friendship patterns and group dynamics that had already developed in the class. We had made no real attempt to restructure the class to create different viable working groups. A major reason for this 'inactivity' was a fortuitous development that had occurred in the class. An experienced speaker of English, bilingual himself with German and English, had befriended the less experienced bilingual learners and had helped them with their work. He led discussion and tended to direct the group when they were working on a joint project. Thus, although some degree of integration had been achieved, it had come about by 'accident': this happy accident had prevented us from seeing that far greater intervention would be necessary if we were to fulfil our aims. Fortunately for our pedagogy we were able to explore this more fully when we extended our collaboration to a new Fourth Year class the following year — a class which turned out to have no such fortuitous group interaction.

Our fourth immediate worry, developing strategies to help the learners of English as a second language cope with the work, cannot be completely separated from our other three concerns. We had concluded that it would be counter-productive to give them separate, 'easier' work. To do so would be to reinforce rather than break down the disparaging views other pupils had of their intelligence. Additionally, low-level work and the derogatory opinions of other learners around them would serve to limit the students' own expectations of themselves. Yet, if there was to be no 'special' work, care had to be taken to make tasks accessible. We would have to take meticulous pains, for example, with the language we used in any spoken or written instructions. As for the literature we studied, we did not rewrite parts, but instead we were careful to anticipate difficulties. Indeed, the ESL teacher's experience enabled her to foresee potential language problems for more pupils than just those who had once been 'hers'. Forewarned, we were able to take earlier action to clear up misunderstandings that occurred among pupils.

Another strategy we used, particularly during the early period of the newcomers' time in the mainstream class, was for one teacher to spend time talking through with them what was required, particularly with a written task, and to help them with the introduction. Additionally, other pupils' responses to the work set, and sometimes even teachers' responses, were used as models for guidance. Collaborative tasks were also set which encouraged support from other pupils, for example, making radio broadcasts, and constructing inter- views. There would, too, be small group discussions at particular points of a novel the class was reading to reflect on events, characters, and to speculate and hypothesize on future developments.

These ways of working gradually emerged as we discussed and evaluated our lessons, our aim being constantly to give as much access as possible to students learning to use English as a second language to the learning processes available generally to all the other students in the class. It was natural enough, too, that we should have a further concern in addition to the four already discussed: it was whether or not focusing on difficulties experienced by our developing bilingual students would impair the education of others in mixed ability classes. It is a common concern. We can report with delight a paradoxical (if that is the way one chooses to see it) conclusion. The other students after a while revealed a greater degree of useful tentativeness and were more able to show where they felt less confident than before. They began to demand similar help to that given to ESL learners. Was this a signifier of the sought for equalling out of status? Were they coming to perceive the usefulness of the more structured help their colleagues was getting? Certainly, they recognized that more teacher time was available to them as individuals or as groups. That is to say that contrary to common sense expectation, the advent of ESL teacher and bilingual pupils into our mainstream classroom led to other pupils receiving more help, not less. This became even more the case once those learning English as a second language grew in confidence and experience and felt able to consult other pupils. It was important and reassuring to discover that attempts to improve teaching strategies for bilingual students could lead to better teaching for all.

The Further Development of an Antiracist Pedagogy

We were sufficiently encouraged to continue the experiment into the following academic year, continuing with the same class into the Fifth Year, and also starting afresh with a new Fourth Year class. This new mixed ability English class was made up of pupils from all the Third Year classes so the ESL students did not begin as 'newcomers' in an already formed group. Also, since relationships were unlikely at first to be well defined, we thought there was a good chance to create the interrelationships and milieu which could give them maximum help. There were two very inexperienced users of English in the class, and two others in the group in need of considerable support. Before the collaboration between the English and ESL departments, certainly three, if not all four, boys would not have been in an English mainstream class in the school. The class was small, only eighteen pupils — a chance of timetabling had made available to the Fourth Year an extra teacher of English, although a cut in teachers at the school the following year had the effect of increasing the class size to twenty-two pupils. Nevertheless, such a favourable class size was of obvious help to us in attempting new initiatives. The class was very much a multi-ethnic group. The parents of the pupils had emigrated from many parts of the world: Jamaica, Guyana, Kenya, Uganda, Nigeria, India, Hong Kong, Cyprus, Greece and the Republic of Ireland. A few parents had come to London from other parts of Britain. Kantilal Parbat, one of the most inexperienced users of English in the class, was a Gujarati speaker from Kenya, but he had arrived in England via India. At the time we are speaking of, he had been in England about eighteen months. On arrival he had spoken and understood very little English and could not write it. He had been placed in a Second Year form and had gone to the language centre every afternoon. In the mornings, in school, he had been withdrawn from all subjects except Maths, PE and Woodwork. He was an extremely shy, quiet boy.

Yogesh Patel, the other very inexperienced user of English in the class, had arrived from India only eleven months before. He had no spoken English and, not surprisingly, scored nil on the NFER tests used at the language centre. His first language is Gujarati, and he, too, was an extremely quiet, passive boy. Like Kantilal, he spent some time at the language centre but was similarly withdrawn from it by the school not because he had sufficient competence in English but so that he could experience a variety of subjects in the Third Year, prior to choosing options for Fourth and Fifth Years.

As Third Years in the withdrawal lessons, Kantilal and Yogesh had said little; and in the very early stages in the Fourth Year they were almost completely silent, and totally dependent on each other in the face of this new, intimidating experience. We recognized their strong mutual need, and anxious for Kantilal and Yogesh to feel comfortable, made no attempt initially to interfere with it. Nevertheless, we wanted them integrated into the class. We simply did not know how to make this come about.

At first we let friendship patterns influence the composition of small groups and pair work. Our main concern, at that time, was that there should not be any informal streaming within the class. Fortunately the friendship patterns in this particular class did not make it difficult for us to ensure a reasonable spread of ability in groups. However, it was not long before we were forced to recognize that the combinations of pairs within the groups and the resulting dynamics of the membership tended to be destructive of, rather than conducive to, work. Equally serious was the attitude towards Kantilal and Yogesh. No group wanted to work with them. They were perceived as having nothing to contribute, neither to the work in hand nor to constructing the social dynamics of the class: jokes, comments, teasing, etc. One student referred to them as 'planks' and this seemed to represent the general view. Also very worrying were the racist implications of some of the remarks made about Kantilal and Yogesh.

Yet again we had to appraise the situation in relation to out beliefs. We both thought it important to persevere with group work. Talk, we felt certain, was going to be the key to any success we might eventually be able to claim. Talk means interaction and seeking towards collaboration. Further it was becoming increasingly obvious that this mode of working, of collaborative learning, should be a mode and an attitude of mind that should permeate not only pupil–pupil interactions, but also those between teacher and pupils, teacher and pupil, and teacher and teacher. We ourselves were benefiting considerably from a collaborative approach in relation to the development of our classroom practice. So what remedial action could we take that retained group work as a strategy?

We thought that a major cause vitiating a good working atmosphere in the groups was the existence of several very strong friendship pairs within the class — useful when the boys were working in pairs, but within groups the bonds between friends seemed to lead to the exclusion of other participants. Sometimes, we thought, this was deliberate, but often it was simply the effect of strong bond pairs being able to take so much for granted that there was little need to be explicit, since the other members of the group, often being weaker than the bonded pair, left what they said unchallenged. We still had the problem, too, of how to ensure that Kantilal and Yogesh were given the opportunity to interact with others in the class so that they might no longer be seen by other pupils as peripheral to the class activities, and so that they might no longer be so dependent on each other.

We concluded that it would be worth the risk of rearranging groups and separating friendship pairs. Our hope was that Kantilal and Yogesh, seeing other pairs parted, would more readily accept their own separation. We decided to aim for ideal combinations. As far as possible, groups would be of mixed ability, mixed experience, mixed first and second language users of English and, crucially, multi-ethnic — this last because we felt this would contribute significantly to breaking down prejudice and suspicion between some of the ethnic groups in the class, and especially that directed at Kantilal and Yogesh. We had to take care, though, to avoid combinations which included 'personality clashes'. Not surprisingly there was some resistance when the students learned that they would no longer be allowed to negotiate their own groupings. But we were determined, and the boys saw that we were. One student asked why they could not any longer choose their own groups. We told them we were unhappy with the way the groups had been functioning, and we told them why we were unhappy. We were quite surprised that, despite objections, the boys did agree to work in our groups. Perhaps that could be said to be due to the obvious justice of our case, but it was just as likely due to the following factors: we were *two* very determined teachers, not one; our pupils had been taken by surprise; our relationship with the class had hitherto been reasonably good.

The new groups got on relatively quickly with their work, too. It appeared that some individuals, deprived of their close friend, felt too vulnerable to be aggressive, and were no longer in a position to exclude others from the collaborative tasks they were engaged on. As hoped, Kantilal and Yogesh soon began interacting with others. Furthermore, there was a greater increase of interactions between other members of the class. Following these first teacher-groupings, further experiments were carried out in the composition of groups.

Our intention was that every boy should have worked with most other boys at some time or other.

It was our perception, borne out by comments of various visitors to the class who noticed how prepared the boys were to help each other, that over time, our experiments really had helped improve the atmosphere in the class. Certainly, an increasingly recognizable feature was an increase in good relations between pupils, and, at least on the surface, of racial harmony. There was also a much better attitude towards work. These results are pleasing enough in themselves, but what happened to us as a direct result of taking these risks also needs to be recorded, and that is that we became more relaxed, more confident, and more trusting of the pupils. The fact is that the very strategies of openness, interaction and support for learning which we wanted to achieve for developing bilingual students are equally applicable to the rest of us — the rest of the mixed ability class *and* ourselves. They were unlooked for but critical benefits of what happened when we looked for ways of teaching bilingual learners: we have improved our teaching and learning processes to a point where we believe they can play a part not only in school learning but also in countering racism in education.

Note

1. The principal writer of the section 'The development of ESL work in a secondary Boys' School' is Ann Burgess. The principal writer of the section 'Talk, collaboration, interaction and mixed ability grouping' is Leon Gore. In the first section the pronoun 'I' refers to Ann Burgess; in the second section it refers to Leon Gore.

6
Bilingual Children and their Infant Schooling

Rita Brightmore and Margaret Ross

In 'Bilingual Children and their Infant Schooling', *Brightmore and Ross describe the evolution of a whole school policy to meet the changing population of their school. They build on their already established infant school practices of parent involvement and of active learning for the enhancement of learning, language and literacy development and extend that to English as a second language within a multilingual setting. The school's Family Book scheme is highlighted as is the whole school INSET programme on learning to read on real books. The children are accepted as competent communicators, and the value of children having access to all the learning resources of the school is emphasized. Particularly illuminating for the integration of learning and language development is the observation reported here that learning to read in English aids the development of talking in English, in the same way that spoken language aids learning to read.*

Background

The account which follows is of work developed with young bilingual children in an open plan nursery and infant school in Spitalfields, a part of east London which has been a primary area of immigration for at least three centuries. In the late 1970s, about a tenth of the children in our school were speaking a language other than English, mainly Sylheti, Urdu, Gujarati and Panjabi. Some of them were fluent speakers of English as well; a few entered the school knowing no English at all. Most of the classes in the school had thirty to thirty-five children in them, which meant that about three or four children in each class were learners of English as a second language. We felt that this number of learners of English as a second language was easy to accommodate and, as a consequence, suffered no feelings of anxiety about how best to teach our bilingual children. Later experience showed us how inappropriately complacent we had been; how we needed to have been much more aware of both the children's needs and the strengths they brought to school with them.

Spitalfields has been home to communities from many countries. The Huguenot Society recently planted mulberry trees in the school grounds to commemorate the tercentenary of their settlement in the district. In the recent past, the area has been predominantly Jewish and the school served kosher meals, but by 1976 most of the Jewish families had moved away and only a few Jewish children attended the school. Nevertheless, the school still served a relatively established, largely white, community. Other than that at this time, the community was fairly settled. Brothers and sisters followed each other into the school, with some parents, and even grandparents, having been former pupils.

Very suddenly a change came over the district. Spitalfields had been designated an area for redevelopment. Blocks of flats were emptied, families rehoused. We thought, because our school building was modern, that our school would remain to serve a wider geographical area while other, older, schools closed. Instead, a new community developed in our not yet reconstructed area. Men from India, Pakistan and Bangladesh had lived and worked in the clothing industry in the area for two or three decades, returning to their home countries to marry and have children, then coming back to England to work. Coinciding with the redevelopment plans were serious changes in the immigration laws, so the men began to bring their wives and children back to England with them for fear of being separated from each other for ever. It was the children of this immigration who started coming to our school. In one year, the number of pupils who spoke English as their second language, or who were about to learn to do so, increased from the previous constant 10 per cent to more than 90 per cent (76 per cent Sylheti; 12 per cent Urdu, Gujarati, Panjabi; 6 per cent Sindhi, Somali, Greek, Turkish, and French Creole together). English was the home language of 6 per cent of the children.

Recognizing the Need for Change and Making a Start

From feelings of security about our organization and teaching methods we became uncertain and insecure. We sought advice and help. The advice we received did not reassure us. On the one hand, we were told by some authorities in the subject that learners of English as a second language needed structured lessons and language drills to help them take on the new language effectively. On the other hand, we were told by others that young learners of an additional language only needed a stimulating environment and they would automatically become good speakers of English. The first view derived from the teaching of English as a foreign language to adults and the second from the idea that we are all natural language users with an inbuilt ability to acquire language.

Both of these views were disturbing to us in school. Teaching children in a narrowly structured way was against all our understanding and observation of the ways that young children learn — actively and needing to be involved in their own learning. The structured method suggested to us was a passive model of learning in which children had to take the instruction offered to them. The second view also challenged our view of how children learn. Certainly, they need a stimulating environment in and from which to learn, but we understood that to be only part of the necessary experience of children at school. We felt that they needed, too, to acquire skills and to develop cognitive structures in order to extend the knowledge they already had and to take on new learning.

In the event, we took ideas from both these opposing approaches, using what seemed to us at the time a sensible mixture of the two. The truth is that having some element of structured language lessons gave us teachers a feeling of security. We thought, too, that it might give us some means of measuring children's progress in learning English. In this last, though, we were wrong, since, as a tool for analysis, it caused us, temporarily, to focus on the failures of the children in relation to their learning English as a second language rather than on the ways they found to communicate and make meaning. Quite quickly, too, we began to see that children's linguistic and cognitive needs could not be met by such focused attention on language structure. Looking back, it had been naive of us to seek so simplistic a solution as the combining of two opposite methodologies. Yet the discovery that it was not the answer propelled us forward.

The question we asked ourselves was this: was it inevitable that even very young children learning to use English in school must begin their formal education handicapped on this account in comparison with those for whom English is a first language? Those who would say 'Yes' to this question might, given the numbers of children of Bengali background speaking Sylheti in the school, have come to the conclusion that the children of Bengali background, at least, should have their early education using their first language fully, changing to English as the language of instruction when they were older. We took a different view and so a different path.

We had always been keen to find ways of fostering children's learning and development and of observing their progress so that we could intervene and help at appropriate times. We were, at this time, too, focusing on the ways that the knowledge and abilities brought to school by monolingual English children could be built on and extended. Surely there was no reason why this basic tenet of education had to be suspended in relation to the infant schooling of bilingual children? We reminded ourselves that in our school, the focus was not on what children lacked but upon teaching and support for their development. So quite logically, our next step had to be to look for ways of extending these notions to the newcomers, to look for ways of extending children's bilingualism and of responding to the cultural diversity of the school.

Our first acts were small ones.

We looked at how children were received into school. The teachers made particular efforts to make sure that children knew where to put their coats, could find their way to the lavatories, knew their way about the school generally. A child, or a group of more experienced children, was asked to look after each newcomer, the teachers trying to find amongst the partners at least one who lived near and who shared the same language.

We tried to find ways for the children to use the school learning they already had. Many of the children who came to us had already had one or two years attendance at school in their country of origin.

It was now our aim to provide a supportive environment in which children knew that both their first and second languages were acceptable. Initially, there were no staff in the school who spoke any of the children's first languages. Our support and help at this stage came, therefore, from parents, older siblings, community workers and people from the local Adult Education Institute. All of these people supported us freely with translations, interpreting, home visits and, later, with tutors who worked in the school with children and parents.

We declared what ammounted to a school policy. After much thought and discussion, we took a decision, itself a statement of belief, that we would treat all children, whatever their home languages or their facility in using English, as having the same conceptual and developmental potential. We felt that if we established a multicultural, multilingual climate in the school, we ought to be able to offer the children at least the opportunity of learning English naturally, in the context of and parallel with their new school learning, free use of all their linguistic skills, and, importantly, the opportunity to learn together with everyone else in the school.

The confidence to take this step, the confidence not to allow the additional linguistic aspects of diversity in our classrooms to throw us off course in curriculum work, as it had until then been allowed to do, seems to have derived from what we already knew from monitoring children's learning in literacy — something we had begun to do for monolingual English speaking children and for fluent bilingual users of English. Nevertheless, although our purpose was based on previous experience, there were crucial differences between it and this new approach. These differences were that we intended to work both towards equality of use between English and the home languages of children in the classroom and to extend and develop community collaboration. We would continue our commitment to action research which we had in the past undertaken through INSET and by connections with more formal research programmes and we would draw on research and other relevant work as we developed our curriculum.

Making Links with the Community and Establishing a Multilingual Ethos in the School

We expected and encouraged children to use their home languages in school. We used books, tapes, alphabet charts and number tapes in a variety of languages. It should not any longer be necessary to argue the value of such action: children can be so much more at ease and so open to new learning; they are not forced to make completely separate lives for themselves, a home life and a school life, or feel that their home languages must be inferior; the community is not 'told' by the school that is has no place in it; children can also show early understanding about how languages work and their awareness helps the monolingual adults around them to develop broader understandings, too.

The school was open to parents. Children were free to arrive during the first period with their parents who could stay with them. This staggering of arrival times meant that teachers and parents had a chance of spending time with each other; the children had the opportunity to include their parents in some part of their school day and then take leave of them in an easy and relaxed manner.

Parents helped in school. Some of the parents who stayed in school helped by translating for the children and for other parents. Some told stories to the children and made story tapes in home languages.

Informal parties were held. As well as more formal occasions such as Open Days, there was a party each term for parents, teachers and children, the food being prepared by all the particpants, children included.

Support for home–school links. We also supported home–school links by making time available during the school day for teachers to visit children's homes. This was in addition to the many invitations and warm offers of hospitality by parents to teachers.

The good feelings and connections made through these activities are a considerable part of the background to the success of the family book scheme and to the positive use to which we have been able to put out INSET work for developing our teaching practice for multilingual classrooms, as the next two sections describe.

Family Book Scheme

We wanted to give the children every opportunity to enjoy books and to find them relevant to their own experiences and interests. This led us to make a number of books together with the children, using one, two or even three languages. Sometimes a book was made by one child and a teacher, sometimes by a class or even a small group of children. For illustrations we used photographs and the children's own drawings. The books were bound and used in the class libraries as well as the school library. The work interested parents and they encouraged their children. At times they were amazed at the quality of the books their children produced. They were real authors. The quality of the books was, too, a source of reassurance to some monolingual English parents concerned that the use of languages other than English in the school would be detrimental to the literacy development of their own children.

The books we were making, especially those using more than one language, became known to colleagues in other schools with whom we were sharing work through an INSET programme organized by the ILEA Centre for Language In Primary Education, and in the manner of networks, they were also seen by Heather Sutton, a researcher from the University of London Institute of Education Thomas Coram Research Unit who had been working on the Parent Involvement in Nursery Education Project and who, thereby, had been helping parents at a nursery school write simple books for their children. Because she was seeking ways for the work with parents to continue and we were keen to extend our own teacher–pupil book making, and because there was no doubt that we had interested parents, we suggested that the Adult Education Institute employ Heather Sutton for a day each week to work with parents. Happily, this was financially possible.

Before long, it was not just parents and teachers working on books. Whole families joined in to produce them: parents, sisters, brothers, aunts, uncles, children in the school all helped to write and illustrate the books. The parents who wrote the first books encouraged other parents to write books, too. The school provided paper, pens and instructions for layout in Bengali, Urdu and English. Families were invited to write in all the languages represented in the school. As soon as the first books were made, a parent workshop was set up in school to help reproduce the books in numbers so that they, like the books made by teachers and children alone, could be used as part of class and school libraries. A further function of the workshop was to encourage new writers in beginning their books. We explained that the books would be edited and that there need be no fear that spelling or other errors would be found in the versions published.

Some books were particularly relevant to the children's immediate environment. For example, one book had been written by a parent who had grown up in a block of flats in which many of the children now lived. The story was about the games that children had played near their home in Spitalfields and about a visit to the countryside that the author had made.

Many families of children in our school came from Bangladesh, and sometimes took their children back there on long visits. One book written by a parent about such a visit shared some of the experiences with us in school and helped to enlarge the knowledge of teachers, children and other parents. The book was first written in Bengali by the author and then translated into English by her.

Sometimes the books allowed a very personal communication between home and school. One such book was *Halima's Story*. Halima had needed treatment for one of her eyes. Her mother wrote the book about what happened to Halima and how the family had left Bangladesh and sought help at a London eye hospital. The book was written in Bengali and then translated into English and Urdu. Halima herself illustrated the story.

Although the family book scheme was time consuming and quite expensive for the school — authors needed supporting, translations needed to be arranged, the layout and duplication of books had to be arranged — the value to everyone connected to the school was immeasurable. A warmth and closeness was generated between everyone involved in their children's learning, and the school had a source — unobtainable elsewhere at the time — of books relevant to the children's interests and literacy levels in most of the languages used in the school. About eighty books were produced in all.

The INSET Programme

The formal aspect of our INSET work had begun earlier with the reading project previously mentioned, initiated by the ILEA Centre for Language in Primary Education, which was looking at the nature of learning to read, through reading real books. We had abandoned graded reading schemes for the children to learn to read using what have come to be known as real books. The focus of the project was then to improve the way that progress of beginner readers was recorded so that our teaching, in what at first appeared to be a less structured methodology, could be fully effective.

Our way of working was for a teacher to read the story to a child and then ask for the story to be 'read' back. We would expect the reading to approximate as closely as possible to the original text but make no demand for strict accuracy. The young reader was asked to read the same text in this way on three separate occasions over a few days. The children's readings were recorded on audio tape and then transcribed side by side so that they could be scrutinized easily for observations about the ways in which the children used the text and any progress observed recorded.

We had not at that time thought to include beginner users of English in the project because of the view, which we than shared with others, that the children needed a good command of spoken English before there was any point in them attempting to learn to read it. Of course, they were not excluded from the book culture of the school, but it had not occurred to us that there would be advantage in inspecting their approaches to reading. That was soon to change, however, when we came to consider the recordings of some of the fluent bilingual learner readers who had been included in the project. Here is one of Mamun's sets of readings done when he was almost 6 years old.

Text of the book	First reading	Second reading	Third reading
Pete had a kite	Pete had a kite	Pete had a kite	Pete had a kite
that flew high	that *fly* high	that *flyed* high	that *flew* high
above the	above the	above the	above the
trees	trees	trees	trees

On examination of Mamun's transcript, the different use of the verb form on the three successive occasions was apparent. The present tense 'fly', followed by the (creatively) overgeneralized past form 'flyed', and finally 'flew'. This progression is one frequently made during the acquisition of English as a first language. The way that Mamun's three readings moved over three developmental stages in the space of a few days made us wonder if reading in the way employed in the project might not also help beginner learners of English as a second language as well as beginner readers. What we had observed happening to the fluent bilinguals' use of English focused our attention on the support to spoken English that books might give them, and then on to the possibilities for very inexperienced users of English, too.

Because of the book culture in our school, we could not fail to recognize that reading books together was as important for children who spoke very little English as it was for those who were fluent users of the language. But was it true — as we felt it was — that beginner users of English were using the text of the books to extend their use of English in both spoken and written modes? If so, the practice of holding back reading in a second language till the learners have some oral fluency did not seem to be a good one.

As a follow up to these observations, as a staff, we decided to mount our own project. We applied for, and obtained, INSET money from our LEA to support our work in collecting further evidence of what happens when children read. Were our children really supported in their acquisition of English by using books in the way described? What were the starting points of the children's reading in English? How did they set about their reading? Which books seemed most supportive to bilingual children? Would our findings be different in any essential ways from those associated with the emerging literacy of other infant age children?

The INSET money was intended for and used to buy in an additional teacher for the equivalent to two teacher days each week, giving permanent staff some time to do their investigative work. They were thus able to work with individual children without the pressure of looking after a whole class at the same time. In addition, as well as studying children in this way, observations were made by all the teachers in their day to day teaching.

In this second reading project, we followed a similar procedure to the first. The children read from the general classroom selection. Sometimes they chose for themselves, sometimes we helped them, or ourselves chose books which they could enjoy and could tackle with success. Once a choice had been made, the teacher, sitting with the child, would read the book to him or her. She would then invite the child to read it back to her. This first reading was taped.

Two further readings were done in the same way, usually a week apart. Some discussions about books were recorded, too, as were some of the stories the children retold. We also recorded children approximating to texts which had come into existence through the children previously dictating the text to their teacher about pictures they had drawn. We transcribed our tapes, sharing the discussion with each other.

Particular points emerged.

— Children expected to make sense of what they were reading.
— Those who spoke very little English as yet, struggled and succeeded in expressing the meaning they perceived.
— They used illustrations in the text to help them read for meaning.
— They experimented with syntax.
— Successive readings brought them closer to the original text.
— They developed an ability to use story language, thus putting themselves in the position of skilled readers whose experience enables them to predict and make sense of texts out of this knowledge.

Making sense of the text. All the children were used to looking at books and hearing stories and so they expected the text to give descriptions or tell stories. When they reread the books to the teacher, we saw that they always tried to make sense of what was before them. *Shirley Sharpeyes* in which a wolf creeps into a house and tries to disguise itself, was read by Sayudez in this way: 'and...and...Shirley girl said "This one funny carpet"' for '"That's a lumpy doormat", said little Shirley Sharpeyes'. In *The boy who cried wolf*, the text is as follows: 'And when the boy came back to the field, the wolf had eaten all his sheep'. Moshed read 'Then he came back to the field and he found...then he cried for his...for his sheep'.

Children who spoke very little English struggled and succeeded in expressing the book meanings. Some of the children whose readings were transcribed spoke little English, yet they brought their past knowledge and experience to bear on what was new in order to make sense of the text. One child who was unable to recall the word 'spade' inventively read 'a big dig' in its place. Afthur, reading *Crocodiles are dangerous* in which a fish is chased and eaten by a crocodile, read in this way:

Text	Afthur's reading
He slid into the water	He runned faster
and swam after the fish	and the fish runned faster

When Lipe was reading *Titch*, she came to a page that read: 'And Titch had a pinwheel that he held in his hand'. She clearly did not know what a pinwheel was. She studied the illustration carefully and then, pointing to the pinwheel, said 'That's like a flower'. Then she tried the text and read 'Titch have a pin'.

Experimenting with syntax and moving closer to the text. The children generally came closer to the text with each successive reading. It was common for them, too, to experiment with syntax in the same way that Mamun had done. Lipe reading *Titch* provides a further example.

Text	First reading	Second reading	Third reading
Titch was	Little is	Little Titch	Titch was
little	Titch	was	little

Using the illustrations to read for meaning. The children took clues from the pictures in the books, substituting their own vocabulary and syntax where words and structures were unfamiliar or forgotten. Always they strove for meaning. Bimbla read 'Sean smiled a little smile' for 'Sean smiles a teeny weeny smile'. Mahmoud read 'He have nowhere to sleep' for 'He didn't have a home or a bed'. Lovely, on seeing an illustration of a child using *Breakthrough to literacy* apparatus, read 'I am doing my Breakthrough' for 'I made a book about my dad'.

Using story language. Beginner readers need to know the ways that spoken language differs from literary language. The children whose readings were recorded had a good understanding of this. For example, Aziz, reading *Meg and Mog*, read 'They whispered the magic word' for 'They all stirred the cauldron'. Mahmoud, in his first reading of *A fairy story*, read 'Once there lived a boy' for 'Once upon a time there lived a poor boy', and, at the end, when the book gives 'He lived happily ever after', Mahmoud was stuck for a minute. Then he began. 'He . . .', he hesitated. The teacher prompted. 'What happens at the end of stories?' 'He lived happily ever after', said Mahmoud.

All these examples, and much of the rest of our recordings, showed us that reading — as we practised it in our school — from the earliest stages of learning English was a good thing, that bilingual children were using, as emerging readers, similar strategies as their monolingual English peer group. Further, we felt that we had demonstrated that reading, undertaken as a developmental process, offered real support for developing fluency and confidence in spoken English. Finally, the children had natural access to, and were learning the words, structures and intonations of, the special language of narrative in English.

Endword

Although the INSET programme focused on reading, the observations made began to spread to other areas of the curriculum. By focusing on the developmental nature of children's learning, by linking into and seeking the support of our specialist teachers' centres, by being active in our own professional development, we gained enough assurance to follow through ways of working with young bilingual pupils not dissimilar from those we would count as good practice for speakers of English as a first language. Children should not be expected to leave behind knowledge and experience gained outside school when they enter school, for these are their foundations for new learning. They should feel comfortable to use their full linguistic range in school and the maintenance and development of the languages they know should be actively pursued. Developing a use of English is best achieved through the curriculum since that allows linguistic and conceptual development to go on side by side, and in company with their peers. A school should be membershipped to its community.

Our work had helped us to turn aside from the idea that had come to us as received wisdom that children who are unable to speak English come to school knowing nothing and ill equipped for learning.

Children's Books Mentioned in this Chapter

(See bibliography for complete source listings).
BEGUM, SUFIA and HALIMA, *Halima's story*.
BIRO, VAL, *The boy who cried wolf*.
BREINBERG, PETRONELLA, *My brother Sean*.
CATTINI, FAY, *A visit to my aunt's house*.
HUTCHINS, PAT, *Titch*.
KNOWLES, FRANCES and THOMPSON, BRIAN, *Shirley Sharpeyes*.
MACKAY, DAVID and SCHAUB, PAMELA, *Crocodiles are dangerous*.
NICOLL, HELEN and PIENKOWSKI, JAN, *Meg and Mog*.
RAHMAN, REHANA, *Jabin's Journey*.
SCHAUB, PAMELA, *A Fairy Story*.
THOMPSON, BRIAN, *My Dad*.

7
'Baby Wasn't Accident':
The Learning of Pupils and Teachers in
Natural Conversation in an Infant School

Valerie Emblen

In ' "Baby Wasn't Accident"': the Learning of Pupils and Teachers in Natural Conversation in an Infant Classroom', *Emblen takes us further into the learning environment described by Brightmore and Ross. Working with lively, enquiring children thriving in the multilingual ethos established in the school, she carefully inspects the conversational strategies of three infant age bilingual learners as they undertake an active learning maths assignment. Creative striving with the English language is the keynote of their endeavours. They switch from Sylheti to English as the teacher joins them. To work with children in this 'ordinary' conversational way, Emblen notes, is to realize their abilities, their already well-developed conversational competence, to recognize how their progress in developing a use of English is fostered by the possibility of using* all *their linguistic resources (and not by shutting out their home language) as they go about their school learning. It is also to take on the odds against which so many bilingual learners have to fight because these children do not learn in ideal and harmonious circumstances, even in schools and classrooms like this one. Quite the opposite. Violent acts of racism are ever personally in their lives, ever personally involved in their learning.*

> *Afna kola kaitaini?*
> (Are you going to eat
> bananas?)
> *Oi ami kola kaimu.*
> (Yes, I am going to
> eat bananas.)

Five year old Momtaj has invented a game. 'Are you going to eat . . . ?' she asks. To which I have to reply, 'Yes, I am going to eat . . . ' or 'No, I am not going to eat . . . ' in Sylheti. Today, she has just got me to say *Oi ami chair kaimu* (Yes, I am going to eat chairs), and this has caused a lot of fun, 'Miss say she eat chair', Momtaj tells her friends in English, 'Miss say she eat chair'.

This is a very ordinary game to play with young children. They are amused by anomalies and will laugh uproariously at the thought of a small giant or a chair sandwich. But this game is also part of Momtaj's plan to teach me Bengali. 'We know Bengali', she told me one day, and went on to ask, 'Why you don't know?' Apart from the game, her programme includes drills and exercises. I often forget them, and when, yet again, I cannot remember our last lesson, she looks sorrowfully at me, sighs deeply and says not — as one might deservedly expect — 'I learn English, why can't you learn Bengali?' but 'Miss, I *tell* you'. In Momtaj's life in school, it is normal to speak Sylheti and English. She certainly does not see herself as a second language learner, nor as a poor speaker of English. She is a great communicator and aware of her real language competence.

Nobinul is 6 years old. He is circling the classroom slowly, thoughtfully. He does this when he has something important to think about. The previous time, the question that burst forth from him was, 'Who this man Jesus, then?' This time, having circled for some fifteen minutes, he said, 'But *they* don't talk you English. *We* talk you English, but *they* don't. They don't know English'. I had just told him that I was going to Bangladesh and he had become anxious. Did I know things would be different? Did I know that cooking was not the same? And fishing was not the same? And, above all, just because Bengali people spoke to me in English in London, I really could not expect that in Bangladesh. This is an enormous and caring leap of the imagination on Nobinul's part, trying to tackle the world from my point of view. Not only that, he is doing it in 'my' language, consciously switching languages to include me in his thinking directly.

Both Momtaj and Nobinul are behaving very differently from the expectations bred in us by the conventional view — however kindly the approach — that the 'ESL child' has a lack that must be remedied before it can take part in normal lessons. In a school full if lively communicators it is difficult to see the teaching of developing bilingual children as plugging gaps or remedying poor language. The children, whatever their knowledge of English, cry out to be treated as people with questions to ask and things to find out and explain. With this recognition comes responsibility. How *do* we provide for bilingual children's further intellectual growth? How do we provide opportunities related to *all* their abilities, not just the ability to use English? It was with questions like this in my mind that I set out that day to look more closely at three bilingual learners tackling the mathematics curriculum. That was *my* purpose as a teacher researcher, a very one-sided purpose, one-sided in the sense of appropriation of significant conversations, as we shall see.

Bilingual Children and the Development of Mathematical Concepts

When I first set out to look at bilingual children's mathematics learning, despite the fact that I held the 'right' notions about the children and their learning, I have to confess that my first hope was that I would find that someone had devised a set of techniques to do the job, even that a pack of materials had been devised that already addressed the 'problem'. Implicitly, I was expecting these materials, should they exist, to be different from those I would normally use in my classroom. Yet with all the lively interactions going on around me, it is difficult to believe that the learning of bilingual children should be catered for differently from that of native speakers of English.

As teachers we cannot close our eyes to the appalling racist and separatist implications of offering a separate or different curriculum to those whose only 'handicap' is that they are not yet fluent in English. When we say 'learn English first, learn the other stuff later', when we find areas of the curriculum to be 'going on with until they have more English', we are denying them the right to learn those things considered important to their classmates, learning that both parents and children are entitled to feel is their right.

Having pursued my research over time, looking closely at how children worked in mathematical situations, I found children going about their work in a lively and enquiring way, using *all* their language resources — and with an enviable facility to switch from one language to another as appropriate. They are constantly striving for clarity, both of ideas and language, and over time, they move closer to the English of their English speaking peers. The transcript and notes which follow do, I think, demonstrate all of these things except the last, which cannot be shown by a single event, though, even in this extract from the much longer tape, we can see the children trying out new words (e.g., *high* in utterances 33 and 34, and *climb* at utterance 48).

The transcript is taken from a video tape of a session of three Sylheti speaking boys, Nobinal, Ali Amjad and Nadimul, building with bricks. It begins at the point where I, the teacher, join them. The boys have been working independently. They have chosen to work with each other and have also chosen to do this using the bricks. (They were initially very interested in the camera and the technician working it, but had become involved in their mathematical play with the bricks, and for some time since seem to have forgotten the video equipment.) They had been using Sylheti among themselves, only using English to ask for a set of toy people to extend their play. At the point where I join them, they change to using English. My intention as teacher and researcher is to check some of the ways they have of expressing mathematical ideas, in English, to support and help develop both mathematical cognition and the expression of that cognition in English. The plan is to talk shape, size and comparisons.

When I join them, though, I can see I will have to suspend this idea for the time being. They are involved in their own game, and as I had not made clear that it would be my purposes and not theirs that we would be following that morning, the session consequently goes the way the children take it.

While the brick building is going on, the main talking points of the conversation are bananas, coconuts and the fire nearby which occurred the night before. The themes arise in the conversation in a way that is normal in any informal conversation between an adult and young children when the children are passing on genuine information to which the adult does not already have access. So my questions are often real questions rather than those classroom questions by which teachers check that children have retained given information. I believe that it is because of this reality that the children feel free to experiment with ideas and with forms for expressing them, and that, in turn, this is the reason for their liveliness and confidence.

When the theme changes to the local fire, this is the first I have heard of it and only gradually during the course of the conversation do I realize the seriousness of what the children are telling me. The fire weighed heavily on them and they did not at this point know if everyone concerned was safe. In particular, Nobinul's house is very near the one that caught fire.

Nobinul was just 6 at the time of the recording. He had been in school nearly two terms; not more, because he suffers from alopecia. His family had been understandably reluctant to send him as he had no hair on his head. They were afraid that he would be teased.

Nadimul and Ali Amjad were both five. They were both in their second term in the infant school, having spent two terms in the nursery. Nadimul's mother, on being told that her son had been talking about Bangladesh, laughed and said that he had been born in England, and had been to Bangladesh only once as a small baby. 'But', she said, 'we get letters and photos from our family and we talk a lot about our home'. Family memories loom large in the minds of children and are, in their own way, as real as direct experience.

In the way that conversation in learning and play goes, the children bring in, use, connect and distance their experience, thoughts and observations. The children are playing with the sounds of words. The sound of '*dollah*' in the words 'Million dollar man' reminds Nobinul of the word for banana, *kola*, in his own language. They want to explain to me what *kola* means. Nobinul leads the way. He wants to keep his teacher's attention. See how he shifts the topic to Pakistan (utterance 6) when it looks as though I might take up Nadimul's comment (utterances 4 and 5). When that move is not as successful as he would like it to be, he tries again (utterance 13) and succeeds.

1.	NOBINUL	*Kola, kola.*
2.	TEACHER	*Kola, kola.* That means lots of bananas.
3.	NOBINUL	*Kola, kola.*
4.	NADIMUL	My mummy say . . . Miss, my mummy say '*kola, kola*'.
5.	TEACHER	What? When did she say that?

6.	NOBINUL	On Pakistan they say '*vola*'.
7.	TEACHER	*Vola?*
8.	NOBINUL	Yeah.
9.	TEACHER	And that means 'banana' in Pakistan? What is it in Bangladesh, then?
10.	NOBINUL	*Kola.*
11.	NADIMUL	*Kola.*
12.	ALI AMJAD	*Kola.*
13.	NOBINUL	Coconut on the tree, miss, in Bangladesh. Coconut on tree.
14.	TEACHER	Coconuts growing on the trees?
15.	NOBINUL	Yeah.
16.	TEACHER	What do you have to do then if you want a coconut? Can you just go and pick it?

Nobinul is equal to this. His 'No, you have to pull' (utterance 17), shows that he has understood the implied meaning of 'it's not as easy as that' behind the teacher's 'can you just go and pick it?' (utterance 16). Now Nadimul and Ali Amjad can join in as equals in the building of the conversation, although in the event, it is Nadimul who takes up the option most strongly. In this next section (utterances 17–29), we can see the children behaving like competent conversationalists. They take turns, they support each other, they help each other develop ideas, and Nobinul can negate ideas and come in with a correcting fact (utterances 17 and 23). These metalinguistic skills are not language-specific and it may be that the most confident and fluent speakers of Mother Tongue as young children become the most confident and fluent speakers of their subsequent languages.

17.	NOBINUL	No, you have to pull, you have to pull.
18.	ALI AMJAD	Climb up.
19.	TEACHER	You have to climb up?
20.	NADIMUL	With ladder and you pull it.
21.	TEACHER	Um.
22.	ALI AMJAD	And coming.
23.	NOBINUL	No, you have to cut it. It's strong, Miss. It's strong.
24.	NADIMUL	It's strong. You have to cut it.
25.	NOBINUL	With knife, Miss. It is strong, very strong.
26.	NADIMUL	And you . . . and you chop it and eat it.
27.	TEACHER	What do you chop it with?
28.	NOBINUL	With knife, strong knife.
29.	NADIMUL	With strong knife.

On two occasions (utterances 23 and 28) Nobinul, with Nadimul picking up from him (utterances 24 and 29), introduces the word *strong*. On neither occasion is it the word likely to have been chosen by a native English speaker; yet, each time it conveys clearly enough the meaning intended. At utterance 23 we are told how firmly coconuts are attached to trees and, therefore, the difficulty it presents to anyone picking them; and in utterance 28 *strong* means 'sharp' and 'heavy'.

This device is one used by all of us. For instance, there are times when we may hold a concept without having access to its accepted or technical terminology. Therefore we use related but 'imprecise' terminology to convey our understandings. This can, of course, be viewed as a lack of vocabulary, but for all of us, Nobinul and Nadimul included, it is usefully seen as an ability to use the language we have at our disposal creatively. It is this kind of striving that allows us to learn and use new words.

The children now need to express a comparison of height.

30.	TEACHER	How . . . is the tree up high?
31.	ALI AMJAD	Yeah.
32.	TEACHER	Or just a little bit high?
33.	NOBINUL	No little bit high. This big high. This big high.
34.	NADIMUL	This big high.
35.	TEACHER	Um.
36.	NOBINUL	No, this big.
37.	NADIMUL	This big.
38.	TEACHER	Uhhuh.

How do you explain how tall a tree is? This would be a problem for most 5- and 6-year-olds. Again, the children bring all their resources to bear. They get up and demonstrate what they mean. Between them, Nobinul and Nadimul solve the problem by creating a ratio: 'We'll call this high. If that's high, then a coconut tree is right up there.' The children stand up and stretch high to show what they mean. Inevitably, they need to use non-verbal means of communication — and, perhaps, but only perhaps, more often than their English speaking classmates. It is important, therefore, to build up an expectation of understanding and being understood.

Note, too, that Ali Amjad is again the first to respond to the initiation of new subject matter (previously at utterances 18 and 22; now at utterance 31), and that on two of these occasions first Nobinul (at utterance 22) and myself (at utterance 33) press for greater explicitness. Throughout this section of the transcript it is noticeable that Ali Amjad says very little. This is not typical behaviour for him. Although I am not worried by this for, as his teacher, I know that he is usually a lively conversationalist, nevertheless, I do try to press him into the conversation. It is only right for a teacher to do this at times, as it is equally right at other times to respect a child's decision not to speak. Later in the interaction, as it transpires, Ali Amjad says to the other two children in Sylheti 'I wish you two would stop talking and get on with the game'. The rest of the talk about coconuts procedes without Ali Amjad's *verbal* participation, despite the fact that, at utterance 40, I deliberately invite him to join in.

39.	NOBINUL	From there . . .
40.	TEACHER	(*to Ali Amjad*) What do you do? You have a ladder . . .
41.	NOBINUL	Yes.
42.	TEACHER	. . . or do you climb up the tree?
43.	NADIMUL	Ladder.
44.	NOBINUL	You have to . . . this big ladder (*again, indicating size by gesture*) from there up there, and you have to, you have to cut it.
45.	TEACHER	(*taking a toy ladder*) Like this one. That the . . . Pretend that's the tree. You put the ladder up there.
46.	NOBINUL	Yes.
47.	TEACHER	Show me what you do then. Look, there's the man. Make him go up the tree and see what happens. Show me what happens.
48.	NOBINUL	You have to go . . . climb up there and cut it.
49.	NADIMUL	You have to . . .
50.	NOBINUL	You get coconut with knife.
51.	TEACHER	Um.
52.	NADIMUL	You have to cut it and . . . and you . . . and you . . . and you cut it with strong knife and you eat it.

Nobinul, at utterance 44, again uses the successful ratio device (gesture plus the words 'this big') to begin a sequence which tells with increasing explicitness about the harvesting of coconuts. He shows, too, that when he knows a better word, he will not be satisfied with one that is merely in the right semantic field, for example, his substitution of 'climb' for 'go'. See, also, how Nadimul contributes, at utterance 50, to making the talk more explicit by improving on Nobinul's 'You get coconut with knife' with his hard won utterance at 52 '. . . you cut it with strong knife and you eat it'. This creative striving contains much hesitation. When children are putting this much effort into making their meanings, it is bound to do so. He is working things out, and this takes time. The other children are prepared to wait, and so am I. Children just beginning to use another language need the space to be hesitant and to make false starts, free of the fear of this natural behaviour being counted as them failing to communicate or failing to think.

In the next section, Nobinul hears my utterances at 54 and 59 as different kinds of nonsense. How could I not know what was inside a coconut, he might be saying at utterance 55. Whereas he is bemused by my question at utterance 59 about the outside of the coconut. Apropos this, at utterance 60, he might well be saying, 'What could a question like this mean?' His apparent lack of comprehension forces me to stop and try to make my meaning more explicit. Later, when we watched the video together, he said 'I thought "outside" was in the playground'.

53.	NOBINUL	You can see inside, Miss.
54.	TEACHER	What's inside?
55.	NOBINUL	(*astounded*) Inside the coconut!
56.	TEACHER	What's . . . what's inside it?
57.	NADIMUL	Coconut.
58.	NOBINUL	Lot's of coconut.
59.	TEACHER	What's outside, then?
60.	NOBINUL	(*puzzled*) Outside . . . outside?
61.	TEACHER	Pretend that's the coconut. What's there? What's that bit on the outside?
62.	NOBINUL	Um . . .
63.	NADIMUL	Looks like grass.
64.	TEACHER	Grass.
65.	NOBINUL	No. Like a little bit dirty, Miss.

It is important to create inside the classroom the kind of atmosphere in which children may be confident enough to indicate that things have stopped making sense for them. It may be particularly necessary when we are making heavy and tangential cognitive or linguistic demands of them. When a teacher can depend upon the children to stop her if the ideas or the language she is using stop making sense, then she is free to engage normally with them; she can listen to the quality of the ideas being expressed and to their development, and she can speak normally herself. Participation in normal conversation in this way, I believe, provides the best models for children's speech. And the cognitive effort the children are putting into creating this conversation is not in doubt.

Having looked very closely at these techniques, I am struck forcibly by the very ordinariness of what we are doing. It is a very ordinary conversation and we are doing the things that people do when they are talking together: exchanging ideas, taking turns, building on what has been said before, sometimes listening to others, sometimes pushing our own point of view. Another strong impression is of the competence of the children and of the wide range of their previous experience. I am reminded of a teacher who once viewed the videoed lesson with me. 'Oh,' she said, 'what they were saying was so interesting I'd forgotten they didn't speak much English'.

It is often said of children of Asian backgrounds that they lack experience in constructive play and, therefore, by implication, of the sort of experiences that are helpful to Western child centred school learning. There can be no doubt, surely, that these children have a wide variety of experience, knowing and constructive play to draw on and that they have already developed many learning skills. Perhaps we should consider it possible to learn a language by getting on with school learning — if the social environment and the teaching make it natural to do so.

A third point I should like to emphasize is linked both to this point about language development and also to the development of mathematical concepts and to curriculum research. How wrong I was to think that we had necessarily to follow *my* lesson plan for me to find out whether the children could give expression to some mathematical ideas or whether the basis for further work was there!

The conversation about coconuts continues for many minutes more. The children take great pleasure in exercising their growing skills and we can appreciate Nobinul's relish for words as well as for coconuts.

96.	NOBINUL	No. White, It's good. It tastes like . . . when you taste it, it's good.
97.	TEACHER	Um.
98.	NOBINUL	Delicious, Miss.

The final section of transcript I want to look at here is when Nobinul, apparently suddenly, changes the subject. He introduces, at utterance 113, the topic that must have been in the forefront of all the children's minds throughout all the lesson time that day, 'Miss, today was fire'.

109.	TEACHER	And where do these trees grow? In your garden?
110.	NADIMUL	My tree did grow already.
111.	TEACHER	In your house? When you were in your house, it was already there?
112.	NADIMUL	And coconuts now.
113.	NOBINUL	Miss, today was fire.
114.	ALI AMJAD	Fire.
115.	NADIMUL	Hanbury Street.
116.	ALI AMJAD	Hanbury Street.
117.	NOBINUL	Not my house. My sister's friend.
118.	TEACHER	Oh. Did the fire engine have to come?
119.	NOBINUL	There's big . . . there's a big fire, Miss. There's a big fire.
120.	NADIMUL	*Manush cor anni* (Somebody did it).
121.	NOBINUL	*Nah* (No). There's a gas coming. Miss, lots of gas.
122.	TEACHER	Um.
123.	NOBINUL	And two houses was burning.
124.	TEACHER	Two houses?
125.	NOBINUL	Yes. And Joynal's shop come gas. Gas.
126.	TEACHER	Really.
127.	NOBINUL	Yes.
128.	TEACHER	Is Joynal here today?
129.	ALI AMJAD	No.
130.	NADIMUL	No.
131.	NOBINUL	You see, all the gas come.
132.	TEACHER	His house is on fire? Joynal's house or Joynal's shop?

133.	NOBINUL	Yes, it full of gas.
134.	TEACHER	Oh.
135.	NOBINUL	Joynal's shop.
136.	TEACHER	Oh.
137.	NOBINUL	My . . . .
138.	TEACHER	Your house is OK?
139.	NADIMUL	*Manush cor anni* (Somebody did it).
140.	NOBINUL	There's little baby. Little baby wasn't dead.
141.	TEACHER	Was he OK?
142.	NOBINUL	Yes.
143.	TEACHER	Did someone rescue him?
144.	NOBINUL	Yes. Fire engine. Quickly they climb up the stairs and they get the baby out.
145.	TEACHER	The firemen?
146.	NOBINUL	Yes, baby wasn't accident.
147.	TEACHER	Oh, dreadful, isn't it? Must be frightening to have your house on fire.
148.	NOBINUL	And daddy . . . daddy's burned, daddy's burned.
149.	TEACHER	He gone to hospital?
150	NOBINUL	Yes. Daddy's burned.

As I have said before, this is the first time I have heard of this fire, and only gradually do I realize the seriousness of what they are telling me.

From Nadimul's comment at utterance 120 (*Manush cor ani* [somebody did it]) I know that he has already heard expressed about this fire the Asian community's ever present and justified fear of wanton racial violence; and possibly, that deliberate acts of racially motivated violence have already become so 'natural' a way of thinking for him that he does not need to have heard an adult express this opinion for him to hold it quite independently himself. Nadimul repeats this idea three times more, always using Sylheti, once at utterance 139 when I am still part of the group, and again twice more it appears on the tape after I have left them to check on Joynal's safety and the children have returned to using Sylheti. Earlier, at utterances 120 and 139 the use of Sylheti to reflect this most terrifying and painful aspect of his community's experience may be additionally significant. It is easy to see why he might unconsciously choose the language which is closest to him for the pain which is his own and his community's. It is perhaps less easy to accept that already at 5 years of age, again unconsciously, he may have learned not to speak of political matters of this kind with members of the dominant white group — however sympathetic they may be to the situation — since as far as his community is concerned very little benefit accrues. Even in Sylheti, Nadimul's anxiety is not taken up by the others, perhaps because it is too frightening for them to do so. But it is plain that he takes no reassurance on the point of whether or not this particular fire was a deliberate act of racial violence from Nobinal's reply to him at utterance 121 '*Nah*, there's a gas coming'.

Two men died in that fire. Investigation later established that the fire had indeed been caused by leaking gas. In some ways this was a relief for the community but a relief tainted by yet other layers of the ever present racism. Because of the death of one of the men it became necessary for his wife to fight for her right to stay in this country. She was deported two years later.

Yes, I did learn from my research that day. And I think by describing the children's school work that day we can easily confirm that children are committed, involved learners who respond very well indeed to the demands of school learning; confirm that these children daily develop their creative use of English within an interactive environment which attempts to facilitate children's learning.

We can also show how important it is to give children space, and to listen to *all* of what children have to tell us. And we can also see that as teachers our interactive and communicative responsibilities by no means begin and end within the narrow confines of a maths or any other curriculum area. The issue that resounds is how also, in our responsibilities as teachers and human beings, to confront the racism and threats to personal safety that are a central part of these young children's lives.

8
Yogesh and Kantilal:
A Case Study of Early Progress in a Mixed Ability
English Class

Ann Burgess and Leon Gore

Burgess and Gore's second contribution, 'Yogesh and Kantilal: a Case Study of Early Progress in a Mixed Ability English Class', focuses on a typical concern for teachers in secondary schools once they begin a partnership to support bilingual learners in the mainstream — especially the most inexperienced users of English: Are pupils really benefiting from the new mainstream structures? What if they do not appear to contribute much in mainstream group activities? If they contribute very little, will their development of English suffer? Burgess and Gore's concern for their two most inexperienced pupils was high, despite the fact that support lessons for bilingual learners were structured into the timetable in close relationship with the mainstream teaching. The ESL teacher of the mainstream partnership taught the support lessons. Studying transcribed tape recordings of their pupils' working conversations, Burgess and Gore discover the value for inexperienced users of English of the use of the tape recorder in 'going back over' work. Such opportunities give students the chance to express what they know, think and feel. The silence of Yogesh and Kantilal that so worried the teachers in the mainstream working group proved to be a listening silence, an attentive silence to the talk going on around them — a stage in their developing ability to interact actively with their working group. As much as speech, listening is part of the interaction process that helps internalization.

Background

Kantilal and Yogesh were members of the class described in Chapter 5 of this volume 'The Move from Withdrawal ESL Teaching to Mainstream Activities is Necessary, Possible and Worthwhile'. That chapter is part of the context of this study. In summary, having established a structure in which developing bilingual students can take part in mainstream activities, having benefited from acting on the belief that talk and interaction are central to learning in mixed ability classes, having found ways of fostering and improving intergroup relations, and having seen Yogesh and Kantilal, the least experienced users of English in the class, appear socially more at ease in the class, we nevertheless remained greatly concerned about their language development. Frequently in group work they would contribute very little. They themselves had expressed concern in support lessons over difficulties they were facing, not only in English but across the curriculum. There was little sign of the hoped for increase in academic confidence by the end of the first term of their work in the Fourth Year class. We felt great anxiety for Yogesh and Kantilal and, indeed, wondered if they might not have been better off, academically, in a withdrawal class, despite all the known limitations. This case study is the result of our not succumbing to this temptation. It records events in relation to work undertaken by the class at the beginning of the second term on a play, *Speech Day*, by Barry Hines — work which proved to be a significant marker for us of the validity of our approach.

Curriculum Context

In addition to the changes already discussed in our earlier chapter in this book, to be hospitable to learners of English as a second language in mainstream classes, we knew it was necessary to implement a multicultural curriculum. That is, one which allows pupils to draw upon their cultural capital[1], one which deals with issues of race, class and gender, one which is problem solving rather than didactic. We introduced into our lessons, for example, such topics as the position of women in society, images of women in the mass media, language and dialect, stereotyping, nuclear power and weapons, immigrants and emigrants, policing, the use of leucotomies for the treatment of mental illness. Our principal method was discussion and sometimes role play. Our materials included articles from newspapers and magazines and also literature which dealt with these serious ideas. Our aim was to encourage critical thinking. Amongst the literature we favoured was *Walkabout* by James Vance Marshall, which, to our minds, questions and undermines notions of Western cultural superiority; *Kes* by Barry Hines which raises issues about school and society, and the nature of freedom; *A Clockwork Orange* by Anthony Burgess, which asks questions about the part played by religion in society, the concept of morality, and the possible form of a not-too-long-in-the-future society, and again, freedom and control.

Speech Day, which was so important a marker for us and our two pupils described in our case study, puts forward the view that schools prepare pupils for the outside world by ascribing to them a status within the school commensurate with their likely future positions in society. This is achieved through the use of streaming and differentiation of the curriculum, the process being aided and abetted by discriminatory attitudes of the teachers. In the play, this is signalled in the choice of lower streams to perform such menial tasks as setting charis out and tidying the school grounds for its speech day. One small incident from the play underlines this point. Ronnie Warboys, the 'hero', mows the grass outside a classroom where a mathematics lesson is being taught. An altercation occurs between Ronnie and the mathematics teacher annoyed at the disruption caused by the noise of the mowing machine. The teacher returns to his class saying:

> It's all right for him: he's nothing better to do with his time. I've got
> to get you lot through an examination at the end of next year.

The school's speech day is the symbol of the whole differentiating process. At this function, the headmaster details the academic success of pupils at the school, and of those who have gone on to university. Ignored is the success of a former lower stream pupil who has started to play regularly for the first team of a famous football club.

In the play, scenes from Ronnie's school are intercut with scenes from Ronnie's family at home and at work. At school Ronnie's class are taken out of English and woodwork lessons, the girls to prepare food for the guests and the boys to help the school handyman smarten the place up. In another scene, we learn that Ronnie's father is in danger of being 'thrown off work' with the consequence that Ronnie's mother takes a boring job 'doing seams all day' — though she enjoys what is to her the more fulfilling occupation of dressmaking. Reference is made on a number of occasions to the danger of unemployment for both skilled and unskilled workers. Two teachers praise the pupils' work in the school art exhibition, and talk of the general potential that will be wasted, and how the rigours of earning a wage can destroy creative energy. Later, as the teachers prepare themselves for the speech day function itself, the woodwork and physical education teachers sardonically comment on their own lack of academic gowns. Thus the teachers are shown as being as trapped as the pupils they teach in social and academic structures which are intended to indicate their positions in the hierarchy. The academic curriculum is seen by many of the teachers as not having necessarily to engage pupils' interests. Yet, pupils are expected *ipso facto* to work at it to pass exams. The play ends with Ronnie being sent out of the hall for laughing at a boorish speech by the Mayor — a former trade union militant, now with 'more' sense — in which he tells everyone that he now realizes there are 'two sides to every question'.

The play is complex and Barry Hines frequently makes use of irony. We did not expect all our pupils to grasp all the intricacies of the play, but we did hope that their reading and discussing of it would lead them to ask the basic question, What are schools for?, to analyze what takes place in them, and to link that more broadly to what goes on in society. The class read the play in two groups, each of the teachers working with one. They were also able to watch a version on video of a Thames Television 'English Programme' production of the play. Following some preliminary discussion the class, provided with assignment sheets, split into small groups for deep discussion of the play. On this occasion, no longer so worried about groupings as we had been, we put students together more or less according to where they were sitting.[2]

We design our worksheets as scaffolding. That is, as Moy and Raleigh state in their article on comprehension in the *The English Magazine* (Autumn 1980), as support for students working on a text, a structure that students are free to take down if they do not need it.

Speech Day: Questions for Discussion

1. What did you think of Ronnie's school and why?
2. Are there any important ways in which it is different from our school?
3. Would you criticize any of the teachers in the play? Why?
4. What was the local employment situation like?
5. How was it affecting Ronnie's family?
6. What were Ronnie's job prospects?
7. Why didn't Ronnie's parents come to speech day?
8. What was important about speech day to the school?
9. How did Ronnie and his friends see it?
10. How did or didn't Ronnie's school prepare him and his friends for the outside world? In discussing this, make use of the term 'status'.
11. Why did the author make Ronnie the central character?
12. What was the author's purpose in having a headmaster quote from Martin Luther King's 'I have a dream' speech?

As you can see from this set of questions, our intention was firstly to help students make connections between their own school and the *Speech Day* school, and then to help them engage with some of the ideas of the play.

Using a Tape Recorder

By this time we had begun to record the discussion of the groups on tape. It was a logical step once we had made talk a central learning mode in our teaching. In the context of the classroom it is difficult for teachers to detach themselves from what is happening, to interpret, to understand and evaluate processes of interaction and learning that are taking place. Additionally, teachers cannot be present nor should they wish to be, in all the group discussions all of the time. For full profit from this mode of learning students benefit from their teachers' absence as well as their presence. Tape recording can, therefore, provide a useful record of talk and give teachers time and space to analyze and evaluate events and processes — particularly those pertaining to the collaboration that occurs between students searching for understanding and attempting to articulate and make explicit their knowledge. It can refine teachers' perceptions of the ways students respond to assignments, to teachers' language, and to the language of their peers. Teachers can, too, develop insights which help them to improve on what they do in their classrooms. They can see, for example, who initiated or changed a particular topic or issue, who strayed intentionally or unintentionally off the subject, the length of any individual's silences; and they can try to interpret the meanings of such silences. This last, as you will see, was particularly significant in our thinking in this case study of Yogesh and Kantilal.

The Students and the Mainstream Class Discussion

Kantilal and Yogesh were together in a group containing bright, lively pupils: Xenophon, Clinton, Yuet Ming and Kevin. The group discussion, as was by then normal for all groups, was recorded. Xenophon, of Greek origin, was intelligent, well liked and respected. He enjoyed a good argument, was easy going and got on well with staff. Clinton, too, liked a good argument and enjoyed being in the same group as Xenophon. Clinton, though, was frequently in trouble and was disliked by some members of staff who saw him as being too argumentative and as not showing sufficient respect for authority. Clinton thought many teachers discriminated against him because he was black — his parents came from Jamaica — but also because he was big and stood out. Teachers were sometimes exasperated by Clinton's disinclination to put pen to paper, especially as his written work, when he did it, was good.

Yuet Ming, whose family was from Hong Kong, was althogether a quieter person. His intelligence had mainly expressed itself in his written work. Recently he had begun to contribute more, orally, and was developing a quiet insistence in putting forward his arguments. He was accepted and liked by all the boys.

Kevin, like Clinton, also belived that teachers discriminated against him. He is black. His parents come from Guyana. He himself has spent time in Guyana and Canada. We think, though, that he was born in Britain. He is highly intelligent, capable of very sharp insights, and has a very wide vocabulary. He was, however, at that time, prone to moods and got upset easily, both by treatment from teachers he considered unjust and by what he considered to be slights by other students. In such a frame of mind he could be difficult, and of this group of boys, we both found him the least straight-forward to work with. There were boys in the class who were afraid of him, yet he could be extremely cooperative and disarmingly charming. At the time of the discussion of *Speech Day* he had arrived in the classroom in one of his moods.

Yogesh and Kantilal were tacitly accepted into groups by now, but were

3.	TEACHER	(*not having picked up Kantilal's possible meaning intention, and addressing herself to the basic injustice of asking the students to do the work in the first place*) What do you think about that? [*Unclear*] to go and do something like that?
4.	YOGESH	(*responding to the teacher's meaning*) It's not fair.
5.	TEACHER	Why isn't it fair?
6.	YOGESH	Because they not allowed (*meaning = it ought not to be allowed*) to do outside work, they want to...
7.	KANTILAL	(*beginning to talk over the top of Yogesh*) Because they... yes, and that boy was in the fifth form innit? So he was doing his...er...job...er...his...er...his subject, which is important, innit? If...if he don't do the work, right, and he...
8.	YOGESH	(*breaking in on Kantilal*) If he don't do that and do outside work, they can't learn here.
9.	TEACHER	(*not hearing his last words, and thereby pushing Yogesh to a clearly shaped sentence*) They can't what?
10.	YOGESH	They can't learn if they do outside work.

Furthermore, they have a sense of audience and of the value of what they have to say. They are able to monitor their spoken thoughts. They struggle to find the appropriate words to express their ideas. Kantilal, having already, in utterance 2, used the term 'outside' to differentiate between school work and menial work, anticipates a problem when he uses the word 'job' in utterance 7, since, though it is perfectly applicable to work undertaken in woodwork lessons, it could also be used to refer to various types of 'outside' work. Hence, he substitutes the word 'subject' for 'job' which both slightly but suitably changes the meaning and clears up any ambiguity there might be for his audience. They also signal words which they feel to exist, but which they do not know, by repetition, a change of tone, or a 'warning' phrase. In the following quotation from the transcript, Kantilal seems to be looking for a word like 'inspect' at the end of the following passage when he says '...look, how we say?...look'.

| 11. | TEACHER | How, what did he say about streaming? |
| 12. | KANTILAL | Is...er...like...um...two kind of groups. Is...er...group A and group B. And in A group, alright, sir...I mean in B group, sir told the B group boys to some work like painting and do the gardening work when the...when someone come to school to look, how we say?...look. |

Throughout the tape, Standard English and dialect are interposed, and done so appropriately. Both Kantilal and Yogesh are taking on the language of their English native speaking peers — 'you know', 'innit?', 'right' are frequently interjected into the conversation in the appropriate place: to ask for confirmation or agreement, or to signal a tacit understanding of a point, or as a mechanism to gain space to think. The appear to handle this dialect with considerable ease. In addition, where, as in the following passage, it is difficult to express an idea directly, either because of not knowing the appropriate language or because the idea has to be grasped for and needs expression to clarify it, they, like anyone else engaged in the same kind of intellectual struggle, use anecdote in a hypothetical mode to make the point.

13.	KANTILAL	One boy is very naughty, right?
14.	TEACHER	Yes.
15.	KANTILAL	He everytime make...er...trouble, right? (*Now moves into exemplification by anecdote*) Yogesh is a bad boy, alright...everytime...
16.	TEACHER	(*interrupting, making a joke of Kantilal's statement about Yogesh; all three know Kantilal's statement at face value to be patently untrue*) We know Yogesh is a bad boy!
17.	KANTILAL	(*taking his turn back very quickly to make absolutely clear the status of his utterance*) Miss, we are just saying that, innit? If he *was*, right?...and...er...if I hit him, right?...and is my fault, innit...
18.	TEACHER	(*encouragingly*) Yes.
19.	KANTILAL	...and he hit me back, and I went to sir, right...say 'Yogesh hit me', right?...and...er...sir believed that, innit, because he's a bad boy, innit, because everytime he's making trouble, innit?
20.	TEACHER	So what are you trying to say, Kantilal?
21.	KANTILAL	Is...er...ah! What's that? (*He struggles for expression*)
22.	TEACHER	Are you talking about people's reputations?
23.	KANTILAL	Um...(*Not sure that the teacher is talking about the same thing as he is*)
24.	TEACHER	Yes? (*Explaining, as she sees that he does not understand*) If you get a name for yourself as a bad boy?
25.	YOGESH	(*who plainly has been following attentively all along*) They mind it, miss. People mind do they.
26.	TEACHER	What do you think, Yogesh? Do you think that's true?
27.	YOGESH	Yes, I think so.

Here the move is from a generalization (in utterance 13, 'one boy is very naughty, right?'), to using Yogesh, who has never yet been naughty in class, as a direct example so that he can personalize a 'bad boy' story to make the point about unfair treatment by teachers. Again, we see Kantilal searching for expression and Yogesh succinctly summing up. We see the teacher, from utterance 20 onwards, also struggling for meaning inside this conversation. In concentrating on Kantilal, she has given Yogesh the time both to take Kantilal's meaning and to formulate a most feeling comment (utterance 25, 'They mind it, miss. People mind do they'); but she has also missed the fact that he has made so pertinent a point and speaks to him at utterance 26 as though he had not yet made it. This is not unfeeling behaviour on the part of the teacher. It is merely an example of what can happen in normal conversational behaviour as three participants engage in creating and understanding the meanings they are making.

We are certain that the overall normality of the conversation is a contributing factor to the boys being so well motivated and taking the discussion so seriously. We are equally certain that studying it has alerted us to those other times when 'normal conversational behaviour' is potentially unsupporting.

Undoubtedly, the boys have perceived that if the function of a speech day in schools is to award prizes for academic achievement, it also functions to demean other pupils who have not won prizes.

28.	YOGESH	They give a prize.
29.	TEACHER	Yes. To who? Who gets the prizes?
30.	YOGESH	Clever boys.
31.	TEACHER	What about the other boys?
32.	KANTILAL	They just watch . . . and in that book, you know, the boys who don't . . . who didn't get the prize, right? Sir told them to do the work.

They have understood the concept of streaming and its implications for the students with regard to teacher attitudes, academic achievement and future job opportunities.

33.	YOGESH	They can't learn if they do outside work.

Kantilal uses the example of boys having to put chairs in the hall instead of having a history lesson as possibly contributing to their lack of examination success, and hence their lack of job prospects;

34.	KANTILAL	If they doing history, right, and Sir say . . . er . . . you can put the . . . all in . . . the chair in the hall, right, and this is the subject he choose in the fifth form, right, . . . so if he . . . if he fail in history, right, maybe he wouldn't get the job because he get the lowest mark, innit?

Both boys understand the dilemma of the pupil Ronnie, who in the play was told by one teacher to cut the grass, and yet got into trouble with another for disturbing that teacher's lesson.

35.	KANTILAL	Miss . . . miss, miss. If the sir say to the boy, right, 'Cut the . . . cut the . . . cut the grass', right, and if he's cutting it anyway he likes, innit? . . . (*correcting himself*) any place he likes . . . because he can say 'That's the grass sir told me to cut' . . . and sir say 'Go and cut it there' . . . and he . . . I don't know . . . he something say. The boy says to sir something, then he say 'Do the hundred words'. Something like that.

If it is true to say that the boys have understood the language and meaning of *Speech Day*, we think, too, that they have arrived at its implications for their own situation in school.

36.	KANTILAL	. . . The boy says to sir something, then he say 'Do the hundred words'. Something like that.
37.	TEACHER	Yes, that's right. What do you think about what Clinton and Kevin and Xenophon have said? Do you want to listen to what they said again? You're shaking your head there, Kantilal. Would you like to go to a school like that?
38.	KANTILAL	No.
39.	TEACHER	Why not?
40.	KANTILAL	Because . . . er . . . if I go to . . . into that school, right and if I was a lowest, a lowest group . . . like Clinton said, there's five . . . five . . . if I was in five group, right, I wouldn't go to this school because . . . er . . . you have to do all the work.
41.	TEACHER	What about you, Yogesh? Would you like to go to a school like that?
42.	YOGESH	No.
43.	TEACHER	Why not?
44.	YOGESH	If I go there, I can't learn anything . . . sir everytime give us work. Do that. Do that.
45.	TEACHER	You do work in lesson, don't you?
46.	KANTILAL	But not that . . . like do the cutting grass and put the all chair in the hall . . . take . . . do the painting on the wall.

Comment

Through the processes of discussion described here (in the mainstream class and in a support lesson with one of the teachers who taught the relevant mainstream lesson) we understood afresh *the centrality of talk*, not only for learning but also for language learning. We had been wrong to think the boys had understood nothing of the mainstream discussion. Their silence was *a listening silence*. Until we monitored their work so closely we had not appreciated quite how important this attentive listening phase is. What they had heard and reflected upon was evident in the support lesson. Nor had we realized quite so deeply, in relation to language development, the way in which *interaction helps internalization* of so called language knowledge.

We have said that Ann Burgess was surprised at how much the boys had comprehended: a great deal more than she thought they would. She said that she had previously gone for simple things, that she had not expected much of them, had not wanted to overwhelm them, and so, she came to realize, she had been setting them too simple a set of tasks at each of their meetings, in support lessons. She came to realize, too, that they had strategies for telling, despite their halting English, that they had opinions and were operating at a high level of abstract thought, entering the struggle willingly, pushing their resources to the extreme. Such resources include: use of concrete examples to represent abstract ideas, often talking at length (seeming sometimes, in the actual interaction, but not on listening to the tape, to be going round and round the point) until that point is grasped, assisting each other when the third person does not understand, anticipating each other's phrasing; they can pick up and distinguish various tones of voice — including the teacher's irony — and turn that into making another point (for example, Kantilal at utterance 17); they often extend their meanings by using a known word to stand in for a word they do not know yet (but feel to exist) signalling what they are doing by a change in voice tone or the introduction of a form of words, e.g., Kantilal at utterance 12.

The transcript of the tape of this support lesson is totally fascinating for what it reveals of these things, but also both for what it reveals of the *conversational strategies* used by the teacher to ease the students along and for the way in which past *listening participation* echoes in the spoken language of the boys in the support lesson.

In the following quotations, one each from the transcripts of the mainstream lesson and the support lesson, we focus on this internalization through interaction.[4]

The first extract is from the discussion in the mainstream lesson, part of the talk which, before we began our study, we thought was not of benefit to Yogesh and Kantilal. The phrases and words in capital letters are those which the students use to refer to various types of work and their attitudes to them.

47. CLINTON   . . . that headmaster, right, he was the kind of person who

<table>
<tr><td></td><td></td><td>wanted THE PUPILS TO DO THE WORK when he could HIRE HELP to do that.</td></tr>
<tr><td>48a.</td><td>YUET MING</td><td>(speaking at the same time as Xenophon and in support of Clinton) Don't seem to encourage them TO DO WORK.</td></tr>
<tr><td>48b.</td><td>XENOPHON</td><td>(speaking at the same time as Yuet Ming and remonstrating with Clinton for being somewhat extreme) Oh, come on man!</td></tr>
<tr><td>49.</td><td>YUET MING</td><td>They don't seem to encourage them TO DO WORK they encourage them TO DO OTHER WORK like... (searches for the word he wants)...</td></tr>
<tr><td>50.</td><td>KEVIN</td><td>(supplying it) LABOUR.</td></tr>
<tr><td>51.</td><td>YUET MING</td><td>LABOUR! That's it!</td></tr>
<tr><td>52.</td><td>CLINTON</td><td>(elaborating now on his view of this kind of work) Encourage them to do MENIAL WORK.</td></tr>
<tr><td>53.</td><td>KEVIN</td><td>(in solidarity with Clinton) True, true my colleague.</td></tr>
<tr><td>54.</td><td>XENOPHON</td><td>(maintaining his earlier position and speaking forcefully to try and break into the argument the others are mounting) WORK EXPERIENCE.</td></tr>
<tr><td>55.</td><td>CLINTON</td><td>(derisively) Yeah! Like cleaning windows, painting walls and you still in school! WORK EXPERIENCE!</td></tr>
</table>

Now a quotation from the support lesson tape. Ann Burgess, Yogesh and Kantilal have just been listening to the extract quoted above.

<table>
<tr><td>56.</td><td>TEACHER</td><td>OK. What do you think about what Clinton said about the headmaster? Allowing his pupils TO DO ALL THIS WORK? What do you think about the head-master?... (She waits for a response, but not getting one, encourages them further) What do you think he was interested in?</td></tr>
<tr><td>57.</td><td>KANTILAL</td><td>In...like...er...if someones came to see the...see the school, right...and he, he didn't have the workmen, and...er...he told the boys TO DO THE WORK.</td></tr>
<tr><td>58.</td><td>YOGESH</td><td>(joining in and speaking the first words in unison with Kantilal) DO THE WORK...clean the window, and everything.</td></tr>
<tr><td>59.</td><td>KANTILAL</td><td>And the boys DID ALL THE WORK...right, and, er...(now Kantilal answers the question last in the teacher's list)...headmaster, headmaster want to be...want his school very nice.</td></tr>
<tr><td>60.</td><td>TEACHER</td><td>(a touch ironically) Isn't that good? Isn't that good for a headmaster to be like that? Have his school looking nice and clean and polished?</td></tr>
</table>

61a.	KANTILAL	(*in immediate response*) Yes, but if he want like that, right, then HE HAVE TO HIRE THE MEN, WORKING MEN.
61b.	YOGESH	(*speaking the words about hiring exactly in unison with Kantilal*) . . . TO HIRE THE MEN.
62.	KANTILAL	He don't allow to told (*meaning = he shouldn't be allowed to tell*) the boys TO DO ALL *THAT* WORK. If he want a clean, clean house, I mean, a clean school, he HAVE TO CALL A WORKING . . . WORKMEN . . . WORKMEN.
63.	TEACHER	What do you think, Yogesh?
64.	YOGESH	(*about to make a distinction between lesson time and free periods in the matter under discussion*) If there was a free period, right, so if the sir say, so that's alright, but if they go to the period and learn, sir say 'Go and clean a window', everything, they can't learn.

If we had on occasions thought of abandoning our mainstreaming principles, we would not have been justified in doing so. The process of working with Yogesh and Kantilal and monitoring them closely showed us what they were able to do, showed us how interaction can foster internalization, proving groundless our fears that they might not be learning — either language or the content of the lessons — in the environment we had established. At this particular point of time in their development, Yogesh and Kantilal needed the time and space the support lessons gave them for the expression of the understandings and analysis of the play. The support lessons worked so well because when the teacher, like the students, also participates in the mainstream lesson, the participants come to the support lesson with shared understandings. The relationship between both types of lesson is not one-directional: the support lesson backing up the mainstream lesson. It works the other way round, too. Finally, it is not only Yogesh and Kantilal who benefited from these arrangements in our mixed ability teaching. Their presence in the classroom provided a focus for thought and discussion about our teaching and gave our deliberations a coherent framework. This focus helped us improve our teaching to all the class.

Notes

1. The concept of cultural capital is Bourdieu's. See Bourdieu, P. (1977) 'Cultural reproduction and social reproduction', in Karabel, J. and Halsey, A. H. (Eds) *Power and Ideology in Education*, OUP.
2. The development of different kinds of groupings in the class is described in 'The Move from Withdrawal ESL Teaching to Mainstream Activities is Necessary,

Possible and Worthwhile', Chapter 5 of this volume.

3. In this section a consecutive number is assigned to each consecutive utterance in the quotations from transcripts. This is so that the authors can refer to them in the text without confusion. However, the quotations themselves do not necessarily follow on from each other in reality.

4. [*Editorial notes*] Here the focus is on a lexical item, but this phenomenon of internalization through interaction seems to operate on very many learning and language learning levels, e.g., genre, style, function, structure, lexis, idiom, intonation.

9
Student Cooperation and Support in Mainstream English[1]

Josie Levine

In 'Student Cooperation and Support in Mainstream English', *Levine describes a series of three lessons of a Fifth Year, multicultural, multilingual English class with the purpose of demonstrating the industrious dynamic of such a class, i.e., the complex range of knowledge, experience and sophistication that obtains in it, and the consulative mode of work between pupils in such a class. The interest is in how classrooms organized in this interactive mode can be said to be natural language learning environments. By analysis of a transcript of a video recording, the conversation of two students tackling an assignment is inspected, and questions of how such conversations work as learning are posed, particularly how such 'real' conversations might assist bilingual learners develop their use of English. The interpretation of the evidence suggests that like all conversations in which the participants are interested and engaged, classroom conversations have, on the one hand, scaffolding elements of reciprocity and mutality and, on the other, areas of struggle which call on the participants to strive for expression and clarity and to negotiate their meanings and understandings. The former lend support to the latter — make the latter possible. Their relationship, one of interdependence and tension, creates the rigour necessary to transform talk into learning and so contribute to language development.*

The Setting

The setting is a Fifth Year classroom in a mixed comprehensive school of working-class pupils in East London. It is a good class, but not goody-goody: all its teachers would testify that they often had to work hard to get and keep them working, yet they would also want to say that they enjoyed working with them, for there was a zest and intellectual excitement in this class. Now, it is the Spring Term of their Fifth Year.

Jimmy has been in this class from the First Year, and Husseyn, a Turkish Cypriot, joined the class at the end of the Third Year. Jimmy and Husseyn are just entering what will prove to be a productive working friendship in a class well versed in mixed ability practices established by a number of the teachers they have had throughout their schooling.

As a lecturer in the English department of a university institute of education, with special interest in the learning development of bilingual children in mainstream classes, I have worked with this class for one double lesson a week for two years in a cooperative-assist role with their regular teachers. Despite this long term involvement, the three lessons that form the major part of the context for the snatch of time which is under discussion in this chapter is unusual in that I acted as lead teacher throughout each of them. They were the three double (eighty minute) lessons of one week.

The class, reaching the final stages of preparation for the CSE English exam, is mixed ability, multicultural and mutilingual. In addition to Husseyn, there are seven other bilingual or developing bilingual students in the class, about the same number of students of Caribbean origin, and a two-thirds to one-third predominance of boys over girls. In this class there is a developing appreciation of the principles and practices of Equal Opportunities as it relates to race, gender and class.

The learning interaction between Husseyn and Jimmy, which we will inspect, comes from the middle of the three lessons — all three of which the regular teacher, the Special Needs support teacher and I had decided should be used to help the class reach a better awareness of the requirements for writing effective discursive essays. The production of discursive writing was one of the requirements of their exam course work.

For reasons which had to do, I recall, with what my colleagues felt to be my seniority, the other two teachers suggested that I might be better placed than they to effect this literary transformation. Although I regarded this as an arguable proposition, I went along with it. I had previously decided, with their approval, that in order to gather research evidence concerning developing bilingual students in mixed ability mainstream classes, all three lessons would be videoed, and each group in the class would also audio-record themselves on tape recorders as they worked. I saw the tape recordings as having a double purpose in that I intended the students to use them to make notes of aspects of their discussion which they might wish to use in their discursive writing. Along with the video, the recordings would also be a data resource which we, the teachers (and some months later the students), would use to help us reflect on the learning going on in the class.

Personally, I was interested to uncover something of the nature of those interactions which are cooperative and involving students developing a use of English as a second language. I had come to know that the kinds of peer and teacher support that were available in mixed ability classrooms organized as this one was — were of the order that enabled the students to go forward both in their learning and their language learning. If I was wanting to claim, as I did and do, that this was a natural language-learning environment, how was it so?

The More Immediate Context

I had free rein to plan the lessons. The overall plan (but much varied in practice by the students and myself) was: to come to grips via pupil group discussion with the first stage of the assignment, then for pupils to make notes about what they wanted to write about, to order the notes, to start writing, to give the writing to a colleague to read and comment on, to discuss each other's work for content and effectiveness, to ammend. The students could consult with a teacher at any stage — an aspect of interaction in cooperative teaching and learning I want to call a *pupil invitation*. It is a mode which sits alongside the more familiar *teacher intervention*, i.e., when the teacher initiates the time and place to work with any group or individual. I should add that in cooperative teaching and learning the teacher is certainly a highly significant resource, but she is no longer the only resource; the pupils are also a significant resource for each other.

But on what basis should they comment on each other's work? First they had to have some understanding of the discursive essay requirements. Indeed, there is plenty of controversy amongst teachers about the vagaries of discursive writing: for example, the whole question of imposing a 'balance of bias' structure on such work. However, as far as their syllabus was concerned, it was discursive writing inclusive of the ability to argue against opposing views that was required.

The students of 5D were quite good at asserting opinions, but did they know that they needed to build into their essays a discussion of the different points of view involved in their chosen topic? Did they know that they had to argue the case for the side they would eventually come down on? I presumed that they did not, or if they did, that that knowledge was tenuously held. If they had had a firmer grip, then, surely, they would be better than they were at writing in this genre? It was quite possible, too, that among the developing bilingual learners, there were students who did know what was required but who needed help to achieve it in English.

I tried, therefore, to build into the work formula and the teaching the kinds of activity which would allow them, progessively, to approach the desired goals. By that I mean that there should be an overall shape and plan to the lessons which would allow students to start from their actual knowledge and skill level but which also encouraged them to engage in rigorous debate — without necessarily arriving at a consensus amongst themselves, or being in agreement with the initial stimulus material.

I knew that they could weigh the material and come to their own conclusions. My task was to get them to marshal the evidence for their case and, further, to refocus on the nature of the opposite case from their own.[2] I thought we might then have a template for both content and structure by which they could measure the rigour of their own and each others' writing, one which revealed both the writer's awareness of having to bring to bear a range of opinions and evidence for and against the topic, cause or issue, and also the degree to which the writer's stance towards it was logically argued. That is, it would take them further than simply being able to say whether they agreed or disagreed with what each other had written, and, therefore, into helping each other craft both their writing and their ability to argue a case successfully.

The First Lesson

I had started the sequence of lessons by giving each of the five or so groups[3] a poster.[4] The posters were captioned or a caption could be inferred. Initially, I did not frame my instructions specifically enough. I only encouraged them to 'Discuss your picture and make notes'. I had certainly not unpacked the specifics of this task in enough detail. For all but the most experienced in school learning what was needed was a better overt framework from which to work. I had to give them that framework later: i.e., describe in detail to each other what was in the poster, discuss all the possible meanings of what they saw, marshal counter arguments to each meaning. Of course, in our teaching as we went around the room, this more specific framework is what we tended to work to. And it was this more specific consultation model which we were covertly providing for pupils. Jimmy can be seen using the more specific focusing techniques as he works with Husseyn in the second lesson (for example, utterance 9, and utterances 51, 57, 59 of the transcript below). So, undoubtedly, we had been modelling the approach. Nevertheless, the lack of overall specificity for a class of such diverse experience probably also led to there being an even greater gap than one might normally expect between interesting and committed discussion — by no means lacking in ideas — and each student's first attempt at capturing their ideas on paper. I had certainly not unpacked this task as well as I might have done.[5]

Each group had a tape recorder on its table to record the discussions. They were told that they could play back their discussions if they wished in order to help prepare their notes. When it came to it, however, this last activity was not a happy part of the lesson as I had failed in my own mind to take account of, and thus make provision for, the noise that this would inevitably create! Our judgment was so affected by the experience brought on by my not having thought, in any way, about organizing for playback that we spent a considerable part of the latter portion of the lesson shouting at the students for 'messing about' and not concentrating. We were astonished, therefore, to find, on listening to the tapes of the discussions, playing back the video, and reading their notes that almost everyone had taken the assignment seriously. It was a classic case of imputing to the students bad behaviour when, as here, the teacher herself had unwittingly constructed the circumstances. (Surely, few would fall into this same trap today with the greater use of tape recorders now).

The Second Lesson and its Working Groups

In the second lesson, all except one group of students were moving towards a first draft. In theory, they were doing this on the basis of the notes they had prepared in the previous lesson. In practice, no one was being required to do this without some kind of intervention on my part. This intervention mostly took the form of a written response to each individual's set of notes. Even so, only the more assured students were to write directly to what they had done in the first lesson. For the rest, I had prepared fresh starts: new material (although based in some way on what had occurred in the previous lesson or on my knowledge of them prior to that: consulting with them on an interest of theirs or a return to a theme from an earlier lesson) and a worksheet intended to offer an overall framework for their work. The content of the new assignments was various, as it had been on the first day. This time, though, it was more closely tailored to each group.

A description of the class on this day should give an impression of the students and of the classroom organization typical of many of their English lessons (see Figure 9.1).

The three students who had been absent in the first lesson formed a new group. They sat at a table at the back of the room with the Special Needs support teacher who, like me, worked to support in the mainstream. They were Kay, shy but persevering, Tabassum and Derek, both bilingual, both ebullient and voluble. The three were used to working together and enjoyed the good challenge they offered each other. They were to start the whole assignment from the beginning, working with the same poster ('Conditions are never just right') that Jimmy and Husseyn's group had had in the first lesson.

In front of them were Saifullah and Kun Sung, notable workers, bilingual and developing bilingual respectively, engaged jointly in building up a piece that comments on the statement: 'The grass is greener on the other side'.

A third group comprises Ghul, Turkish Cypriot and not long in the country, alert, working wih Monica, black and then the commanding young woman in the class, and Zhora, talented dancer who, till now, has seemed so confident, but who has been rocked by a proposed arranged marriage she is unwilling to agree to. These three girls, Ghul, Monica and Zhora, detach themselves from the boys with whom they usually work, Maurice and Mac. They want to listen again to the last lesson's discussion, to see if it will confirm and help them write about their feeling — which, when I listened to their tape, I came to share — that the boys had shut them out of the discussion

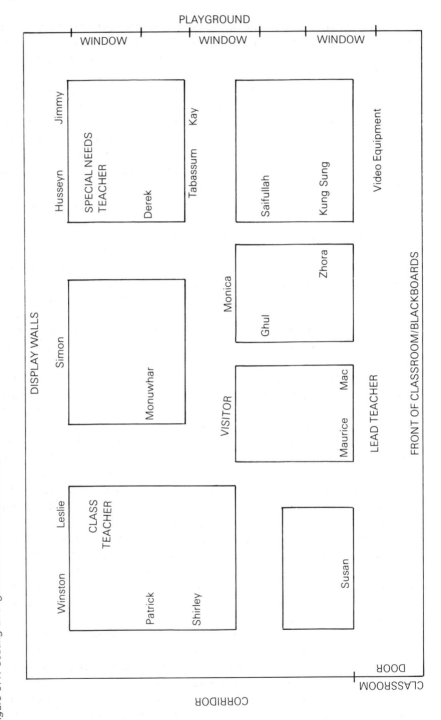

Figure 9.1: Seating arrangements in the second lesson

These boys, Maurice and Mac, both sophisticated and knowledgeable black students, are in this second lesson debating with a visitor the relative merits of capitalism and socialism. It is this question which has arisen for them from the poster they had been given in the previous lesson, the caption of which was: 'There is no such thing as a free lunch'. They are doing their work, so to speak, engaging in discursive argument, but they are also deeply involved in stringing the visitor along, seeing how far they can push the boundaries of an argument in opposition to the visitor's offered opinion. It is politely and elegantly done and they can and do push the boundaries considerably, as the tape of the discussion verifies. However, all this militates against them getting much writing done. I hope to see evidence in the third lesson of them demonstrating in writing their undoubted powers of argument and their proven ability to articulate a number of different points of view.

Susan has to go the dentist half way though the lesson and has decided to sit near the door and get on with her writing by herself.

Behind her Shirley and Patrick work together. This has been normal practice to date. What is less characteristic today is that they have begun work immediately. (Is this the value of my having written a close response to their work?) Usually, they are among the hardest to get going. It is no accident, therefore, that Shirley will turn in the most competent piece of the whole week, having, for a change, put her intelligence and concentration to working to the full.

I have asked Winston to continue to work with Leslie, the only pairing I have directed the entire week. They are friends, but Winston doesn't always choose to work with his pal, so I am taking a risk. If it comes off, Leslie will have sound support in his work, and Winston in having to be explicit (as he will need to be in the assignment I have offered them) may perforce find himself writing in less complicated forms than usual. However there was another reason for asking them to work together. It is simply that Winston is more likely than I am to successfully control Leslie. At the time, I was not acknowledging that one to myself, though that had not fooled Winston. Some months later, he told me that he had seen through me there and then.

Winston and Leslie sit at the same table as Shirley and Patrick. Not surprisingly, given past experience of explosion in this area of the room, their regular English teacher sits down at this table first. He spends a great deal of time with Patrick and Winston and Leslie. Shirley, after a very short period of reading my comments on their work together in the previous lesson, 'abandons' Patrick so she can get on with her writing.

At the table at the centre back of the room are Monuwhar and Simon. Like Husseyn, Monuwhar has been in the country and the class only since the Third Year. Together, he and Simon inspect the tape recorder which is intended both for them and for Jimmy and Husseyn. In the previous lesson, the four of them, with the Special Needs support teacher, had been working on the poster that Kay, Tabassum and Derek are about to use at the adjoining table in the back corner of the room. But the Special Needs teacher has moved over to Kay, Tabassum and Derek today. Husseyn and Jimmy move across with her, taking with them, but not yet having looked at, their share of the new material offered to their original group. It is not clear whether they do this because they like to be with this teacher and are 'trailing' her, or because they are following the poster they worked with last lesson and are not yet aware that their current work no longer involves it, or because they do not want to work with Simon. Monuwhar, by their shifting, has been left, also perhaps unwillingly, to work with Simon. He buries himself deeply and intently in reading (although reading is still a very slow process for him) a copy of the edition of *Issues in Race and Education*[6] that I have supplied as imput for their new assignment. By moving across, Jimmy and Husseyn are left without a tape recorder. They do not at first address themselves to their given work. Instead, they watch and listen to the group which now has 'their' poster, Jimmy, bit by bit, coming to realize that he and Husseyn are not part of this group today. They watch wistfully, if not resentfully, the animated, excited discourse before them, and then, receding quietly into themselves, slouch back in their chairs, lethargic. Ten minutes or so into the lesson, they call me over to complain of their lack of equipment. To make good this lack, and to their laughing consternation, I bring the video microphone to their table. It has its effect. They lean forward and towards each other, put the work I have given them to do between them, and, looking at it for the first time, begin.

Perhaps I have now said enough to capture what is in this second lesson: some of both the complexity, the range of experience, knowledge and sophistication the pupils possess, and the industrious dynamic of this classroom. I hope I have also given a useful impression of the lesson mode of consultative work between students and between students and the adults in the room. I want also to indicate that although students sit in groups, some of them are now entering a phase of individual attention to their writing. Thus we can see that talk in the classroom on this day serves diverse and essential purposes: to begin and pursue a debate prior to writing; to work through a joint assignment or individual work, to chat, gain trust and further understanding of the task, to check, to read something through and comment on it. No one yet, in this second lesson, is discussing another's completed piece, although what they will go on to do in the third lesson is either to complete something already begun or write a discursive essay chosen from a list of topics drawn up for the use of the English department by one of its members.

Jimmy and Husseyn's Assignment

Jimmy and Husseyn's assignment (in my original planning, to have been shared with Monuwhar and Simon) is to explore the pros and cons of an aspect of some then newly introduced nationality legislation. An aspect of this legislation is dealt with in the article in *Issues in Race and Education*,[6] which is accompanied by a cartoon. It is the issue of 'fishing' — a practice of entering places of work and demanding from black people evidence, including their passports, that they have the right to be in Britain. This article, and the cartoon, speculates about the implications of the extension of these 'fishing' exercises to schools; the worksheet is minimal.

1. *Talk together*
   What does the picture mean?
   What would be the opposite things to say?
2. *Write down*, each person for her/himself, the things you want to say arising from your discussion.

The assignment bears upon their previous work in the following ways: the manner of doing the work is generally familiar to them in that they are expected to work together and use talk initially as the central mode for tackling the assignment; it follows up the previous lesson, specifically, in that they have a picture stimulus and they are asked, first, to work out what they think is the meaning of what they see, and then to marshal a case for an opposite point of view; the topic of the assignment, in that it bears on Equal Opportunities and on an issue of race, is not strange to them, even though the specific content is. I expect them to be able to get quite far into their task, given all these different levels of familiarity.

Jimmy and Husseyn Working Together

It is, perhaps, now time to say why I have chosen to focus in this chapter on the interaction between Jimmy and Husseyn rather than on any other interesting and generative partnership available for inspection from the data collected over these three lessons. Certainly, I had more inside information about many of the other groups from working with them in the lessons than I had of this pair. But that was the point, really. They were on their own that day, working together with no teacher either intervening or with them by invitation. It was noticable, too, that although they had never worked in quite this relationship before, they were comfortable together. This, therefore, looked like the kind of socially supportive partnership that, in our experience, was proving to be fundamental to our students developing their knowledge, understanding and skills, in both finding their own voice and taking up their school learning.

Furthermore, these two happened to have their voices, as Jimmy says at the end of the transcript, on the video all the time, thus offering to anyone wishing to inspect some of the dynamics of collaborative learning excellent and accessible data.

The time span of the extract is from the microphone being taken to Husseyn and Jimmy's table till they settle down to make individual notes of their discussion. Comments about and within the transcript focus on the movement of the topic, and Jimmy's almost teacherly structuring of the discourse. Further levels of interpretation are discussed in the final section of this chapter.

Transcript of Husseyn and Jimmy Working Together

The two boys together look at their copy of the newspaper. Jimmy seems to take in at a glance the thrust of the headline and illustration (and, possibly, of the article itself) and assuming responsibility, speaks first.

1.	JIMMY	Er...soon we'll have to go in...to mo...to move into every school, right? And separate the black, and see if...their parents and them have got the right to live in England. An' if this 'appens...it will...er...cause uproar in the federation, won't it?
2.	HUSSEYN	Yeah. (*The rest of the utterance is indeciperable, but it leads to Jimmy saying:*)
3.	JIMMY	Er...do you...do you agree with it? (*and to him urging Husseyn to do what's expected of him in the lesson*) Talk. Just talk to me. Like, do you, do you...agree with me?
4.	HUSSEYN	Don' think so.
5.	JIMMY	Why?
6.	HUSSEYN	'Cos...um...I think we're all right, y'know.
7.	JIMMY	Wha'? (*It would seem that this is not the response that Jimmy is expecting; how could it be, how could Jimmy expect any member of the black community to feel 'fishing' to be all right?*)
8.	HUSSEYN	(*thinking Jimmy has not heard him rather than that Jimmy thinks he has got it wrong, makes a great effort to speak more clearly*) I think we're all right.

Since his friend seems to have got hold of the wrong end of the stick, Jimmy decides on another tack. He sets out to help Husseyn reach a more correct reading of the evidence by employing the strategy his teachers used in the previous lesson, which was first to get people to tell themselves what they saw in the picture and then to move on to its perceived meaning.

9.	JIMMY	(*drawing Husseyn's attention to the picture*) All right. Look, because...oh...'ere's the coppers. One, Two, three, four, five, six, seven. Right? And they've put a rope...and to the

[indecipherable] is all the black people 'n' Pakistanis, an' all that.

10. HUSSEYN   (*following Jimmy's 'lesson'*) Yeah, yeah.

11. JIMMY   True enough.

12. HUSSEYN   Tha's true.

13. JIMMY   (*continuing the strategy*) 'm . . . plus 'ere's the teachers in the [indecipherable] and they couldn't care less.

14. HUSSEYN   (*about to initiate an addition to the list of events and people that Jimmy has been making*) The Pakis . . .

15. JIMMY   Wha'?

16. HUSSEYN   The Pakis . . .

17. JIMMY   Wha'?

18. HUSSEYN   (*he has perceived a need to make a distinction amongst the teachers, between black and white teachers, i.e., a finer distinction than Jimmy has yet made*) The black people teachers . . . (*but, under Jimmy's persistant questioning, Husseyn can't formulate what he wants to say about the black teachers being treated differently from the white; and, further, how, of the black teachers, it might be misplaced to say that they couldn't care less; instead, he aptly uses a quotation from the newspaper to make his point; he starts to read paragraph 8*) . . . 'The white teachers in the staff room enjoying an extended break under . . . '(*he hesitates over the reading of the next word*).

Jimmy now employs another teacherly strategy, this time to help Husseyn read his aptly chosen paragraph.

19. JIMMY   (*supplying the word*) 'surveillance'.

20. HUSSEYN   (*picking up from Jimmy but without halting the flow of his reading*) ' . . . surveillance . . . '

21. JIMMY   (*encouragingly*) Yeah, yeah.

22. HUSSEYN   (*still reading*) ' . . . The black teachers will be . . . (*He hesitates again*)

23. JIMMY   (*supplying the word*) 'elsewhere'.

24. HUSSEYN   (*concluding his reading*) ' . . . elsewhere being questioned.'

25. JIMMY   (*accepting the reading as a contribution and summing up*) So . . . so, they're going to be, like, questioned?

26. HUSSEYN   Yeah.

Jimmy, seemingly satisfied that this phase of their work has concluded in agreement about what is happening in the picture, initiates a move to apply this (assumed) understanding to what he further assumes is a shared circumstance — only to find himself, after a very short time, again confounded.

27.	JIMMY	Yeah, yeah, but what about . . . I mean, do you think this would 'appen, like, in our school? Do y'reckon it would 'appen in our school?
28.	HUSSEYN	Nah, I don' think so.
29.	JIMMY	(*pressing Husseyn to clarify*) Why?
30.	HUSSEYN	'Cos in this school everything's free.
31.	JIMMY	(*finding this an astonishing answer, and not understanding that Husseyn is talking out of his original different 'reading' of the picture, simply repeats the word in a puzzled way*) Free?
32.	HUSSEYN	(*as if being asked for confirmation of his statement*) Yeah.

Jimmy then takes a little time out to recover his equilibrium — by listening in to the group in front of him — before getting back to Husseyn. He seems to have given up on trying to get Husseyn into his, Jimmy's, frame of understanding. Of course, it does not occur to him, as the dominant member of the pair, the — as it were — 'natural' leader in this enterprise, the speaker of English, that he should try to enter Husseyn's frame of reference for interpreting the drawing they are discussing. He goes on to do what most of us do when, in a facilitating role, we do not know what to do next. He moves on to something else, in this case, the next bit of the assignment, and in the course of it, finds himself inspecting his own ideas, as well.

33.	JIMMY	Just a minute. (*He turns his attention for several seconds to the trio sitting in front of him; then back to Husseyn and the worksheet they have before them, and reads*) Orright, 'What would be the opposite . . . things to say?'
34.	HUSSEYN	(*responding at once*) The opposite is . . . the police are . . .
35.	JIMMY	(*interrupting Husseyn as he chimes in almost as quickly with his own idea*) Is that the police interrogate the white people, innit?
36.	HUSSEYN	Yeah.
37.	JIMMY	(*checking up in his own mind*) Is it? It is, innit?
38.	HUSSEYN	[inaudible] . . . black people . . . [inaudible]
39.	JIMMY	(*ignoring Husseyn and adding a rider to his statement of an opposite case*) An' is this right then? They would also have to interrogate the white teachers. (*He pauses for further thought, this time about the position of half caste people*) 'Arf a mo' . . . Just the mi . . . Just the middle group. What would 'appen then?
40.	HUSSEYN	(*trying to respond*) Erum . . .
41.	JIMMY	(*forestalling interruption as he pursues his thoughts*) Like . . . quiet! . . . if the middle way . . . er . . . consisted of half caste people an' all that, right? Right. Then,

		what . . . then what would 'appen to the middle group?
42.	HUSSEYN	(*uncertainly offering his first full statement of the discussion*) Think . . . they're going all together? (*Then with greater certainty*) The police are asking the question the black and white together.
43.	JIMMY	(*agreeing, tentatively, perhaps to encourage Husseyn to go on or perhaps making a personal stab at hearing out an oppositional view*) Yeah. Yeah, might be that, ain't it? (*but then deciding that in his reading of the issue, that wouldn't be the case*) Wait . . . 'arf a minute. I haven't got a right really to say that.
44.	HUSSEYN	(*mentally in his stride now because on his reading of the issue, as we shall see, his statement could be the case*) I think . . .

At this point, Jimmy is distracted back to the animated discussion taking place in the group in front of him. What he hears is them drawing conclusions which, if not exactly wild are certainly different from those drawn by his group when they worked on the same poster in the previous lesson. He intervenes excitedly.

45.	JIMMY	Scuse me! It ain't that! It means that nothing's perfect. No! It means that nothing's perfect.

Meanwhile, Jimmy's attention to the other group has given Husseyn valuable space to continue to work out what he wants to say that is true to his reading of the illustration. He has seen before — or knew of its possibility — police questioning children, only then it had had a benign purpose: in time of civil war, if parents were not able to look after them, their children might be evacuated to a camp in a relatively safer region.

46.	HUSSEYN	. . . the police asking [inaudible]. The hope is your parents think they can.
47.	JIMMY	(*his attention back, he urges Husseyn on*) Yeah Go on.
48.	HUSSEYN	(*taking his opportunity*) If the children's parents' circumstance is not good, right, the policemen are going to take the child off them, putting the child in a camp . . . er . . . school camp. Right? I think this going to be.

All this is completely beyond Jimmy's comprehension, as was Husseyn's earlier talk about being free. Again, Jimmy does not attempt to penetrate Husseyn's statements. Instead, he starts to operate a different imperative. He yawns. On the surface, it looks simply as though he needs a change of activity. He resorts to a previous strategy of moving on the the next thing.

| 49. JIMMY | (*pulling out of his yawn, and referring to the worksheet*) Er . . . shall we do number 2, or what? |
| 50. HUSSEYN | Yeah. (*Reads from the worksheet*) 'Write down each person . . . |

There is a long pause. When Jimmy speaks again, he seems to have decided to have one last go at getting Husseyn to understand the thrust of the article and discuss its pro and cons. Although he has never understood, at any time in this interaction, either what Husseyn's interpretation actually is — of the police, in time of war, separating children from their parents for the common good — nor from where it is coming, he seems to have sensed that he should offer Husseyn a better context for changing his understanding than has previously been available to him. Focusing on Husseyn's Muslim faith rather than his country of origin, Jimmy continues.

51. JIMMY	Oi! Oi! Just had a thought, right? In case, right . . . we was in, like . . . er . . . Bangladesh, like . . .
52. HUSSEYN	(*politely*) Yeah?
53. JIMMY	. . . what would 'appen then?
54. HUSSEYN	(*completely flummoxed*) If be in Bangladesh?
55. JIMMY	Yeah.
56. HUSSEYN	(*playing for time*) Yeah . . . right . . .
57. JIMMY	(*realizing that to imagine being in Bangladesh does not help Husseyn, a Turkish Cypriot, at all, but only confuses the issue, he attempts to improve the context*) No . . . or Turkey.
58. HUSSEYN	Yeah.
59. JIMMY	(*finally getting it right*) No . . . or Cyprus. What would that mean?
60. HUSSEYN	(*repeating, mumbling Jimmy's words, perhaps to gain thinking time*) What would that . . .
61. JIMMY	Eh?
62. HUSSEYN	(*unable to work out the intention of what is, to him, Jimmy's opaque questioning*) Dunno.
63. JIMMY	(*prompting, offering him for the first time a key word and, by now, a little impatient*) Would that also be racialist?
64. HUSSEYN	(*with no real conviction and still mumbling*) Think so, yes.
65. JIMMY	Wha'?
66. HUSSEYN	Think so.

There is a long pause. It seems they both want to move on, get some relief from this impasse. A change of activity would help. I certainly think that their discomfort with not quite understanding each other is a greater motive for moving to the next part of the assignment than the fact that they believe themselves ready to start making notes. Besides, they have an assignment sheet

31. KHALID   (*muttering incomprehensively together*)
    and
    METIN
32. LEE SAI   ... people on the ship, and to go away from island from south.
33. FEMI   (*seeing a way of making a complete escape from the previous difficult ideas, shifts allegiance again*) That's it! We can move to the south.
34. LEE SAI   (*pleased at having been taken seriously and been regarded as sensible*) Yeah.

Metin, however, does not want to lose his case and attempts, at utterance 35, to take the next turn. Lee Sai, confidently but wrongly taking him to be in agreement, completes Metin's sentence for him as though it were part of the discourse of his, Lee Sai's, own suggestion. But then Khalid returns to the fray at 37 and an argument about who will speak next ensues between him and Metin, the most entertaining part of which is the way they, with conscious irony, turn the polite bidding phrase which I have taught them, *Excuse me*, to the purpose of closing off space from each other — a device not unknown in more sophisticated debating chambers.

35. METIN   Look, we must ...
36. LEE SAI   Try.
37. KHALID   Excuse me! Excuse me! METIN Look! Look!
38. KHALID   Excuse me! Excuse me! METIN Look, I'm talking man.
39. KHALID   (*laughing*) Excuse me!
40. METIN   (*serious, insistant*) I'm talking.
41. KHALID   (*mocking*) Excuse me!
42. METIN   (*still serious about his own suggestion*) You can't believe me, right?
43. KHALID   (*intensifying the mockery*) Excuse me! Excuse me!
44. HALIM   (*turning to Femi and reprimanding him for his loose chairing of the discussion*) You can't let them talk ...
45. KHALID   (*turning now on Halim, exasperation and disgust added to his earlier mocking*) Excuse me!

(*At this point the tape recorder is switched off while they sort out the quarrel.*)

Talk, Reflective Thinking and the Tape Recorder

It seemed a pity to resign the achievement of these discussions to the oblivion of the summer holidays, and I wondered doubtfully whether more could be drawn from our island when we returned in September. The interest of a few boys who were prepared to consider ways of facing famine and relationships with the outside world was sustained. However, the others had lost interest and gleefully accepted 'death' with the failure of the crops: a signal that they 'did not want to play' any more.

This, then, was the death of the island idea. Its success had been entirely oral. Little had emerged in written form: indeed it was valuable because it had been taken seriously as a verbal topic that did not require justification by written work. It had served its purpose and proved a point. Relationships had opened up, risks had been taken, verbal skills in English had been developed. The students had also demonstrated that they could be better at understanding one another's meanings in English than I could: often a speaker of one language would explain to me the English of another pupils with a different language. Nor was it infrequent during the rest of their language centre time for students to choose to record discussion, explanation and oral composition of stories. They came to know a lot of things about talk through the use of talk as a learning strategy and the range of situations in which they could function developed through their active participation in them. They could help each other to speak, show solidarity, as well as compete and sabotage; they knew how to claim space and also be facilitative; they were learning to recognize the importance of turn taking, to chair, to bring themselves back to a central point, to summarize; they could complain and argue, interview to elicit opinions and information.

The use of the tape recorders has proved to be invaluable. They legitimize oracy from the beginning so that class, group, or an individual's talk can always be regarded by the students as a valid activity. Considerable practice and experience is gained that contributes to an ability to organize thought through English: aiding the dissociation processes leading to more explicit writing. The obvious value of the written word in supporting the development of reflective processes of thought comes from the convenient possibilities for re-examination, rehearsal and rearrangement while refining both thought and its expression. This, not surprisingly, has led to a pedagogical prominence for writing. The increasing practicality of audio-visual equipment in capturing speech allows talk to become subject to similar reflective use. Researchers into natural speech are wary of the effect on their production of speakers knowing they are being recorded. They therefore take the trouble to minimize this influence when making tapes. However, when recording talk as a deliberate alternative to using writing as a developmental medium, the intention is to heighten students' awareness of what they are saying and of the effectiveness of their communication.

Over the period of their existence as a group, the people I have been describing here became increasingly adept at controlling the equipment. They learned both to plan ahead and remove unwanted instrusions; they corrected and rephrased. They played back to examine what had already been expressed when hesitance, interruption, uncertainty or confusion stopped the flow; they listened to recapture the feeling for the topic after a break. The consequence was that members of the group became increasingly critical of their work and in particular about its form and content. They strove to improve as they became aware of more possibilities. These are all activities known to writers.

In the following extract, they are all in the act of negotiating a rounded conclusion. We can say, I think, that they are showing signs of planning an ending. In the space between the last quotation from the transcript and this which follows, Tam Ho has had time to make a suggestion that he could grow a strain of super-grass, so that if they remained on the island during the flood, there would be food to eat after the disaster had receded. Metin, too, had added another idea: about escaping by plane. Femi initiates and efficiently undertakes a reinspection of the ideas that have been put forward.

46.	FEMI	You know, if we, if we discuss this to ourself, it'll be much better. You know. Mr Lee say about this . . . er . . . about this ship. Mr Tam say about eat grass.
47.	TAM HO	Yes.
48.	FEMI	Mr Halim say about the . . .
49.	HALIM	(*whose island name is Jungle Boy, hurriedly pushes away the conversation turn he is being offered — he has not got round to putting a suggestion yet*) Not me! Khalid!
50.	FEMI	(*holding on tightly to the shaping of the discussion summary*) Mr Khalid who will say about the water flooded, about, you know, about the water. And I say about the . . . if we make a brick to stop the water coming. And you here, Metin, say about . . .
51.	METIN	(*insisting on his island name*) Mr Tarzan.
52.	FEMI	(*accepting the correction*) Mr Tarzan say about that, about . . . er . . . train.
53.	METIN	(*correcting him again*) Aeroplane.
54.	FEMI	Aeroplane. And Mr Halim . . .
55.	HALIM	(*insisting, in turn, on his island name*) Jungle Boy.
56.	FEMI	And Jungle Boy say about what he doesn't know what to say about that!

It looks as though this last cutting remark could sting Halim into spoken involvement. He seems, with Femi, anyway, to be aware that the relative merits of the suggestions have not yet been decided. The discussion continues, still ably led by Femi — even down to maintaining the island names of those who have been insisting on them.

57.	FEMI	First, let's do about what everybody said. First because Mr Lee said about the ship, because the ship might sink. (*meaning: I'm not sure that's such a good idea, after all*).
58.	HALIM	Yeah.

59. FEMI   That's what I'm worrying about, Khalid is saying about the . . . er . . . what was it? About the underground thing and the . . . the water might sink over there . . . we might have an earthquake, and Mr . . . er . . .
60. HALIM   Metin?
61. FEMI   Tarzan (*he remembers Metin's island name*). He said about the aeroplane . . . er . . . (*about to make his own assessment of the suggestion*) . . . the aeroplane was really dangerous anyone flies on people in aeroplane, that's in . . . that's in . . . that is into something (*meaning: the aeroplane might fly into something*). You can't do that . . . (*and then he foresees further drawbacks to the suggestion*) . . . and the animals? What are we going to eat? Because we can't stay in the air for long. (*Making a decision*) We can go to another country.
62. HALIM   Yeah. It is . . .

(*Indecipherable talk of several voices, out of which Tam Ho's emerges*)

63. TAM HO   (*reminding everyone of his earlier suggestion about super-grass*) . . . glass (*his pronunciation of 'grass'*)
64. FEMI   (*picking up the threads and still performing the task of weighing one idea against another*) Mr Tam said about the super-grass, but how can we get super-grass from?
65. TAM HO   I can make it. For a long time I've been making super-glass.
66. FEMI   (*sardonically*) You been making it a hundred years, eh?
67. TAM HO   (*Defensively, beginning to see that the others think his idea is not feasible — daft even*) No!
68. KHALID   (*cackling, mocking, laughter*)
69. FEMI   So you have . . .
70. TAM HO   (*anticipating the kind of question that might be coming, and going into aggressive defence of his idea, status and ability as a scientist*) Yes, Many years ago.
71. HALIM   (*this is Halim's first real contribution to the debate other than to agree with a previous speaker or to pass on the speaking 'buck'; presumably, that is why he introduces himself, even though it is now well into the discussion; he then goes on to make a considerable challenge to Tam Ho's idea*) Excuse me. My name is Jungle Boy. I'm sure that one man says that, I'm surer that wrong.
72. TAM HO   (*taking up the challenge and denying its implication at once*) No!
73. HALIM   (*not to be deterred*) I think so.
74. TAM HO   (*calling for reasons, not assertions*) Why?
75. HALIM   (*beginning to give his reason*) See a long time the bottle . . .
76. TAM HO   (*no idea what Halim is talking about*) What? What bottle?

77. FEMI   (*neither has Femi any idea what Halim is talking about, and he can see the good work so far done towards drawing together the threads of the discussion going up in the smoke of a new argument, and so he tries to prevent a diversion, calling for them to think hard about what will and will not work, what will be a more or less dangerous thing to do*) No, let's do everything right. We got to make a machine, a machine can do this. I don't know why this thing, even if we make anything, right, we might cause an earthquake. That's what we worry about. You don't want any fire . . .

78. TAM HO   (*persisting and still refusing to accept their aspersions on his scientific ability*) Do you know I'm a scientist? I can make it because . . . (*indecipherable few words*) . . . glass.

Recorded talk, then, both spontaneous and formal, I think we can see, provides a means of becoming more conscious of ordering thought. For pupils inexperience with literacy in English can be a barrier to conscious ordering of thoughts taking place through that mode. Recorded discussion is, therefore, a particularly useful tool. It also prepares them for explicit writing by helping them to order and reorder what their thoughts are. Listening to taped stories and taping their own readings helps them to recognize that reading involves learning a voice. For pupils unfamiliar with the sound of that voice, this is most supportive, and again permits increased access to reflection on the meaning of texts.

As a group, they also began to listen to each other more carefully and critically so that, increasingly, they interacted effectively with others rather than aiming primarily for their own personal performance. Is this akin to an inexperienced reader becoming aware that a book's voice can creatively evoke and mingle with personal ideas and experiences to generate new understandings?

Sometimes, I collected their ideas from tapes and wrote a summary of them for them. This not only demonstrated how their ideas could be drawn together in written form but also provided material in which the validity of their talk could be recognized. The familiarity of the content encouraged fluent reading.

Talk, Tape Recorders and Teachers: a Summary

I have tried to demonstrate the value of recording talk for pupils and of their taking active responsibility for that recording. Finally, I should like to draw together what it is that I think is the value of recorded talk for teachers. It is this.

— It provides clues from the beginning as to the English already available to a student, the areas of interest, the angles of interest

— It helps teachers to get to know students as people and as users of English
— It helps to signal to the students that the teacher values talk; doing it legitimizes it as a learning activity.
— It provides a means of assessing and reassessing what happens in a lesson/activity/outing, often with surprising results (e.g., lessons that appeared to be chaotic had been creative and productive)
— It provides a means of sharing knowledge about students' capacity to negotiate and communicate successfully long before their grasp of English spoken forms are maturely established; reveals the strategies they use to achieve this; shows their limitations and, therefore, where they need help or focus to move forward.
— It provides information for the learning to be based appropriately on students' needs and interests.
— It provides a way for the students to communicate indirectly with their teacher when it could be embarrassing or compromising to do so directly.
— It provides data which teachers and students can use as a memory bank, which they can reflect on, which can be turned into written texts directly or summarized.
— It allows teachers to derive a record of students' verbal attainment, of their pattern of development, and assess their needs more aptly.
— It allows students both to know their teachers and their peers better because interaction is essential.

Notes

1. Utterances in the transcript quoted in this chapter are numbered consecutively for ease of reference. The transcripts themselves do represent consecutive events. However, utterance 1 of this chapter is not the first utterance of the original taped discussions.
2. [*Editoral note*] But what if his use of the word was a slip? What if he meant '*and we will be able to walk above the level of the waters?*' That would keep his argument for building above water level sound. But does that account for why Femi appears to use the word *high* to mean *deep* between utterances 21 and 25? Perhaps it does. Perhaps we all governed in heated discussion in this way, building our understandings both from the words which are to us salient and also by our own personal understandings of their meanings. Intruding into and intensifying the process for these discussants is the fact that they are at the beginning of their process of developing a use of English and may well have been taught or come across the words expressing these opposite meanings, *high/low*, *under/over*, *above/below*, very close together, if not at the same time. In such cases, learners of a new language often find the sounds representing the meanings of the words they are being taught harder to remember than the concepts they

represent, and quite often, at a point of early acquaintance with new words, they use them seemingly at random, in a way that is regarded in the customary speech of the language as the wrong way round. Yet, the relationship between sound and meaning is generally agreed to be arbitary. The confusion seemingly generated here has possible interpretation as a manifestation of this particular feature of language.

11
'C'mon Shabir, Get Out All Your Ideas'
or Recognizing the Limitations of Our Teaching

Susan Werner

In ' "C'mon Shabir, Get Out All Your Ideas" or Recognizing the Limitations of Our Teaching', Werner carefully describes the internal detail of central areas for teachers' attention if bilingual learners developing a use of English are to get maximum benefit from mainstream classes: the teaching/learning environment, social context, curriculum content; going on to spell out and closely inspect 'lesson' plans, materials and transcripts of tapes of a wide ranging Humanities collaborative learning curriculum project in Development Education in terms of teaching objectives, lesson content and procedures, talk contexts, language activities, class organization, and whether there was a satisfactory level of student cooperation. By this introspective means she offers a practical tool for checking on the efficacy of important features of the learning environments we establish. Satisfied that the Humanities project, and its methodology, has largely met the collaborative criteria established for it (and having seen how practice within it could be further enhanced), she finds that her observations of it also reveal a signal 'failure' within it of one learner. By means of analysis of a support lesson conversation she has with her student in 'learning difficulties', Werner discovers that she has been underestimating this pupil's knowledge and thinking because of his struggles with expression in English, and that she has been overestimating the degree to which she has been lending support towards this development; and in so doing, contributing to his difficulties.

Introduction

The School

The work described in this chapter was undertaken between 1980 and 1982 with colleagues in the Humanities Department of one of Waltham Forest's multiracial junior high schools (age range 11–14).[1] Its intake consisted of a large number of children of Caribbean origin, of Pakistanis, of indigenous white children and smaller numbers of Cypriots, African-Asians, Africans, Indians and Bangladeshis. A significant number of the school population had a first language other than English — Panjabi and Urdu being the main language groups with Gujarati, Tamil, Greek, Turkish, Italian, Cantonese and Twi also spoken. The staff as a whole had espoused an antiracist, antisexist stance (although no written policy was developed) and an active multicultural working party existed whose aim was the development of a multicultural curriculum. There were two teachers from the borough's West Indian Supplementary Service (WISS) working in the school, as was one teacher from the borough's Remedial team and two from the borough's English as a Second Language team.[2] All were seconded full time to the school and worked widely throughout the school, something which, at this time, was exceptional, as was the general flexibility and supportiveness of the school staff who, by and large, encouraged throughout the school the involvement in the mainstream curriculum of bilingual students, their specialist language teachers, and the other supplementary staff.

The Role of the ESL Department

Throughout preceding years, the role of the English as a Second Language Department had broadened from only teaching in withdrawal groups, moved through accompanying Third Year students into Science, to a much more active involvement in mainstream classes. At the time of which I am writing, the year of the school's closure, I, as a teacher of English as a Second Language, was also a member of the Humanities Department, and my ESL colleague, who was Science trained, was also a member of the Science Department, each of us having mainstream whole-class teaching responsibilities. By limiting the number of students we taught in small groups to those at the early end of the bilingual continuum and to those whose mainstream work we supported, and by participating in two main areas of the curriculum where we met a wide range of developing bilinguals, we hoped to use our time most effectively and contribute to the speedier social and educational integration of the bilingual students into mainstream school life.

The Humanities Department

Humanities was a two year course in the First and Second Year, taken by all pupils. The department consisted of a Geography, a History, and an RE specialist, the two WISS teachers and myself, the English as a Second Language teacher. The classes were mixed ability. In the Second Year, two classes were taught at a time, split three ways so that class sizes were reduced to 14–18 students. Each class had two double and one single period of Humanities each week. In the Third Year, students began to work in the subject specialisms of History, Geography and RE in preparation for the examination orientation of the senior high school. The Humanities Department saw itself as having a vital role to play in the field of multicultural education. As a result of the interests of individuals and the very democratic structure of the department, thorough discussion of teaching methods and curriculum content was possible. Towards the end of my first year at the school, I accompanied a group of developing bilingual students into the class and took part in the 'whispering over the shoulder' mode of teaching described in the next section of this chapter. It was quickly and easily decided that this was unsatisfactory and I was formally invited to join the team, taking responsibility for a full class, some of whom were also withdrawn from other areas of the curriculum for work in English as a Second Language. Several other of the students in the class were bilinguals fluent in English.

Developing Bilingual Students and Mainstream Classes

Traditionally, developing bilingual students were withdrawn from certain lessons in order to join a small group at a similar stage of competence in English: withdrawn to an ESL teacher so she can 'teach them English'. Along the continuum of bilingualism, pupils who were just beginning to operate in English were withdrawn from many lessons and pupils who had a fair degree of competence from few. My concern in this study of a course of Humanities work was with students who were withdrawn from a few mainstream lessons.

In my withdrawal group, I had a group of Second Year students, who in accordance with the traditions of the department, had not yet attended any Humanities lessons and were keen to go. I was hopeful that they would benefit from the lessons, and aware that their continued withdrawal would be damaging. Students became alienated from 'ESL' peers and teachers, some-times from school altogether, when they begin to feel they are not being provided with a stimulating enough environment, that they are being deprived of the mainstream curriculum by continued attendance in ESL classes. Hand in hand with this reaction there is often a consciousness of stigma attached to their withdrawal. However positive the image of ESL students and teachers in the school, withdrawal from lessons implies to peers and other teachers an inability to cope — an implication which may exacerbate racist attitudes, students' self image being undermined. It is also harder for them to build up social relationships beyond the withdrawal groups.

One option open to me was to place the students in a Humanities class and attempt to liaise very closely with the subject teacher so that I could support their learning in withdrawal lessons. Another was to invite myself into the class with them. I did the latter. By being in class, alongside the students, I reasoned that I would be able to become properly aware of what was taught and how. I would be readily able to help bilingual students with difficulties as they arose and, in the withdrawal group context later, could reinforce the subject learning, and develop appropriate language structures and vocabulary practice. This list alone shows that there are some positive aspects to working in this 'whispering over the shoulder' mode. One significant drawback, however, is again the potential — certainly as high as with withdrawal lessons — for reinforcing bilingual students' isolation and confirming a sense of their inability to cope; it can be taken as a demonstration of this supposed inability, and have an effect of creating and/or reinforcing racist views within the class. Another is that if there are only a few students in the class in the process of developing a use of English, ESL teachers can easily consider this not the most efficient use of their time. Thirdly, the method does not affect the curriculum in terms of inviting students to participate in it more easily.

What is the Solution for Developing Bilingual Students to Gain Maximum Benefit from the Mainstream Classes?

For developing bilingual students to gain the maximum benefit from the mainstream classes, three areas need to be closely scrutinized: the teaching/learning environment, the social context, and the curriculum content.

Teaching/learning environment. Fundamental to the success of the project which will be described below, is a commitment on the part of all the staff involved to mixed ability teaching. In this context, developing bilingual students are simply part of a mixed class in which collaborative learning and group work can be established as the norm. In this way, just as, for example, better readers can help less experienced readers, so experienced users of English can help developing bilinguals. The teacher's task is to organize the class in such a way as to encourage such collaborative learning, to devise materials which are accessible to all students and build on the knowledge and experience of individuals in the class, involving the students in meaningful tasks where their *active* participation is required for learning to take place. Talk is a vital activity for such collaboration. In this kind of working environment, students are motivated and their confidence in their own powers grows.

Social context. The social context is a mixed ability working environment where the students know that the groups are organized so as to facilitate the participation of all members, and that it is the responsibility of each member to be 'hospitable' to the others, to recognize the contributions, value the talents and experiences of the others. In this a teacher has a vital role to play as model and guide. It must be further said that the working environment must be seen to be antiracist and antisexist. Whatever the prevailing attitudes in the wider community, the school needs to be unambiguous in its statements and practice in relation to offering equal opportunities for all to learn. Students have to know that no individual or group will be marginalized on the basis of gender or ethnicity. Racist and sexist attitudes need to be openly discussed as part of a whole school philosophy for the education of its students. There is no way it can operate successfully unless every student can feel confident to express her or his point of view without fear of ridicule on either of these two grounds.

Curriculum content. Just as one needs to analyze carefully styles of teaching and the materials used to encourage the active participation of all pupils, so attention must also be paid to content. Too often our reasons for selecting what we teach (and how) are not sufficiently considered. Yet this area is vital for students' motivation and participation. The content of the curriculum should not be exclusive to the interests and experience of one particular sector of the school community, but should have relevance to all and be presented in such a way that all members of the group can learn from it.

Ours was a multiracial, multilingual, urban working-class teaching environment. We were operating in a deteriorating Victorian building that looked more like a prison than a place of enlightenment. We had certain advantages, however: a highly committed staff; a flexible administration which had an explicit commitment to antiracist, antisexist education; and enthusiastic students. In planning this project, we considered the three points discussed above, namely, the teaching/learning environment, the social context, and the subject content. The result was the Panjab Project.

The Panjab Project

Background and Aims

Each member of the Humanities team was allocated overall responsibility for a half term's unit of work. My contribution was to the redesigning of part of the Second Year course — originally on the syllabus as *The Third World*. In 1980–81, we drew together the general shape of the unit establishing the working principles and discovering the weaknesses. The following year, after a great deal of discussion both within the school and more widely,[3] the unit was restructured and much improved upon, though because of changing circumstances, it was never finalized. However, I firmly believe that the evidence of the success of the 1981–82 version is a strong case for collaborative learning and just as strong a case for the participation in the mainstream of bilingual students developing a use of English.

Responsibility for redesigning this unit gave me the opportunity of proving that the principles I had raised at so many departmental meetings were workable. Below are a list of my aims in becoming involved, as a teacher of English as a Second Language, in the Humanities Department: aims which I hoped the successful development of this unit would go some way to furthering.

1. To foster the confidence of the students developing a use of English as a Second Language new to Humanities, and also of bilingual students already taking the subject, so that they participate more actively in the learning situation.
2. To devise materials and an approach to teaching the subject which encourage this.
3. In doing so, to provide models for subject teachers to encourage more active learning which can be developed in other areas of the syllabus.
4. In a department where a readiness continually to reassess course content areas, to focus attention on the language needs of all pupils and the accessibility of course materials to all pupils.
5. To extend the multicultural content of and approach to the subject.

How the Planning Decisions were Made

My task, for reasons explained earlier, was to provide the learning environment, social context and curriculum content, actively to engage all the pupils in learning something of the issues related to the term 'Third World', and what the notion of 'Development' might mean in that context. This was to be achieved in a short half term of four to six weeks!

We were very clear about the social context and learning environment we wanted to achieve. Students already were in mixed ability classes where they were expected to cooperate with each other and include those learning to use English — although it had taken us a year firmly to establish this mode of behaviour. We quickly decided that a simulation exercise would be an effective way of breaking down barriers, concentrating on important issues relating to Development. It would help us to shift the focus away from fairly mechanical written tasks to presenting other more purposeful tasks which could only be resolved through talk, interacting, discovering, negotiating, deciding, planning, and presenting *collaboratively*. Solutions to the practical problems related to implementing this ambitious design came slowly, by trial and error and by discussion.[3]

One of the more difficult decisions we had to reach was over content. The reason for wanting to revise the unit came in the first place because the staff had expressed dissatisfaction with the materials which had been used previously. It was suggested that the reason they did not engage the students' interest might possibly be because they were so remote from their experiences. We decided, instead, to choose a Third World country more closely related to the experiences of, at least, some of the students, and to focus on a particular area as a case study. Eventually we chose India because, while it experiences many of the text book 'problems' of the Third World, it is a country so richly diverse that stereotypes can easily be challenged. The location of the case study in the Panjab enabled us at least to touch on the question of the Green Revolution to the local population. Further, many of the school's students originated from Pakistan, part of which was once part of a larger undivided Panjab, and it was felt that they would be familiar with much background information, e.g., village life, farming methods. It was felt that they would be able to make a positive contribution based on their knowledge. Also, there were two Indian teachers on the staff, one of whom came from the Panjab and who was, therefore, in a position to give authoritative information.

The Panjab Unit

The Panjab unit was half of a term's work for a second year's Humanities course. The purpose of the first part of the unit was to place the Panjab in its context within India and give the students some idea about its particular features, e.g., its predominantly Sikh population, its relative prosperity (attributed to the success of the Green Revolution), its high wheat production. The first time we did the unit, we used an assortment of workcards and a students' booklet to get this background information across, all in the written mode, creating a considerable lack of variety through excluding other modes. Learning from our mistakes, we provided more visual stimulus the second time round, cutting down considerably on the written work and trying to make research activities a communal operation. This generated more enthusiasm for the 'high spot' of the unit, the simulation. The material presented here is from the second time of doing the unit. For the simulation in the last weeks of the course, the students 'became' Panjabi villagers, initially making a decision through their representatives on the village council, the Panchayat, about whether they wanted to sell village land to build flats for emigrants returning to the village. Cue cards were provided and pupils divided into groups of three or four. The groups were teacher selected to be mixed ability, mixed gender and multilingual. The flats proposition was rejected. The villagers, in their groups, were then allowed a week to decide whether to take up an alternative proposal by the Block Development Officer to build a cloth cooperative, a sugar factory or farming school. They were given a further period of time to organize their case for their chosen scheme, to present it to him and to convince him of their argument. (See Tables 11.1 and 11.2).

Table 11.1: A sketch of the procedure, organization, learning and talk contexts.
Part 1: Preparation

Teaching objectives	Lesson content and procedure	Talk context	Language activity	Class organization
	introductory talk with slide-show	input of information by teacher students contributing experience and knowledge	*listening* to teacher and peers to clarify understanding of information and opinions *talking* to give information and opinions	two full classes together in formal setting
Students take on information in a variety of ways and get used to working socially	mapmaking using outline map and atlases for reference follow-up group talks to class	sharing out work borrowing reference work representation work formal exposition to whole class	*talking* to pool information and negotiate tasks; complaining; some formal talk *listening* for instructions and information and to others; to chatter; to formal talk *reading* to extract information and organize on map *writing*: labelling maps; making notes for talks	small groups within whole class
	gathering information, gaining experience, tasks and opportunities to use displays, artefacts re: climate, crafts, industry, agriculture, education, religion and village life	research recording	*speaking* to access, negotiate, share information; decide relevance; give informal reports *reading* for instructions, information; locating specific information *listening* for information and instructions; to other points of view about relevance, etc. *writing* to take notes from a variety of sources	in 2s + 3s moving around displays in classrooms and hall

Table 11.2: A sketch of the procedure, organization, learning and talk contexts. Part 2: The Simulation

Teaching objectives	Lesson content and procedure	Talk context	Language activity	Class organization
Students to take on roles, gain an understanding of power relations and democratic processes; students work collaboratively	interest group (family) meeting with role cards	using role cards: –to identify with own interest group –to decide on group view of BDO's proposal –to help spokesperson to prepare to represent group at Panchayat	*reading* from role cards to identify own group interests; to comprehend opinions *listening* to gain information and understand arguments *speaking* to formulate opinions and mount argument; to clarify understanding; to decide how to represent views at the more formal Panchayat meeting; to interrupt to gain access to discussion and/or formal debate; to challenge views, disagree, contradict; to question politely in formal and informal context	interest (family) groups of 4 or 5
	Panchayat (meetings of families within village)	conducting the Panchayat meeting so all views are expressed and listeners participate appropriately		whole class with 5 Panchayat reps and Sarpanch (head person) and audience in formal setting
	3-village meeting with BDO	spokespersons present the views of their villages (arrived at at each separate village Panchayat); audience participation		two classes (i.e. 3 villages with BDO in formal setting

Did the Students Collaborate? Transcript of Some Evidence

Some Contextual Points

Two points need mention here. The first is that there had been a good deal of pre-publicity to encourage the students' interest in this unit — from the sight of several teachers setting up unaccustomed displays in and around the Humanities rooms, through the obvious interest of the Head and outside agencies[3] in what was happening, to my own earnest request to the various groups at the opening sessions to view this work differently, to see it as a kind of experiment which depended on their cooperation, an experiment in which talk and student collaboration were essential. The second is that the situation had been carefully structured to make it necessary for students to work together, from the initial activity of map making, through joint decision making at family group and Panchayat (village meeting) levels, to the preparation and presentation of materials to the Block Development Officer. The problem, fatal to a simulation on this scale, of students consistently 'opting out' in large numbers did not occur, although, of course, there were occasions when some students were less involved in the tasks than others. We shall see, though, in the final section, how a student, even in the reasonable and encouraging circumstances that obtained through this unit of work, may still *appear* not to be learning.

The Setting for Transcript 1

Extracts from the transcript of my group's first Panchayat meeting (in the simulation they were the village of Chak Zinda) illustrate the students' active participation in the simulation. They also show how much information about the context they had absorbed both from the two weeks' background work and from their role cards. The 'village' had approximately ten minutes to spend reaching its decision at Panchayat level on whether to sell land for the building development, then the Head Person (Sarpanch) had to convey that decision with an explanation to the Development Officer at a public meeting at which all three simulated villages were present. Shortage of time was added to by our Panchayat, at least, being interrupted several times by the Development Officer urging us to make our decisions!

Chak Zinda assembled for its Panchayat meeting. The Sarpanch and the family group representatives sat in a semicircle at the front of the class while the rest of us (nine or so students and myself, having the role of village lawyer) were sitting informally on chairs and desks facing them. It is not without significance that no other conversations were pursued in the course of the meeting. The villagers were attending to what their representatives were saying. This listening silence was only broken by laughter, occasional interruptions for clarifications of a point, and by murmurs of agreement and such like. Only at the end of the session, when they were summoned to the hall for the public meeting, does the class potential for noise become apparent!

The device of casting ourselves, the teachers, in the role of village lawyers was to enable us to participate in the simulation as facilitators, to clarify procedure should that be necessary, and to aid villages, again where necessary, to make their points, but without undermining the students' role in the simulation. As the transcript shows, I found myself intervening rather more than I had expected to, particularly at the beginning, where I felt responsible for 'getting the ball rolling' as each group representative was invited to put her or his group's point of view. With hindsight, I realized that the difficulty would have been overcome if the Sarpanch had chaired the meeting.

Representatives at the Panchayat meeting

Name	Sex	Ethnic origin	Other Information
Sevgi	F	Turkish Cypriot	academically able; fluent bilingual in Turkish and English
Andrew	M	White Walthamstow	bright; unmotivated academically
Paul	M	White Walthamstow	hardworking; shy; withdrawn from French lessons for remedial work
Alfie	M	White Walthamstow	participates well in oral work; underachieving in written work; low self image academically
Aubrey	M	Ghanaian	bilingual; able; well motivated; helpful

Andrew, Alfie, Aubrey and Sevgi were used to participating orally in class and, presumably, that is why their groups chose them to be spokespersons. Paul was selected by even shyer members of his group, who, it should not be allowed to pass without note, were both bilingual learners and female. There is still much work to be done in the area of gender expectations.

Transcript 1

1. TEACHER   (*taking it as her task to introduce Paul and then in the action changing her mind and starting to guide him into making his opening statement*) So, perhaps, um, Paul, who represents . . . well, tell us who you are and who you represent, please . . .
2. DEVELOPMENT OFFICER   (*interrupting*) Ten minutes more, OK?
3. PAUL   (*tentatively: too quietly*) Muzara.
4. TEACHER   Hm?

5.	PAUL	(*more firmly*) Muzara.
6.	TEACHER	(*trying to guide Paul into a shaped statement*) Mention who you are. (*Pausing briefly, then deciding on another prompt*) What are the Muzara?
7.	PAUL	(*not quite 'with' things yet*) Hey?
8.	TEACHER	(*encouragingly*) What are they? (*Pausing briefly, then adding another prompt*) Are they potters or farmers or what?
9.	PAUL	(*muttering unconfidently*) Landless.
10.	CLASS	(*not having caught Paul's statement*) What?
11.	TEACHER	(*answering for Paul, wanting to get things moving*) Landless. No land.
12.	PAUL	(*launching himself into a statement of his group's viewpoint which is that after the flats are built there will be little hope of future employment because the building of the flats will have destroyed the farmland*) We don't want the flats because, um, if we get jobs building the flats . . . flats . . . we'll be paid for a year building it. So, when we lost our ground, like, building it, we won't have much jobs. Um, so we don't want it, don't want the flats really . . .
13.	TEACHER	(*encouraging him to go on*) Uhhuh.
14.	PAUL	Because . . .
15.	ANOTHER	(*agreeing with Paul's statement*) That's it.
16.	TEACHER	(*at one and the same time, as teacher trying to help Paul, and as unofficial chair feeling the need to move on and so taking over from him and summarizing*) You think it's just short term — it'll give you work for a while . . .
17.	PAUL	Yeah.
18.	TEACHER	(*continuing*) But once the flats are built, it won't make you any better off and it won't make the village any better off? OK? (*Making a transitional move*) Mm . . . what about the small farmers? Aubrey, is that you?
19.	AUBREY	(*easily introducing himself on the model the teacher tried to use above to help Paul get started and capably summarizing for the rest of the village the information on his cue card, and his group's dilemma*) Miss, uh, we're the Malhotti family. We own a small piece of land — fifteen acres — and in the family one side wants, um, the flats, and the other just wants to keep the land. So, we're not really sure yet, um, I think most people [*indecipherable*] would like to keep the land . . .

20.	TEACHER	(*as village lawyer perhaps*) You would like to keep the land? You don't want to sell? (*Reminding all of them, in addressing Aubrey, of the protocol of decision making in this system of local government*) Well, remember, you're the person with the deciding vote. If they can't make up their minds, the rest of the family, then it's your decision. OK? (*Making next transitional move and choosing Alfie's family group*) Right, who else have we got? Alfie.
21.	ALFIE	(*attempting the same introductory pattern, but with less fluency than Aubrey*) Um, the Dadi family.
22.	TEACHER	(*offering him the pattern she has presented before*) Who are you? Who do you represent? What do the Dadi family do?
23.	ALFIE	We're, um . . . (*He is interrupted by the Development Officer who has returned to the room to find out how much longer the Chak Zindra village will be before leaving for the district meeting*)
24.	DEVELOPMENT OFFICER	Sorry to interrupt again.
25.	ALFIE	(*continuing*) . . . craftworkers.
26.	TEACHER	(*encouraging him to go on*) Uhuh.
27.	ALFIE	(*almost inaudibly, launching into an argument against the flats in which he, too, draws on the information on his cue card to give a general impression of living on a knife edge*) And I think they shouldn't put . . . build flats on the land, because if we . . . we get our cotton from the farming, um, thingy, farming, um, land and if they sell and have flats on their land and put flats on all the other land if we ain't got enough money to buy land — because we would need it to grow our cotton on, but we can't afford it, like we need machinery but we can't afford it. (*About to imply, now, the moral responsibility of the rich towards his, poorer, group*) And if the farmers do sell their land, we won't have no work or anything, and we're just hardly living now with what cotton we get. So, I reckon they shouldn't sell.
28.	TEACHER	OK. Thank you.
29.	SEVGI	(*who is also the Sarpanch, begins, without the need for overt transition, the introduction to her family group*) We're the Purewell family and we think that, um . . . (*but she is interrupted by the teacher who is, rightly, under the impression that Andrew is the spokesperson for this family*).

30.	TEACHER	Can I . . . could I just suggest that Andrew told us, or is Andrew going to say something in a minute?
31.	ANDREW	I'll say something in a minute.
32.	SEVGI	(*continuing confusedly, but clear on the point of being in favour of building flats as an investment*) We . . . we were going to . . . we suggested to have some flats because we could buy some . . . buy land and they could invest that money and the work — we could get the farmers and people that work in the village to work on the flats, and they'd be working and getting good wages, and (*she has absorbed the argument of the others against the flats and continues persuasively*) they'd be working and getting good wages, until its built, and then we could, if we made a profit out of it, then we could build more flats.
33.	ALFIE	(*politely of the teacher/village lawyer*) Could we butt in on her for a minute? (*Making his challenge*) Uh, I think that's not right, because you ain't thinking of other people.
34.	AUBREY	(*making an alliance with Alfie*) Yeah, you're just thinking about yourself.
34.	ALFIE	Yeah, your the richest family, but . . .
35.	ANOTHER	(*joining the argument against the rich*) What about the poor?
36.	ALFIE	What about us?
37.	AUBREY	(*making the argument personal; in fact, the land to be sold is village land, not Sevgi's family's*) If you sell the land, you'll still be rich, wouldn't you?
38.	ALFIE	(*in support*) Yeah.
39.	SEVGI	(*disputing the truth of these statements and offering a palliative, but openly now acting as a landowner*) No! We'll pay you more of it.
40.		GENERAL OUTCRY
41.	ALFIE	(*quickly interpreting the power positions: the rich will be able to build up their capital to no benefit of the poor*) You'll get rent from those flats and you're gonna say you want more, because you can just keep getting [bigger?]. What about the land we own?
42.	SEVGI	(*continuing her argument that everyone will benefit financially*) Well, we could give you, uh . . . higher mon . . . You can sell it for higher money . . .
43.	AUBREY	(*starting to respond to this suggestion*) Yeah, but . . . (*is interrupted by Alfie*).
44.	ALFIE	(*only too aware of the dependence of his landless*

		group on the rich farmers for cotton) Yeah, but that money can't last us for ever. Anyway, we ain't got no land, so what we gonna do then? (*Sarcastically*) You gonna give us some cotton then, or something?
45.	SEVGI	(*not to be diverted from her investment argument*) You could invest it from us.
46.	ALFIE	(*believing his point has not been taken*) You're gonna have, you're gonna have all flats on the land, so how . . .
47.	SEVGI	(*denying that the flats will take all the farming land*) Not all of the land. Not all of the land. Part of the land is still . . .
48.	AUBREY and ALFIE	(*forcefully*) You shouldn't sell. You shouldn't sell.

The meeting, having begun as a simple statement of each family group's viewpoint (utterances 1–32), initially with considerable teacher support (utterances 1–16), but which, nevertheless, offers models for ensuing statements, moves, as a result of the reporting of incompatible viewpoints and power relationships between the rich and poor, into a challenging debate with positions taken and alliances formed (utterances 33–48). The students are absorbed and engaged and enjoying themselves. The discussion, of course, continued. Eventually, a vote was taken, and Andrew, the rightful Purewell representative, abandons the view put by Sevgi, the Sarpanch who usurped his place, and votes against the flats. Aubrey and Alfie continue to put the case against the flats with such strength that eventually, they find themselves as spokespersons at the public meeting.

What the Students Showed Us They Could Do

Using this transcript as evidence, it is fascinating to see the use the students make of the information given and also what information and experience of their own they bring to the development of their arguments. For example, Alfie saw through and beyond the information he was given on the cards. His main arguments against the flats were based on the need for land on which farmers, i.e., not his family group, could grow cotton to supply the craftworkers. They were not directly related to the points on the cue cards, viz., that the flats would provide a bigger market for the sale of cloth, and that the flats would be the beginning of modernity and industrialization and, therefore, a threat to the craftworkers' traditions. Yet, as well, he frequently referred to the fact that they could hardly make a living now that they had not the money to invest in machinery, that if the flats were built it would lead to the ruin of the village. These were all opinions or pieces of information expressed on the two cards for his family group (the Dadis).

Similarly, Sevgi's group developed its own line of argument regarding the flats, going for a profit-making-for-further-investment approach, using village labour for building, rather than the (less sophisticated) cue card suggestions that the flats would attract people and make the village look successful, and that the government's employment of labourers would present a threat to wage levels.

Once the discussion developed, Sevgi proposed to employ village workers and let them live in the flats for a given period of time which caused Aubrey, Alfie and Andrew to speculate on how viable this would be. This, in turn, led them to a discussion of the rights and wrongs of getting further into debt. In other words, the students selected and used what they saw as relevant points, but were not bound or limited by the cue cards for their arguments if other factors occurred to them which they considered as important. The fact was that there had been a very limited amount of recording of factual information before the beginning of the simulation, and a very short period of time to absorb that information and the limited information on the cue cards. Yet we were at last realizing our students' abilities to draw on a variety of information, selecting from where they felt it appropriate, making their own decisions about what was relevant to a developing argument, and using the information to further their line of argument or oppose someone else's.

Considering their relative lack of experience in such a context (in school, at least), it was surprising to note how many students were able to operate in this way and to provide opportunities and models to aid each other's development. We do not have the data to draw hard conclusions about these particular matters. However, take Paul, for example: my instinct is that it benefited him to be his group's representative and to have expressed (in the end) their view coherently. I believe, too, that although he did not contribute to the ensuing discussion of Sevgi's proposal, the fact that he was there, on the Panchayat, listening and physically close to the others, would work towards building his confidence for another time when he might perhaps feel more strongly the need to make a contribution. From this occasion he has a model for future occasions. In another incident, it would seem that my admitting, as village lawyer, to some confusion about a point being made was all the example needed to encourage a bilingual girl recently arrived from Pakistan to volunteer to be spokesperson for her group next time.

These methods of working give our students the experience to develop the confidence and the techniques of participating in group discussion, learning from more experienced or 'daring' people, the language of the great variety of speech acts that we need to call on in discussion. The methods also enable us to realize just how capable our students are when presented with the right opportunities.

Shabir in the Mainstream Humanities Class: Extracts from a Case Study

Background to Transcript 2

If the work I have described above, about decision making and development in the Panjab, was broadly successful, I have to admit to grave concern about one boy who seemed not to be gaining, certainly from the second part of our unit of work. Shabir was a student from Kashmir who, at the time of this work, had spent about four years in Britain. His languages were Urdu, Panjabi and English, and he was fluent in the first two. Popular and sociable at school, it was difficult to understand, given his range of friendships, that he often worked hard, and mostly seemed to understand what was going on, why he was experiencing so much difficulty in moving from understanding to expression in both spoken and written English. Unsurprisingly, his standard of reading and written work does not reflect his true ability.

Shabir's participation in the Panjab Project was enthusiastic. He entered heartily into the spirit of the first two weeks' scene setting activities. He brought in cassettes of Urdu songs as background music, enjoyed the displays, borrowed books and, in an informal way, explained to non-Asian students about items on display — particularly delighting in directing the spice tasting activities. He was an expert and enjoyed the status of that position. In the simulation itself, however, he took very little part in group discussion, even when part of a (family) group discussion of only three who, as can be seen from Transcript 2 below, were very hospitable, not only in allowing him the opportunity and granting him the time, but also in urging him to contribute.

Participants in the family group discussion

Name	Sex	Ethnic origin	Other information
Alfie	M	White Walthamstow	participates orally but has low self esteem academically; underachieving in written work
Kehinde	F	Nigerian	fluent speaker of English; academically able; tends to participate orally in class only when asked
Shabir	M	Pakistani	trilingual in Urdu, Panjabi and developing English; the latter is very hesitant; in England about four years

Transcript 2

This extract is from the initial stage of the simulation where each family group in the village is to decide whether it wants village land to be sold for the development of flats. The meeting takes place prior to the first Panchayat meeting part of which we looked at in Transcript 1. Taking these two transcripts together it can be appreciated just how reliable a representative of this family group's views Alfie was. Here, he is very much the organizer of the group, while Kehinde puts him straight on matters of information — and some other things he has not thought about: for example, utterances 3, 7b and 14. They work cooperatively, together developing ideas, as in utterances 9–19 and 21–25. They even on occasion complete each other's sentences (utterances 17 + 18) and 22 + 23). However, at the same time, Alfie is aware of a responsibility to include Shabir in the activity, and he does so encouragingly, with generosity (utterances 25 and 27). It is clear that Shabir wants to participate but cannot articulate his thoughts (utterances 8, 20, 26 and 28b). Study of the end of this section of transcript (utterances 29–34) indicates that had he been able to make his thoughts known then Alfie and Kehinde might have had to deal with an argument that ran somewhat counter to their own. Might he not have wanted the modernization, been willing to take the risk of change? It is certainly possible that this could have been so both from what he picked out to read in response to Alfie's 'C'mon, Shabir, get out your ideas' (utterances 27 and 28b), and from his responses to the contribution of the teacher who intervenes in their discussion at utterance 29 to put some alternative, entrepreneurial views.

1.	ALFIE	(*taking charge of the proceedings*) C'mon, we gotta...sort of...talk about...em...this, innit? (*He takes a cue card as focus and starts to read from it*) '---people with a lot of money---'...(*Shabir also has a card and is following Alfie's lead, reading with him*)
2.	ALFIE and SHABIR	(*in unison, Shabir much the quieter*) 'to live here'.
3.	KEHINDE	(*realizing they have so far neglected to allot role-functions*) Who's Representative?
4.	ALFIE	(*happy to volunteer*) I'll be it, if you want.
5.	KEHINDE	(*equally happy to agree*) Yeah.
6.	ALFIE	(*returning to the direction of the discussion with an all embracing invitation to contribute*) Right, then. You got any ideas? (*Kehinde meanwhile has been reading her cue card. Her next utterance and Alfie's are spoken together*)
7a.	ALFIE	What do you reckon?
7b.	KEHINDE	(*indicating her cue card*) Here's some ideas.
8.	SHABIR	(*also attempting a response to Alfie's invitation*) Mmmm. (*Alfie pauses for him, but nothing more ensues*).

9.	ALFIE	(*setting to work with Kehinde to sort out their ideas*) Right. If they reckon they're going to bring us some more money, right...there's no way that we...it...*can* bring us more money.
10.	KEHINDE	No, but if they bring us flats, right...
11.	ALFIE	Yeah, but we're going to have to pay money to live in them, aren't we?
12.	KEHINDE	If we build your flats, right, how're we going to do any more work? (*Meaning = 'How are we going to be able to carry on our traditional work?'*) 'Cos we need the field to grow our...plants.
13.	ALFIE	And we're going to need money to move in them, or something. That's what they're probably going to get at. Right. If we sell our land...
14.	KEHINDE	(*reminding him that it is village land, not their own personal land; the craftworker family are landless*) We haven't got any land. We haven't got any land.
15.	ALFIE	Yeah, I mean, what we gonna work on, you know?
16.	KEHINDE	We'll need money to buy, uh, cotton.
17.	ALFIE	Yeah. So...
18.	KEHINDE	(*they seem both to have had the same idea at the same time; Kehinde finishes Alfie's sentence for him*)...it's a bad thing.
19.	ALFIE	(*confirming*) Yeah.
20.	SHABIR	(*apparently wanting to say something about the conclusion they have so far come to, but again unable to articulate*) Mmmm.
21.	ALFIE	(*beginning to develop a justification for their decision against the flats*) Yeah, should just leave it the same and don't change any ideas. Just keep it like it has been for years.
22.	KEHINDE	If they change, we can't have...
23.	ALFIE	(*his turn to complete Kehinde's sentence, and then go on to broaden the argument*)... a lot of things...like same for other villages.
24.	KEHINDE	(*adding more fuel to their argument*) We can't afford to buy more equipment.
25.	ALFIE	(*expanding on this theme*) Yeah, we're just about living now. Um, the other villages...some of the other villages are troubled like this as well...um...(*Here there is a pause; then Alfie invites Shabir to state his preference*) C'mon, Shabir. What do you want?
26.	SHABIR	(*shows willingness, but again struggles and fails*) Mmmm.

27. ALFIE   (*seeming to understand that the problem is one of articulating the ideas rather than of not having any*) C'mon, get out all your ideas. (*He then goes on to explain the situation; Shabir, meanwhile has sought the security of the cue cards; unable to articulate a statement, he makes his response by reading from the card; he and Alfie speak together*).

28a. ALFIE   We're going to have to make an arrangement, ain't we?

28b. SHABIR   (*reading from cue card*) 'These flats will bring people with a lot of money...' (*Here, a teacher arrives and intervenes in the discussion*)

29. TEACHER   Don't you think (*now looking at a cue card*), it says here, um, if more people come to live in the village with a lot of, more money, then that will be good for you, because you'll have more people there to buy your goods...?

30. ALFIE   (*responding immediately and oppositionally to the teacher's offer of an alternative view*) Yes, but... (*to be interrupted by Shabir*)

31. SHABIR   (*seeming to like the suggestion the teacher has put forward*) Yeah, yeah...

32. TEACHER   (*completing her utterance*)... and your clothes, and so on.

33. SHABIR   (*apparently continuing in support of this alternative view*) Yeah.

34. KEHINDE   (*giving a reason for maintaining opposition*) If we build the flats... but we can't have any fields to grow them... (*The discussion and argument continue a little; Shabir takes no more part verbally*).

From the point of view of this structure of lesson being a way of involving developing bilingual students in active learning with their peers, this extract offers much food for thought. What could it be offering Shabir? I was extremely pessimistic that he was getting anything out of the experience. And yet...

1. It shows that English Mother Tongue speakers and more experienced other users of English are capable of generosity and encouragement of people with less experience in using English than themselves, and that sometimes, perhaps because they are in such close interaction, they seem to be able to diagnose a student's difficulties with more accuracy than the teachers can or do. Certainly, Alfie recognized well before I did that Shabir's problem was more of articulation than lack of comprehension.
2. We learn, too, not to take it for granted that a student unsuccessful in

articulating his points of view on a topic, as Shabir is in this interaction, will always be alienated by the experience. Shabir showed no obvious signs of it, if indeed it was the case for him. Throughout, he listened attentively to the views the others were expressing. With the benefit of having studied tapes of the interaction I set up after seeing Shabir in the present plight (Transcripts 3 and 4, below, are extracts from it), I conclude that while too much of this kind of experience would be alienating, sometimes being an interested, listening participant is as important a contribution to language development as expression is. The choice of content certainly helped maintain his interest and motivation. I believe now that this particular experience was for Shabir of the same order of usefulness as Paul's experience of being spokesperson at the first Panchayat meeting (Transcript 1).

3. It was at the time, though, very uncomfortable for me to observe Shabir in his first part of the simulation. Shabir's case was, perhaps, extreme; nevertheless, his apparent difficulties showed us clearly where we would need to provide better support the next time this or another unit of work like it was undertaken. First, we saw that the reading level and the language complexity of the materials needed attention; they created difficulties for a number of students, not all bilingual. Secondly, we saw that we had not built into the unit any kind of check on understanding of concepts and associated terminology (e.g., Green Revolution, farming cooperative); if, for example, students had given short talks to the rest of the class about their research they would have been more confident of the terms before embarking on the simulation. Because they were not required actively to use the terminology in Part 1, some never had the opportunity to do so before they were in role when they had, in addition, quite sophisticated arguments to communicate. (Note, though, that Shabir was not without the means to mount a hypothetical case, as I was to discover later; see Transcript 4, below.) Thirdly, there appears to be a need to structure some of the interactions more carefully so that procedures are easier to grasp for those students to whom they are not yet familiar. The ESL group would have been an ideal place to allow developing bilinguals to check out new ideas, terminology and the procedures of the Project. It was an opportunity which I failed to exploit to maximum effect.

4. All that I have mentioned so far of what we learned was deduced from the observation in the actual progress of a lesson or reflection on group talk by means of tape and transcript. Without this reflective means of understanding better what happens in our lessons, I would not have access to Shabir's in-class experience, and without that I might not have taken him aside nor recorded our conversation (see section below, 'What Shabir knew'). And had I not done so, I might have gone on construing my student with lower expectation of him than he deserved.

What Shabir Knew

Till now, then, in relation to this unit of work, we had no idea what Shabir knew and did not know nor what he could not do. We thought he could do very little. As his ESL teacher observing him in the early part of the simulation, I was concerned that his initial great enthusiasm for the unit might not be sustained. Certainly, I felt that we had not equipped him to take part. Appalled at this oversight, I decided to spend my next double period available as a support lesson with Shabir, checking information, recapping, generally making sure that he had grasped what was going on, and helping to prepare him for what was to come in the next Humanities lesson so that he could participate. I tape recorded most of the conversation of just over an hour. The conversation falls into three stages.

In the first section, with the cue cards on the table in front of us as prompts should he wish to refer to them, I tried to draw information about the context of the simulation from him. Very early on in the conversation, Shabir makes a fairly lengthy, but to me an incoherent and incomprehensible, utterance.

> Then richest have a big field and flats, and they . . . paid money. When some people going to their village, and they said, 'Do something for us, and live in our flat'. Poor people live there, and there some money, and, uh, . . . if Dadi family (*the family of craftworkers, the family group to which he belonged*) haven't to got nothing. Their only small money. Then, if . . .

Only much later, after I had listened to the tape of the first Panchayat meeting, did I realize that what he was attempting was a summary of the views expressed at that meeting. Not seeing where his conversation was leading and determined to proceed with my plan of helping him to do better in the next lesson, I cut him short. His responses then become much more stilted. He allowed this information recap, generally acquiescing to statements of information with many 'Yes, miss's', and often echoing my words. He did not drop out of the conversation, but he had stopped initiating. What I was doing was explicitly telling him what I hoped he already knew. This type of conversation is not very conducive to a teacher gauging how much a student knows and can do. Implicitly, I was making him aware of how little I thought he understood. Realizing this, I decided on a change of tack and encouraged him to talk about his own knowledge of making a living in Pakistan and of farming in Kashmir. I did this initially, because, viewing him as I did as having fared so poorly, first with Alfie and Kehinde in class, then in my initial questioning, I saw in it a way of making him feel that he had something to contribute. Our conversation ranged over possibilities for employment: working in a sugar factory, leaving the village and finding employment in town, returning to the village and opening a shop. Shabir had a realistic understanding of his interest group, the craftworkers, as having a precarious living, and it is to this that our discussion about employment relates, rather than to an appreciation of the choices for development facing the villagers. I bring the conversation back to my view of the matter in hand.

Transcript 3

1.	TEACHER	(*bringing the conversation back to her agenda*) Ummm . . . so if you look at all the possibilities, either a sugar factory, or a cloth cooperative, or a . . . a school in your . . . a farming school in your village of Chak Zinda, which do you think would be best?
2.	SHABIR	(*confidently*) Farming . . . farming school.
3.	TEACHER	Why?
4.	SHABIR	(*begins to explain*) Because they teach us how to . . . whassname? . . . grow things.
5.	TEACHER	(*encouraging*) Mmmm.
6.	SHABIR	(*continuing explanation*) And . . . whassname? . . . dig land.
7.	TEACHER	Mmhm.
8.	SHABIR	(*elaborating further, developing his own pattern of speech, to talk about crop rotation and irrigation*) And, ah, I would like to put water in the land or not. Which year we put water in there, which year we not put there. Which year we grow things here. Which year we grow things there. Which, eh, fruit, vegetable grow in this land.
9.	TEACHER	Uhuh.
10.	SHABIR	(*expanding into a new topic of crops and soil*) Some land is like sands land and stones. They have a big . . . whassname? . . . uh, boley in there.
11.	TEACHER	(*not understanding the word 'boley'*) A big . . . ?
12.	SHABIR	(*persevering despite this setback*) Boley.
13.	TEACHER	What's that?
14.	SHABIR	(*showing that he has the ability to gloss words, trying to make sure that she understands*) Boley . . . like wheat.
15.	TEACHER	(*finally taking his meaning*) Oh, barley! (*then continuing to encourage him further*) Uhuh.
16.	SHABIR	(*showing his further knowledge of farming*) Yeah, that' little thing. If you grow in tha' . . . whassname? . . . sand and . . . stone land, you can get big wheat.
17.	TEACHER	Good quality?
18.	SHABIR	Yeah, good quality.

(*The conversation continues*)

In this section of our conversation, Shabir was much more animated and fluent, and it became clear to me that he had got a contribution to make and opinions which were relevant to decision making in Chak Zinda. These were not mere family reminiscences, but pertinent points to support his argument for the foundation of a farming school in the area now that the flats project had been turned down. Because his points did not relate to his role, as I saw it, and to the views I anticipated he and others like him might have, as a craftworker in Chak Zinda (for this was the narrow frame in which I was operating), I was slow to realize the significance of his choice of farming school to the larger questions of choice and development in the area. In this next extract, Shabir is talking confidently in support of his choice of farming school, but because I have not yet come fully to appreciate his view that craftworkers might do well to think of their days in this trade as numbered and look for other means of support, take on other skills, I find it hard to follow his complex argument about why it would help craftworkers to attend a farming school. He explains.

Transcript 4

1.	SHABIR	(*making a hypothetical case; putting himself in the position of being a member of a rich family*) . . . If we are rich family, for example, and then when I have money, and I am fed up in our country . . .
2.	TEACHER	Yes.
3.	SHABIR	Then I try to go in other country for holiday or something. And then when I go, and maybe they (*he means the rich family who are possibly going abroad*) need you, and you say you need work, and they know about you, and you know how to work, and maybe, they choose you, and you, say, work with them, um, (*he has paused to correct himself, and does so, accurately for the preposition, but no longer certain which way the pronouns should go to maintain the hypothetical nature of his explanation*) for me. I mean for them.
4.	TEACHER	(*checking that she has understood*) Oh, I see. Right, so if the richest family . . . somebody decides to go away, they need somebody who's going to manage their farm for them?
5.	SHABIR	Yes, miss.
6.	TEACHER	Be in charge of their farm?
8.	SHABIR	Yes, miss.
9.	TEACHER	'Cos you'd still be in the village, and you'd know how to do it?
10.	SHABIR	Yes, miss.
11.	TEACHER	I understand now.

12.	SHABIR	(*wanting to add strength to his case bringing in personal experience*) Because my father was working like this when he was in Pakistan.
13.	TEACHER	Uhuh. He was looking after somebody else's farm?
14.	SHABIR	Yes, miss. And he is saying how to grow things . . .

The lesson is drawing to a close. Realizing, at last, the logic behind Shabir's decision, I urge him to work out his arguments and put the case to his fellow group members. It is possible that my effort to help him to participate did, that day, have the opposite effect from that intended, for Shabir was absent that afternoon! His colleagues had to do without the benefit of having heard his opinion — for the record, they went ahead and decided in favour of a cloth cooperative.

What the Teacher Learned from Shabir

Focusing on the participation of Shabir in this project reveals its strengths and its weaknesses. Our choice of learning content had been a marked success. Shabir was excited that he already knew so much about farming and village life which was new to others in the class. He thrived on his position of 'expert' in the initial stages and it was perhaps this confidence in his understanding of the context and issue of development in a rural area of the subcontinent which sustained him through the frustrations of the simulation itself.

Whilst the choice of topic was of patent relevance and interest to Shabir, it also engaged the other students in our multiethnic class. In the second run of the course, the interest and commitment of the majority of the students was sustained throughout. Significantly, there was no undermining of the project because of racist attitudes. In great measure this was due to the general ethos of the school, for though there were individuals within it who held racist views, they were well aware of what was acceptable behaviour within the school. But I would suggest, more importantly, that the challenge to us as teachers was to ensure that the energies of all students should be channelled into the simulation — a challenge partly because it was novel, but largely because it was entirely open-ended. The students had the power to influence the outcome. This was in marked contrast to the style of so much of the rest of their Humanities course which frequently consisted of literal reading comprehensions demanding little reasoning ability.

In this positive atmosphere, then, when the majority of the students were intrigued to find out more about those things about which Shabir was already knowledgeable, his motivation and status were high. Less extrovert Asian students were encouraged by all this. Whether or not their understanding of the questions of development in a rural economy was as sophisticated as Shabir's, they all had something to bring; a knowledge of Sikh or Hindu religions; dress, cooking, language, agriculture.

It would have been interesting to have made a study of how the other students engaged with the project. Some appeared to draw on their knowledge of the class system in Britain judging by the attitudes they displayed in the simulation, as did Alfie, for example, as a member of the landless poor in relation to Sevgi, the Sarpanch and representative of the rich landowners. To this extent, we did breach some 'rich-world/poor-world' stereotypes in that it was plain from the simulation that village people are not necessarily an homogeneous group, but people with a variety of interests. Our students were able to see, too, that while there are mechanisms which allow people to exert some control over their lives, there are others which limit the extent of that control — mostly quite considerably; for example, the power and influence of outsiders like the Block Development Officer. Students were also able to discern parallels between the urban area in which they actually lived and that of the rural, simulated context, as was revealed by the comments they made at the debriefing at the end of the project.

However, are we getting away from the point: what the teacher learned from Shabir? I think not. Shabir showed us that we got much of what we did right in terms of content and social context. In stressing talk and the sharing of ideas and information in Part 1 of the project, we gave Shabir the opportunity to strengthen his position. He was able to share what he knew relatively freely and gain further respect from others. Had he been required to write everything down it would have held up this process. The informal learning environment was one in which he could operate well. However, it might have benefited him had Part 1 had some more public outcome; for example, if students had been required to report on their findings in talks, interviews, displays and articles.

In the simulation itself, I learned a great deal from my observations of Shabir. Like others, he found the role cards difficult to read. They were, indeed, unnecessarily complex, particularly since the students were so unconfident of much of the terminology relating to the project. The fact that interest groups were teacher chosen enabled us to match Shabir with students who recognized his value and who would be encouraging to him. However, if Shabir had been paired with another speaker of his first language, he would have been able to communicate his ideas more quickly and effectively, gained confidence, maybe gained an interpreter-friend, and been helped to win over the group to his point of view. It is such a simple solution that it is difficult to imagine how I did not think of it at the time.

Even so, that would have been an answer to only part of Shabir's difficulty in the situation. Other questions concern the role of the ESL teacher. An important aspect of her job is to help set up situations in classrooms so that bilinguals may better understand the lesson content and experience increased motivation to learn. We had achieved this with Shabir. It is also her job to ensure that students have access to the kinds of English which enable them to participate. This I failed to do.

I was shocked to discover just how difficult he found participating in the simulation — even in such an hospitable group. Most of the students had both sufficient command of spoken and written English and also enough interest in this way of working to enable them to learn from the models presented by their peers and teachers. Thus, unlike Shabir, they were able to take a full part in the simulation. The degree of their oral participation varied according to a number of factors that included personality and each individual's grasp of the information offered. However, Shabir, I believe, was precluded from participating in the simulation not by timidity nor, as I discovered from my conversation with him, by lack of comprehension, but simply by a situation of 'limited English' which I had helped create. Through not anticipating the kinds of English which would be thrown up in the lesson situation — any lesson situations. His difficulties arose just because his personal experience was so relevant and because he had a thorough grasp of what was being asked yet disagreed with the rest of the group. He needed to convey sophisticated and, to his hearers, unexpected ideas to people who had already had quite a different line of argument. He knew what he wanted to say, but because it was not what we, the other participants, were expecting to hear, it required more skills than he yet possessed in English to enter the debate on the terms on which he needed to.

I had not taught these skills relating to argument and persuasion. In the small group situation in which I also taught, I gave the students the opportunity to express themselves and I tried to reinforce classwork, subject content, lexis, structures, etc., but I did not provide for sufficient practice at a functional level for developing skills in English of, for example, persuasion and argument. There was plenty of time for personal anecdote, and in the transcript of our conversation it is clear that Shabir gained in confidence when he was able to operate in this mode. However, this has to be seen as a starting point. Other types of talk need to be tried out in the security of small group work if they are eventually to be used with effect elsewhere.

Of course, at that stage, in 1982, in that school, as in many others, talk had still to come to be viewed as a positive force for learning by many teachers and students. I was at a stage of trying to get it so viewed, and this project was almost our first venture into enacting our commitment to it. As one of the students, Noorjahan, commented after the project:

> . . . This course was different from the other work we done, because the other work we done was only really reading and answering questions. But for this one it was more practical.

She went on to say that she thought this was more interesting but that she did not think that she had developed any new skills. Another girl commented:

> . . . by speaking to each other I learned more than just writing it down on paper . . . I enjoyed the part of the course when we were deciding

what we wanted to happen in our lives and arguing with the BDO . . .

And having taken on our emphasis on collaborative learning, she told us that the skill she had learned was to work together.

Perhaps it is not surprising that I had not yet thought carefully enough about the varieties of talk styles that would be required of the class and specifically of the bilingual students within it, nor of how I would structure my ESL lessons to help develop them. The Panjab Project was an innovation for which I had not properly prepared my students. Some were able to model themselves on peers and teacher, but Shabir was not. Like many teachers, I suspect, I am not sufficiently analytical about the language demands of the curriculum nor how the students can be taught so as to meet those demands. In putting so much effort into designing a course which would motivate the majority of the class, I overlooked the specifics that would need to be taught to some, at least, of the students. These specifics ranged from understanding terms, like 'Green Revolution', to acquiring the techniques of interrupting a conversation firmly, but politely, in order to express one's views.

In Shabir's case, he was being asked to hypothesize about what he wanted as a member of a cotton weaving family in the village called Chak Zinda. He wanted to use conditional clauses with 'if', but floundered, it seemed, because he did not know what tense to follow up with. He wanted to describe his own knowledge of farming but felt his knowledge of suitable vocabulary in English to be too limited to do so. Paradoxically, he might have been able to say something if he had known less. It could have been his knowledge which stumped him, especially since, in addition, he wanted to contradict the others in his group.

Reflecting on these events and on Shabir's 'failures' has taught me the necessity of providing opportunities in the ESL class for students to practise strategies for participating in the many English language saturated situations they encounter. If we are serious about our aim for students that they gain power to use language and analyze information so that they may have some control over their lives, then our teaching and the way in which we think about our teaching must in themselves be a demonstration of our intentions.

Since this work was undertaken in 1982, advances have been made in the teaching of bilingual students in schools. There is a great deal more work done in subject classes in secondary schools. Such work as described here is no longer quite as unusual as it was when we did it. Furthermore, there is an increasing recognition of the validity of the students' use of their first language in the learning process. However, I fear still that important questions relating to the students' real involvement in subject learning have not yet been thoroughly tackled. I fear, too, that unless we take care to attend to them, they could disappear under the requirements of the 1988 Education Reform Act.

Whatever the shortcomings of the Panjab Project, one thing it did demonstrate was that setting up an educational environment that values talk as a learning mode benefits all students. This is not just a device to provide greater opportunity to those learning to use English as a Second Language to do so, although, of course, we believe that without it they cannot do so as well as they might when all their teachers take responsibility for them. Nor can harmonious intergroup relations be expected without action and interaction in the mainstream. Developing bilingual students do need the support of small group work and of the particular kinds of opportunities for language practice and experience that ESL teachers can provide, but also subject teachers need to consider their teaching context, how it facilitates learning and productive social interaction. The choice, too, of subject content is as important as the style of learning in inspiring students into their learning.

Notes

1. The authority has since reorganized its secondary provision into 11–16 all-through schools.
2. These two services have now been amalgamated into the borough's Multicultural Development Service.
3. This work was undertaken in collaboration with Don Harrison, Archway Development Education; Stuart Scott, ILEA; colleagues in the school and more widely in the borough; colleagues in the School's Council Programme Three Activity, Language for Learning; Second Language Learners and Mainstream Curriculum Group; members of the Panjabi Sikh Community in West London.

12
Political and Moral Contexts in English and ESL Teaching

Helen Davitt

By means of comprehensive contextual analyses of a discussion lesson with a group of bilingual learners Davitt, in 'Political and Moral Contexts in English and ESL Teaching', *is able to offer a multi-level critique of discourses within the teaching of English in particular, and of schooling in general. She shows how discourses stemming from conservatist-liberal ideologies discriminate against the educational achievement and intellectual and moral development not only of bilingual learners but of the majority school populaiton of working-class pupils.*

Within her critique, Davitt outlines three main theoretical models of contemporary English teaching, the traditional, the progressive and the cultural analytical. She also shows that an underexamined interactive 'language for learning' pedagogy based primarily on fictional texts produced within a middle-class, conservatist-liberal milieu, cannot achieve equal educational rights, nor a rigorously political moral analytic education. What is needed is a discursive analytic practice based more on factual materials relating to the pupils' contemporary world.

She is able to show that, contrary to the general expectations of teachers operating from within a conservatist-liberal ideology, the provision of factual information relating to contemporary issues and an analytic mode of education within English teaching provides a motivating and rigorous educational model for pupils, incorporating the development of language, thought, skills, intellect, and moral and political understanding. In teacher action research terms, the difficulties that teachers experience in seeking to effect such transformations in educational theory and practice in the face of the dominant ideology is also demonstrated.

The chapter offers an incremental analysis necessarily built in the follow-ing sections:

1. *Political and Moral Underachievement in Education*
2. *Particular School Contexts*
   - (a) *The local education authority*
   - (b) *The school's intake*
   - (c) *Teachers' status, political positions and curriculum development*
3. *English Teaching*
   - (a) *Practical circumstances and theoretical premises of English teaching*
   - (b) *The English Literature theoretical premise*
   - (c) *The progressive/creative theoretical promise*
   - (d) *The development of the analytic mode of English teaching.*
   - (e) *Overlap and disagreement between the traditions*
4. *Equal Opportunities Education*
   - (a) *Policies, practices and materials*
   - (b) *Multicultural teaching in the English department*
5. *The School and Antiracism*
   - (a) *Multinationals and Apartheid*
   - (b) *Developing materials on Apartheid*
6. *Analytic Education*
   - (a) *Some crucial questions*
   - (b) *The Apartheid materials*
7. *A Consideration of Appropriate Learning Materials for Bilingual Pupils*
8. *Background to the Lesson Analyzed*
   - (a) *The class*
   - (b) *The group members and group dynamics*
   - (c) *The teachers*
   - (d) *The lesson content*
9. *The Discussion Lesson*
   - (a) *Comment on the transcript*
   - (b) *Follow up*
10. *Conclusions*
11. *Appendices*
    - (a) *Materials used in the lesson*
    - (b) *Transcript of the lesson*

Political and Moral Underdevelopment in Education

The following is a description of the preparation, reception and evaluation of one fify-five minute lesson with a Fourth Year group of five pupils learning English as a second language. The lesson took place in a modern inner-city comprehensive school of 1400 pupils and ninety teachers.

The original intention was to write a case study of this one lesson since it provided evidence that developing bilingual pupils, given a discursive, communicative and interactive environment could handle complex material in learning English as a second language. This in turn provided evidence that pupils' language itself is developed in such a context. It was also proof that 'language itself is a tool for learning'.

But language for learning *what* exactly? As an English teacher, being caught between the exigencies of helping pupils to literacy with texts that on the one hand might promote reading development, but frequently did the opposite as far as intellectual development was concerned, the concept of 'language for learning' presented the same problem: for learning *what*?

Having experienced it — indeed, as a teacher, being complicit in it — I knew that traditional and authoritarian education took away from pupils, particularly working-class pupils, as much if not more than it gave. So, while happy to produce transcripts and descriptions of lessons which might help to confirm and legitimate educational theory and pedagogies based on interactive communication, i.e., 'language for learning', I knew that doing so also served to increase awareness that this was also to continue to skim the surface of the very fundamental issues of education.

'Language for learning' seemed to be the theoretical flavour of the decade, but a flavour, particularly as far as working-class children were concerned, sprinkled liberally over perennially suspect substances. Since it was theory and practice about curriculum *methods* rather than about curriculum *content*, or, and never more than tangentially, about curriculum outcomes, as such, it helped maintain a comfortable conservatist/liberal status quo diffuseness as opposed to more intellectually rigorous ways of thinking about and practising education.

'Language for learning' was taken up by teachers because (a) it helped to legitimate the talk that always went on in their classrooms anyway and (b) because it legitimated development of more humane learning environments based on communicative interaction.

It was practised by teachers within a continuum of competencies, concerns and criticisms. Competent teachers were criticized for the 'noise' emanating from their classrooms as they tried to organize discussion based learning for their pupils. There was also criticism, rightly, of teachers who interpreted their function in 'language for learning' pedagogy as mere hosts of a mêlée, disobliged of carefully structuring a discursive learning environment. There was concern about what to do when discussion based learning in multicultural classsrooms (read multi-group) got 'serious', i.e., when they generated more heat than light or when the issues taken up spilled outside the confines of curriculum matters into highly pertinent opposition. There was also a concern, with a major focus on oral work, about when you got the reading and writing done; until it dawns that what you do is try to integrate the most appropriate balance of speaking, listening, reading and writing for the development of each pupil, or group of pupils. No easy task; but, of course, many teachers had always been trying to do just that — often enough without anyone to tell them they were on the right track, or the contrary.

But if 'language for learning' legitimated pedagogies of interactive communication for teachers, it didn't necessarily do so for pupils. It was not the pedagogy they had 'learned', and superficially welcome though it may have been, they had no reason to give it any more fundamental trust than any other.

The fact is that 'language for learning' also, paradoxically, helps maintain linguistic deprivation theories about why children fail in schools. It both incorporates and marginalizes other important ways of learning, e.g., observing, thinking, feeling, experiencing, doing and taking action. It would be nice to be able to make a case that 'language for learning' both improves the whole quality of education for, and significantly alters the rate of exchange in qualifications of, working-class pupils. But, usefully mitigating though it is, and though secured of a place in some future holistic system of equal rights education, since it is the political forces and processes in which lessons are *embedded*, rather than the enlightened pedagogies used in them, which has greatest effect, this is not a case that can be made.

Nevertheless, although the politics of the system you are working in, and the potentials of the one you would wish to see in place, might be clear enough, as a practising teacher - caught up in such a 'moment' of educational theory, juggling the day to day pragmatics of teaching, attempting to develop bits of curriculum, make materials — working out more detailed ways of thinking about and trying to practise education is by no means the clear cut process it might seem to be with the benefit of hindsight. The analytic clarity which hindsight represents is arrived at by reflection and discussion with colleagues who are also both analyzing educational practice and trying to build analytical modes of teaching.

Thus, with benefit of hindsight, it has to be said that while producing a case study proving bilingual learners' ability to sustain a fifty-five minute discussion on complex issues might well serve some half decent purposes, it is hardly a decent enough enterprise if it does not also try to describe and raise basic moral and political issues about the forces in which this or any other lesson is embedded.

In describing the lesson *and* the processes in which it was embedded the intention is to indicate not only the intrinsically moral and political nature of both the production and outcomes of this one lesson, but by implication, of any lesson anywhere. Although the balance of forces will vary in specific lessons, at different times and in different places, comprehensive observation of any five minutes of any classroom interaction, with acknowledgment of the processes in which it is embedded, must inevitably expose the political and moral nature of that specific educational experience. This is despite the odd notion that education could and should be 'free' of politics.

The fact is, of course, that despite the slogan 'politics should be kept out of education' — which reinforces the popular notion that it is both possible and desirable to do so — there isn't a single element of the educational process that is without its political and moral components. Besides contributing to political mystification, ignorance and confusion, what the sloganizers do is to conflate two different issues — the issue of party political indoctrination in schools and the issue of children's right to a decent political education that allows them to understand the political and moral components of any situation, not least the politics of their own eleven years of compulsory schooling. The conflation of these two issues is reinforced by 'naturalized' mis-understanding on the one hand, and by deliberate manipulation of that misunderstanding on the other.

Political and moral components in education are there in the political intentions of Government; in the operations of the local education authorities and school governing bodies; in the influences of exam boards and employers; in the action, or inaction, of parents. They are also there in the nitty-gritty, day-in-day-out political thought, actions and attitudes of school headteachers and management teams, heads of departments and, of course, of classroom teachers themselves.

Explicit and implicit political and moral components are also inside every classroom every day — in the lesson content, in the pedagogical methods used, in the interactions between pupils and teachers and between pupils themselves and, last but not least, in the outcomes of the classroom lessons, in terms of the knowledge, skills and processes developed — or not developed.

The real issue is not whether education is political and moral or, deceptively, whether 'politics should be kept out of education'. The issue is *what variety of political and moral forces does a particular educational system employ*, in what ways, by what means and to what ends? Which political forces exercise the greatest power over the educational process, for what purposes and in whose interests? For instance, precisely whose interests does it serve to maintain a politically underdeveloped population by, supposedly, 'keeping politics out of education'? Which sections of society would have the most to gain if instead of the political 'ghost writing' by which education is shaped, real political literacy for pupils came to be regarded as worthy of the same attention as the three Rs?

Education is, in fact, rife with political acts and intentions, both in the narrowly party political sense and in the comprehensive sense of the word political: the activity, intellectual and actual, whereby who gets what, where, when and how is determined. Trying to suppress, distort, divert attention from the political forces and outcomes of education is itself a politically dishonest act. It is subversive of the human right to political literacy and, therefore, of the right to decent moral, political and intellectual development.

By 'decent moral, political and intellectual development', I mean nothing less than educational development based on the philosophy of political and socio-economic equal human rights, i.e., educational development based on the right — and the responsibility — of all human beings to develop the relationships, social, political, economic and personal that both suit individuals *and* are caring of the human rights of others.

Educationists who purport to adhere to even a smattering of equal educational rights have an obvious fundamental responsibility, in spite of all other overt and covert political intentions, pragmatisms and qualifications to the contrary, to attempt to provide pupils with access not only to the world's knowledge, understandings and skills in the usual sense, but to comprehensive political understanding of the world in which the pupils, and their teachers, actually live their lives.

Access to such fundamental understanding entails not only the development of the usual range of knowledge and skills, but must also include the development of analytical and political understandings and skills rooted in the premises of equal human rights to decent intellectual, moral, political and socio-economic development. Without such access, 'education' is indeed further indoctrination — howsoever subtle, 'commonsensical', covert or unrecognized the means — into whatever dominant, inegalitarian ideology and culture holds sway at particular points in time. The lesson later described attempts to base itself on the above premises. However, it ultimately bears little more than a fragmentary relationship to those premises. For that very reason both the lesson and the processes in which it is embedded seem worth describing.

Particular School Contexts

The Local Education Authority

The school's local education authority is Labour Party controlled, in contradistinction to a Conservative Government. The authority has continuously been berated for commanding too large a budget, overspending, wastage, poor exam results and for being too liberal in its educational policies, particularly its declarations relating to equal opportunities, anti-racism and anti-sexism. (No sight of similar 'iniatives' on class, however.) These merely liberal policies were often characterized as 'extreme left' by a status quo, conservatist media. At the time of the situation described in this chapter, the authority was intermittently threatened with disbandment by the national Government; the richest middle-class boroughs of the LEA were at the forefront of the campaign, amongst their aims being divesting themselves of responsibility for the funding of the poorer working-class boroughs, and reversing liberalized educational policies. The authority, of course, was later abolished in the Education Reform Act of 1988, with responsibility for the city's education being handed over to the individual boroughs that had comprised it.

Teachers (ranging from the reformist to the more radical) in this LEA were often not only in conflict with the management teams in schools, with the inspectorate and with the LEA and their divisional offices, but with each other. Their conflicts were over their own differing educational philosophies or *modus operandi* and, schizophrenically, over the issue of trying to promote changes and developments at all, since to do so, they were told — and also told each other — would involve further endangering an already endangered and unusually 'generous' authority.

Inside the school, there was an overall ethos, or culture, of interest in curriculum 'progress' but also in preventing the institutional boat from being rocked overmuch by anything too critically innovative. This ethos and culture, as in all educational institutions clearly highly political and moral (or, to be more precise, immoral), percolated through the departmental structures in the school. The subject departments primarily concerned with the lesson later described, the English and English as a Second Language Department, were no exception.

The School's Intake

The school is a modern purpose-built comprehensive in the centre of London. the influential section of its intake has always been a strong minority of white middle-class children, whose parents are the most politically astute and vociferous. It is these middle-class parents who take positions as the parent representatives on the governing body, and who share the same liberal political persuasions of the majority of that body who come from the centre and right wing of the Labour Party.

The school's reputation has depended largely on the good examination results it achieves for these middle-class children — and the fact that many of them go on to be accepted at universities, including Oxbridge. This 'achievement' supports a myth that the school's exam results overall are good, which is in fact not the case. In the statistical table of the LEA's exam results for all its secondary schools, based on ability profiles at intake, this school is in nearer the bottom of that table. In effect, the school achieves poor exam results for its majority intake of working-class children, black and white.

At the time I am writing of, white working-class children formed the majority of the school's intake, with a large minority of black working-class children. The school was mixed ability for the first two years, with 'ability' setting or banding in some subjects thereafter, depending on the educational politics of the head of department, or upon the ability of a majority in a department to affect departmental policy.

Although there was some small mix of working- and middle-class children in the upper school top set exam classes, few middle-class children were to be found taking low level exam classes in all of their subjects, while many working-class children were in that position. And if few white working-class children appeared in A level classes, an even rarer appearance was a black working-class child.

There was an 'open' sixth form, open in that it did not confine entry into the sixth form only to pupils of academic ability, but also ran CSE, RSA, O level resits and City and Guilds courses for the working-class children. A look into the sixth form common room would quickly reveal the educational, class and racial divisions amongst pupils. The middle-class pupils generally occupied one end of the common room, the black working-class pupils the opposite end and the white working-class pupils the middle. There was some mingling between the white and black working-class pupils, but almost none between working-class and middle-class pupils.

In the school there were about seventy children for whom English was their second language. Bangladeshi, Chinese, Spanish and Moroccan children formed the largest groups of pupils learning to use English as a second language. Also included were children from many other parts of the world: e.g., Eritrea, Bulgaria, Ghana, Iraq, Hungary, Turkey and Japan. In total, the children possessed about forty different home languages between them. There were about fifteen beginner learners of English, but most of the others had become functionally bilingual, and literate for most ordinary everyday situations.

Like the other pupils, these bilingual learners are learners within the particular educational curriculum on offer, with access, or lack of it, to exam options dependent upon their 'ability'. Unlike other pupils, they are learning in a second spoken and written language, a fact which is seldom taken into account when defining ability — in the same way that a whole host of socio-economic and cultural variables are discounted when judging the 'ability' of children generally. Although many of the pupils learning English may soon appear to be fluently bilingual as far as speaking the language is concerned, their reading and writing of it will not be as advanced as that of their indigenous peers.

For some years now, LEAs have been providing additional teacher support for bilingual pupils learning in English through Home Office Section 11 funding. Historically, the Section 11 funding has been interpreted as a means of providing specialist language teachers who would teach 'extra' language support lessons. In effect, this has meant that bilingual pupils got fewer lessons in the mainstream curriculum, since the simplest means of supporting their learning has, until relatively recently, been seen as withdrawal from mainstream lessons in order to take 'extra' English — rather than to arrange the language support around the mainstream lesson.

The Swann Report (DES, 1985) recommended a shift from withdrawal to mainstream support. The fact remains, however, that whatever the form of provision, and although 75 per cent of the money for the teachers of this 'extra' English comes from Home Office Section 11 funds, rather than from local LEA monies, many indigenous parents and pupils — indeed, even some teachers — have objected to this 'extra' language support provision. They do not recognize the bilingual students' right to it, often seeing language support teaching more as an educational privilege than a right. Racism is obviously part of this perception, a perception that involves belated recognition that indigenous children themselves are not educated according to their needs, which then turns not on the issue that *all* children should have that right, but on the resentment that somehow bilingual children appear to get 'more'. However, bilingual children leave school with fewer qualifications than their indigenous peers. A few bilingual pupils doggedly pursue education into the sixth form and may succeed in achieving exam qualifications two, three and four years later than their peers.

Teachers' Status, Political Positions and Curriculum Development

At the time I refer to, in company with the staffing of all schools, most of the teachers were white, middle-class, grammar school and university educated and of a politically liberal persuasion. Almost all of the teachers, well placed in the management hierarchy (including the few of working-class or ethnic minority origin), support the conservatist-liberal ethos. Those teachers who are the more analytical and critical both of their own work and of the school's curriculum arrangements and practices are, by and large, on the lower paid scales, of working-class origin, or of ethnic minority origin.

There was, in fact, quite a lot of educational debate within the school. But while voluntary working parties, committees and workshops for developing policies and instituting various changes and developments abounded, outcomes did not, most proposals, particularly those that might be construed as 'radical', being blocked at some stage or another. Despite there having been changes in headteacher and management team members, and consequent changes in management 'style', the structual management operations of the school remained characteristically static, supported and kept that way by the bureaucratic functionalism of the LEA Divisional Office, whose perceived priorities were to keep the school running along the traditional lines of the liberal status quo; to make sure the school did not incur the wrath of its most powerful middle-class parents; to keep the school from any innovation that would attract the negative attention of the conservatist/liberal media; and to administer the Government's budget cuts.

The possibilities of teacher directed curricular innovation are quite effectively smothered by the simple expedients of cutting out the teacher time needed to develop such work, and the in-service training time needed to put such work into operation. The will to curricular innovation and development needs a supportive ethos. Furthermore, those teachers interested enough to pursue curriculum innovation are less likely to obtain promotion at the normal rate, more likely not to get it at all. Far from being supported for their efforts, they can expect to be accused of being 'uncooperative', 'oppositional' and the like.

English Teaching

Practical circumstances and theoretical premises of English Teaching

There were fourteen teachers in the English Department, but nine of them also held posts of responsibility outside the English Department — as members of the Humanities Department, the Business Studies Department, as Head of ESL, Head of Community Education and as Heads of Year. So these teachers' energy and commitment could not in any case be focused *primarily* on English teaching as such, and perhaps least of all (even if they wished it to be) on dealing with troubling questions, such as, given the nature of language and thought, what does teaching English to *mother tongue* speakers of English actually imply in socio-political terms?.

Indeed, quite apart from a general unwillingness to address 'difficult' questions (and apart from a serious lack of discussion time for doing so) the department (like many other English Departments at this point in the history of English mother tongue teaching) was thoroughly fragmented even on the status quo theoretical bases for its teaching. These theoretical fragmentations were reflected most obviously in the different teacher-training orthodoxies the teachers had experienced. They were also reflective of teachers' political positions within the department, the school and the educational system, and reflective of their own political and moral biases — conscious and subconscious — towards education, towards the pupils they taught and towards other members of staff.

The English Literature Theoretical Premise

The dominant group of teachers in the department saw and practised English teaching in its most theoretically traditional sense, i.e., based heavily on literature, preferably 'good' English literature, and on the production of 'lit. crit.' type essays relating to a textual analysis of the same. The underlying assumption is that this provides intellectual, cultural and linguistic 'enrichment' and a morally healthy familiarity with the 'universal' values said to be found in such literature. Although within this position it was understood that all pupils for their own good and for the good of 'society' *ought* to have access to this literary education, it was also tacitly acknowledged that, realistically, only a small percentage — the more middle-class pupils — were *actually* capable of 'appreciating' and/or engaging with this literary approach.

This group of teachers held power in the department, not necessarily always numerically, but by virtue of their being either middle-class or assuming conservatist-liberal middle-class attitudes and practices; by being older and possessing more academic qualifications than the actual head and deputy head of department; by having more power and posts of responsibility in the other management structures of the school and, indeed, by their ability to inspire a deferent cultural, social and institutionally prudent consensus in most of the other members of the department.

The Progressive/Creative Theoretical Premise

The second group in the department adhered to the more theoretically 'progressive' tradition of English teaching: the 1960s 'creative and imaginative' model which was itself a reaction to the 'inappropriateness' of the 'Eng. Lit.' model for most working-class children. This 'progressive' model assumes that working-class children need their imaginations 'stimulated'. The theoretical impulse for this was the assumption of imaginative and creative deprivation, resulting in a general inadequacy of the intellect which, in turn, is seen as what causes working-class children to fail in school.

The way to stimulate such a child is to present it with a variety of bits of literature, short stories, poems, photographs, extracts from novels, etc., all pertaining to 'relevant' themes in an ostensibly child-centred pedagogy, all purporting to start from where the child is supposedly 'at' in intellectual, imaginative and socio-cultural terms. The child, supposedly finding this approach more 'accessible', is encouraged to creative expression based upon it, in the hope that this will lead to oracy and literacy skills — not to mention less classroom resistance and, supposedly, greater happiness all round.

It is typical of this 'creative' mode that it may well include (in its attempts to 'stimulate' the imagination) a wide range of outlandish, sensational and even radical materials and approaches. However, the eventual intended intellectual outcomes from the use of this material is incorporation into a status quo conservatist/liberal socio-cultural consensus of the imagination based on supposedly 'universal' values.

Themes (e.g., childhood, school, animals, parents, family life, growing up, poverty, adventure, gangs, old age, relationships and war), plus the intellectual, oracy and literacy tasks emanating from them, are presented as *relevant* to the child's *assumed* experiences, observations, interests and levels of socio-cultural and intellectual development.

However, despite the variety and purported 'relevance' of these themes and literary specifics, because this model, like the 'lit. crit.' model, is also about incorporating and transmitting the values and attitudes of the dominant culture, (ultimately assuming a world of conservatist/liberal emotions, responses, perceptions and agreements) it, too, inevitably precludes properly analytical intellectual development. For instance childhood or old age may well be presented as themes suitable for stimulating a matrix of desired responses about the human processes common or 'universal' to childhood or old age any place, any time. Or poverty might be presented as a state worthy of general lamentation in the belief that its presentation develops a liberal emotional em-

197

pathy, and some consequent, if vaguely defined, sense of social responsibility.

In this model children are to 'attain' an agreed and limited range of values and responses which are seen as valid, more or less, in any conditions, any place, any time, past present or projected. Specifics are used as matters of description rather than matters of analysis. It is outside the theoretical and pedagogical frame of this mode of English teaching to focus too directly or for too long on pupils' *actual* emotional, reflective articulations in relation to such real human questions. On the contrary, indirection and dependence upon second hand, fictional, creative expressions and responses is commonly thought more desirable on the grounds that the child can explore 'relevant' issues yet not suffer the possible psychological trauma of reality.

But truly comprehensive nurturing in education must surely include helping pupils to develop the intellectual, emotional, imaginative and reflective ability and strength to make sustained socio-economic and socio-cultural analyses as to the political reasons for such matters as poverty or wealth, or of the *specifics* of childhood or old age in different conditions: it must include helping pupils make sustained analyses of what political and moral action is needed to eradicate poverty; and helping them find their own and their teachers' place within that moral and political action.

Yet such analyses are no more a focus of real intellectual attention within this model than they were with the old Eng. Lit. model. Just as in the traditional Eng. Lit. model, the creative/relevant model produces only occasional and fragmentary socio-historical contextualizations of the bits of literature it uses. In fact, the creative/progressive model probably does less contextualizing. In presenting literary specifics, neither of these models presents any comprehensive analyses of either the socio-political conditions producing and 'agreeing' those texts, or means of evaluating the degree of social, emotional and developmental worth of these texts to the pupils themselves. Despite psychological, sociological, psycholinguistic and sociolinguistic evidence of the relationship between intellectual, linguistic and social development, that evidence remains politically and morally superficial to English mother tongue teaching as generally practised. The fact is that despite the differences between these two models of English mother tongue teaching, one labelled traditional, the other progressive, both emanate from conservatist-liberal, anti-intellectual perspectives. As such, neither are in serious opposition to one another.

Indeed inside the school, the educational 'debate' over these models by the 'progressives' within the department was characteristically constrained by the more pressing politics of who will be allowed to teach the upper Eng. Lit. level exam classes each year, since 'successful' teaching of these exam classes was seen as improving promotion prospects. Furthermore, classroom management in these classes, consisting as they did of mainly middle-class and aspiring middle-class pupils, was less fraught, and the more academic nature of the work said to be more 'interesting' to the teachers — more comfortable at any rate, since it allowed them to pursue the sort of English teaching with which they themselves were more familiar.

Within the department there was also a 'floating' group of teachers who would affiliate themselves to either of the two dominant groups — depending on the issue, upon their training, upon the politics of which classes has been allocated to them, and upon their need to appeal to or assuage the power of either of the other groups at particular points in time.

Whatever departmental policy disagreements there were over these two modes of English teaching, e.g., over lesson content, pedagogy, nature of tasks set, these were 'resolved' by the convenient assertion that each teacher in the department should be allowed to practise as an 'individual professional'. This notion derived from another conservatist/liberal assumption, i.e., that whatever such 'individual professionals' (their differences notwithstanding) managed to do for pupils, particularly working-class pupils, must all be to the good anyway.

A consequence of this *laissaiz-faire* was that there was little departmental examination of materials, tasks set or pedagogy; little in the way of an agreed policy on the purchase of books and almost nothing in the way of the cooperative building up of teacher produced departmental teaching materials. Indeed, organization overall was minimal: if you were keen to use a particular text at a particular time with a class, the primary means of ensuring that you would be able to do so was to get to the stock cupboard and grab that set of texts before anybody else did.

Departments can, of course, be more organized than this. Indeed, this particular department did develop administratively. But the fundamental fragmentation of theory and practices remained. It is a fragmentation common to English mother tongue teaching. The National Curriculum for English creates various 'shifts' in the balances of this fragmentation, but it does not seriously address fundamental questions relating to the theory of the relationship between language and thought, society and equal rights.

The Development of an Analytic Mode of English Teaching

Finally, there was a minority of two teachers, sometime three, of working-class and/or on the lower scales in the department, who, much to the annoyance of the other groups, made sporadic attempts to pursue the development of an analytical mode of English mother tongue teaching. The consequent attempts to discuss the content, pedagogy and outcomes of the department's English teaching in terms of skills and intellectual development of *all* pupils, and of working-class pupils in particular, could well have remained a mere irritation to the other groups, if it were not for the fact that this group's interests in analytical teaching also involved input into proposed departmental buying of texts, money for the development of materials, input into the department's evaluation systems and proposals for new syllabuses.

This minority ended up in competition over resources for the production of materials, which inevitably put them in conflict with the interests of the other members of the department, and with the generally status quo consensual management of the department. Departmental discussions were, to put it midly, difficult. A major obstacle was the embedded dominant socio-cultural assumption that such an analytical teaching model, rather than having the potential for liberating and contributing to pupils' self-confidence, understanding, skills and integrity, must instead, inevitably, deny the 'creative and spiritual' nurturing of the human imagination.

Also classic was the dominant conclusion that the conflicting theoretical positions were in fact 'personality conflicts', the onus for the said conflicts residing, of course, with the minority interested in analytical teaching — they also, of course, being the only ones with 'personalities'. Either that or they had to be pushing the idea of analytical teaching because of their affiliation to left wing politics. This is despite the fact that none of the minority teachers belonged to any political party, whereas the same could not be said of the dominant majority. And finally, there was the confident assumption that working-class pupils were the least capable of coping with anything resembling an analytical mode of English teaching.

That traditionally trained English teachers just might have a mind-set and vested career interests against proposals for analytical teaching was not recognized as part of the problematics of discussion.

As English teachers involved for 99 per cent of their time in the actual teaching of children, there was, of course, across the department, agreement on broad objectives of literacy and communicative competence — if little on the means to achieve it. Most teachers in fact exhausted themselves daily in their attempts to achieve those objectives. Most teachers with five classes were teaching upwards of 120 children a week, more if they didn't have the relief of small group sixth form teaching.

There was also agreement on the need for children to develop their skills in writing well beyond, for instance, producing summaries of their favourite TV programmes, or indeed of intellectually fairly puerile, if often verbally sophisticated, Eng. Lit. essays. But what children wrote, how they came to write it, the intellectual understanding behind what they produced, their development in thinking and writing, often became subsumed to the pragmatics of getting them to write something, *anything*.

Developing literacy is certainly the ongoing intention and anxiety of all English teachers. But very often it is literacy of a limited kind. It is a literacy produced from the crude compromises of the day-to-day classroom situation in its interaction with popular and not so popular cultures; produced in the compromise between teachers' insistence on and children's resistance to writing; produced in the compromise of getting an exam folder filled with different sorts of writing, sometimes, any sort of writing. It is crude in terms of political and socio-economic literacy and in terms of emotional, psychological, cultural and philosophic understanding.

The question of how to help pupils develop their own powers in contemporary socio-cultural understanding and analysis — in a way that being the receivers and appreciators of Eng.Lit. did not, or being 'stimulated' into 'creativity' by bits and pieces of writing from here and there also did not — remained matters of ongoing concern to the minority of teachers trying to develop an analytic mode of English teaching and the pedagogies that went with it. However, even if the other members of the department might have agreed that some of these points were worth thinking about, now and then, these issues were regarded, by and large, as matters of unnecessary controversy.

Overlap and Disagreement between the Traditions

As time passed, and the issues didn't, the minority teachers' attempts at developing bits of work based on an analytical model of teaching were regarded less and less as the work of a few isolated 'individual professionals' legitimately bothered about the cultural and intellectual effects of the traditional modes of English mother tongue teaching on pupils, especially working-class pupils. Nor was such work seen merely as perhaps an understandable threat to the other two dominant traditions. Instead, it was regarded almost as anathema, a piece of cultural perversion, of left-wing infiltration, a 'communist plot' almost, rather than the piece of progressive liberal practice it actually amounted to — given the ability of the structures of the system not even to swallow it up and spit it out, but simply to marginalize and ignore it.

As with the Eng. Lit. and creative/relevant models of teaching, in the analytic mode, consideration of a text's thematic and technical structuring and uses of language would continue to be a part of the learning. But from quite different dominant premises, premises of socio-cultural analysis, of interaction between reader and text, rather than from 'agreed' premises of 'universal' values and liberal aesthetics.

In the analytical mode of English teaching there needed to be more use of materials that would illuminate texts' socio-historical background. There also needed to be the use of a pedagogy based much more on discussion and collaborative learning techniques, since in an analytical teaching mode the focus on the teacher's range of subjective cultural assumptions about a text can no longer be considered adequate in guiding pupils to a fuller understanding of that text's values. Nor, more importantly, can teachers' subjective cultural assumptions be regarded as adequate to the active intellectual engagement and development of the pupil as an independent individual and as a politically and morally rigourous social being.

This did not necessarily mean that every single piece of literature had to get the 'full' analytical treatment, but it did mean contextualizing enough pieces of work so that pupils had the *means* of analysis at their disposal, to apply to other texts or other media.

All of this was highly suspect, of course, yet unable to be dismissed as far as the traditional and progressive English teachers were concerned, since most would agree that some, though limited, socio-cultural backgrounding of texts is necessary. But what was not acceptable to them is that with an analytical mode of teaching, although literature is included as content material, it no longer constitutes the almost exclusive content material for English mother tongue teaching. In an analytical mode of teaching you are no longer confining English to the 'teaching' of literature or to the teaching of personal 'creative/imaginative' writing stimulated by it. You are in effect trying to encourage and promote an analytical mode of thinking. This is dependent upon a more comprehensive range of content materials, upon more flexible pedagogical methods of communicative interaction, which will help promote the development of more intellectually comprehensive types of knowledge, understandings and skills.

Yet another less than popular aspect of analytical teaching is the necessary analysis of bias. Since bias is inevitable in all texts, in all teachers and in all pupils, analytical teaching inevitably has to teach about the concept of bias, which involves discussing, declaring and evaluating biases, whether texts', teachers' or pupils'.

Equal Opportunities Education

Policies, Practice and Materials

Nevertheless, despite the difficulties over a period of several years, some materials, pedagogy on analytical teaching, and halting discussion on the subject, did become tolerated, if not welcomed as an item on the departmental agenda.

One of the pieces of work produced during this period was a booklet, euphemistically entitled *Work and Movement*, which was a compilation of historical and literary accounts of racist and classist exploitations of labour which, not incidentally, one advisory teacher for the multi-cultural education, himself black, said he 'wouldn't touch with a barge pole' because of predictable parental reaction and accusations of being 'political'. It was a crude piece of work pedagogically speaking (if no cruder than most of the other work done in the department), attempting to give pupils socio-cultural insights into social and economic structures and into literature produced within those structures — insights to which they would not otherwise have had access.

At about this time the school itself was trying to formulate its multicultural (not yet anti-racist) policy. It had got as far as beginning to form its crisis management sections of the policy, i.e., what to do about racist incidents and remarks — what indeed to do about the National Front contingent amongst its pupil intake. (The school was able to transfer, though not to educate, one pupil in the Third Year who was distributing fascist literature, and who later went on to infamy as a National Front organizer). However, in common with other institutions at this time, the school had made virtually no progress yet in forming multicultural *curriculum* policy, never mind appropriate pedagogy for the multicultural classroom.

Multicultural Teaching in the English Department

Proposals for purchase of more multicultural, anti-racist texts were eventually agreed by the department. But these would be primarily for lower school and CSE teaching. Proposals for the insertion of such literature on O level lists foundered on such catch-22 questions in the minds of the traditionalists as the 'dubious' literary merit of multicultural literature on the one hand, and their levels of conceptual and literary difficulty on the other. The same conditions remain true of traditionalists in relation to choosing literature for GCSE. This matter, in our department, was 'resolved' in characteristic fashion: as 'individual professionals' those teachers interested in using such literature in O level classes could do so — 'providing the exam board approved', the threat being that it might not, a threat discovered by the teachers to be unfounded when they read the exam board's regulations. The 'interested' teachers proceeded to use such literature, but were only too well aware of the marginalization of the issue *per se*, the limited number of teachers who would be using such literature, and the limited number of pupils who would be exposed to it.

The School and Anti-racism

Multinationals and Apartheid

At the same point in time, a major incident in the school's political and moral history occurred; an incident which, again, demonstrates issues of morality in education generally. A middle-class parent of the School Association had written to all the major multinational companies in the area asking for donations to the school fund. Three major companies, all heavily involved in the South African economy, had, with some alacrity, donated sums of money to the school — and their company literature to the school library and to the business studies department of the school, literature promoting an image of the companies as benefactors to the world economy, including the peoples and economies of South Africa and Namibia. The head of English who was also chairperson of the School Association was somewhat concerned that one of the companies was in fact notorious for its oppressions and exploitations not only in South Africa but worldwide. Other teachers in the school, and particularly the minority of teachers in the English Department who had been lobbying for anti-racist materials and the space to try to develop analytical modes of teaching, were alarmed that the school would accept monies from these companies. These teachers were also members of the school's Multicultural Education Committee, latterly renamed the Anti-racist Committee. The obvious question was what was the worth of a school's multicultural and antiracist education policy if the school turned around and accepted money from these racist companies heavily involved in South Africa?

The headteacher considered himself strongly multicultural and anti-racist. He did not, however, consider it his duty to advise the School Association that the school could not accept the said monies. The head of English, as chair of the School Association, eventually declared that the monies should be accepted, on the grounds that the parent had asked for the monies 'in good faith' and this sort of parental 'initiative' should be encouraged, rather than censored in any way. The deputy head of English also declared that the monies should be accepted, on the grounds that pupils could be given extra opportunities, e.g., such monies could pay for extra-curricular trips, which would also benefit pupils of ethnic minority origins.

The teachers opposing the acceptance of these monies, none of them with posts of managerial power within the school, in opposing the conservatist-liberal politics and morals of the majority of the staff, ended up in their usual marginalized position. They decided that the only thing to do now was to mount a campaign of information about the operations of these companies, particularly with reference to their dealings in South Africa.

It became obvious that some teachers were very unclear about socio-economic structures generally, inclusive of the concept of multinational corporations. Indeed at that point in time, 1981, before apartheid and South Africa came to be in the news almost daily, there were also some staff who perceived apartheid as an inevitable and ultimately beneficial colonialism: 'I've heard that there are plenty of black people in other African countries who go voluntarily to South Africa to get jobs, because there's nothing for them in their own countries.'

There were no alternative information materials in either the school or the local library. A range of up to date informative materials had to be purchased from alternative bookshops and from the Anti-Apartheid Movement and a display of them mounted in the staffroom. Proposals for returning the monies to these companies were also placed on the agendas of both the union meetings and on the staff meeting. The main union meeting agreed that all the monies from these companies should be sent back. At the staff meeting, his reputation as a multiculturalist at stake, the Head finally spoke against the operations of the most notorious of these companies. However, despite our information campaign which also gave information about the *other* two multinationals, and despite the fact that these companies were also involved in the production of armaments and of weapons of chemical warfare — indeed of the very tear gas used against South Africans who demonstrated against apartheid — the Head of the school spoke in favour of keeping the money donated by them. His reasoning was that they also produced such things as office equipment and brand name antisceptic liquids and ointments.

At this meeting the staff voted *not* to send the money back, on the grounds that, as one teacher put it, 'all these companies have skeletons in the closet, 'but that we had to live with that, or live with 'anarchy'. Sending the money back was also categorized an unnecessarily 'political' act — whereas accepting it was seen as apolitical and 'normal'.

One of the teachers, alarmed at the implications of accepting such monies, discussed the issue with a black parent at a parents' evening and that parent wrote a letter to the headteacher registering his concern. Another discussion with an inspector for multicultural education — although he pointed out that there was nothing he could do if the school decided to accept the money — resulted in him doing what he could do, referring unequivocally to the racist nature of the South African and other economies in the speech he was invited to give at an 'International Evening' of entertainments put on by the school as its contribution to multicultural education.

That one letter by the parent to the headteacher, plus that speech by the multicultural inspector, though it was received with some irritation by an audience of pupils, parents and teachers intent on entertainment, were both important. The head of English, concluding that the issue wasn't going to go away, now decided as chair also of the School's Council that for the proposed returning of the monies to be truly democratic, pupils themselves should vote on the issue. Most children knew little more about economics than their individual experience and/or what the tabloid press encouraged them to believe, and that didn't include knowledge about the operation of capitalist corporations here or abroad. Few of them knew much about South African apartheid either, since there was little or no teaching about these issues in the curriculum. However, the minority of children who elected to vote in this hastily called School's Council election, about eighty pupils out of 1400, surprisingly to some, voted to return *all* the monies to the multinationals.

Much later, another staff meeting was called and finally staff voted also to send all the monies back: partly, one suspects — and as one member of staff, who was previously for keeping the money, but was now for sending it back, said — because they were 'fed up' with having to deal with the issue on staff meeting agendas.

But there were also teachers changing their vote because they did now know more about economic and political structures, perceiving that the economic system was not, after all, a matter of neutral 'interdependence', nor their own relationship to it morally neutral either. To get to this point with a staff of 'well educated' adults in charge of the day to day 'education' of children had taken well over a year.

The story of the school sending the money back to the first company had got into the newspapers, no one quite knew how. The headteacher was then quoted in the newspaper as saying that the decision to send the money back was consistent with the 'school's and the Local Education Authority's policy of multiethnic education'. The same article reported the teachers as 'spurning' a merely charitable offer from benevolent multinational corporations. The teachers were, of course, described as militant and political, rather than, more accurately, as more liberally moralistic than anything else. Sending monies back to these companies was more a symbolic act of moral conscience than an act of real militancy. For a limited number of pupils and teachers it might be said to have had some positive if very limited politically educative and socio-cultural effects.

Educators worth their salt have always been concerned about the life chances of their pupils. So it has never been good enough to perceive the educational system as a philosophical and academic ivory tower that won't dirty its hands with the practical and pragmatic issues of skills related to employment. But the *volte face* of the last few years of forging intimate connection between education and industry has almost silenced questions about the morality of that connection. The ascendance of the bias in education towards producing operators, managers and technocrats for industry out of the 'more able', and towards 'training' for the 'low achievers' — all of it based on the desires of employers interested in profitable exploitations, as opposed to the development of an equitable education, never mind the development of equitable economic, political and moral progress — diminishes further the possibilities of any such thing as decent equal human rights education. The present bias in favour of close links between education and industry can never be what it is made out to be — the answer to the educational 'failure' of working-class children. On the contrary.

Developing Materials on Apartheid

Partly because of the above mentioned school history, partly because 'Peace Education' and 'Development Education' (education about the Third World which backpedalled classist, racist and sexist exploitation and forefronted what was termed as world economic 'interdependence') were now becoming part of liberal progressiveness in education, I, now a scale 2 postholder with responsibility for the development of a Third Year syllabus for the English Department, requested and was given tentative permission by the department to gather materials for a module of work of 'current events'.

However, the more of these materials purchased, the more obvious the conservatist/liberal bias in them became. To make a module of work using these existing materials would mean in effect 'fighting the materials' themselves in order to get to the fundamental issues of socio-economic, psychological and cultural exploitations and oppressions.

The problem was to put together a unit of materials that would try to help pupils to reach comprehensive understanding of those exploitations. In effect, nothing could better allow this than to put together a unit of work based on the politics of working-class pupils' own situation in the here and now.

It was mooted that we might put together a unit on a current strike at a garment factory. But agreement to contribute materials for this produced next to nothing. Moreover, we well knew just how much in-school, governor, inspectorate support such a unit would be likely to get.

Coincidentally, I was at that time a member of the Schools' Council Language for Learning project which was looking at discussion based, collaborative learning. One of the other teachers in the project brought a module of work that she had constructed for use in her school's lower school Humanities Department. The module was based on the life of people in a village in India. Its aim was to present the 'underdevelopment' problems of the village and to show what the villagers did to try to solve the problems. The materials included pictures, reports, statistical information, descriptive and autobiographical materials. The unit of work used drama simulation as its main pedagogical method, the children enacting roles of the people in the village, stating problems, holding meetings to consider solutions, etc., then producing written work from that.[1]

In one Project session the Project teachers were examining these materials specifically for the language structure and accessibility levels for pupils learning in English as their second language. I found a good deal to admire in the construction of this module. It provided a variety of materials, and the pedagogical method provided a variety of access into the problems and possible resolutions of daily life in an entire socio-economic setting, including something of the political skills needed, and it presented ample opportunity for the development of oracy and literacy skills.

What it did not do was offer a comprehensive means of analysis of 'underdevelopment', either in terms of internal or external political structures. Being given an opportunity to enact ways of pragmatically resolving difficulties caused by powerful politico-economic structures is one thing; being given an opportunity to make sustained analyses of those fundamental structures and to hypothesize how they might be transformed is quite another.

Eventually tacit approval was given to put together a module of work on the Third World. But, again, all the materials I could find exhibited a conservatist/liberal bias towards Third World problems. It was a bias almost the equivalent to the benign colonialism evidenced in the history books that 'taught' about that previous era. The one country where that bias was least possible was South Africa.

There was no doubt (despite the spurious objection that South Africa was an anomaly) that South African apartheid provided the sharpest paradigm for comprehending the economic bases of racism and of the role of the state in the maintenance of poverty, exploitation and the oppression of labour.

Having gathered a range of materials, from photographs to reports, autobiographical accounts, the UN Declaration of Human Rights, extracts from Mandela's trial and from the Steve Biko inquest, newspaper clippings, poems, cartoons, information on censorship, plays, short stories, extracts from apartheid laws, novels, a list of British companies operating with apartheid, plus statistics on health, education, tax, land and income for black and white groups, a source book entitled *Apartheid* was produced. As well as a means of developing literacy in the usual way, the teaching materials were also a means of attempting to deal with pupils' political illiteracy, their limited world knowledge, and with classroom racism — all from a vantage point of the formal curricular study.

Since the materials were not confined to 'literature' and made attempts to provide a socio-economic analytical model of capitalist exploitation, for such work to be entertained it would have to be supported by those with more power and influence than I had. The English advisory teachers and an inspector for multicultural education were contacted. They were very helpful, one advisory teacher in particular offering advice on pedagogical method and necessary supplementary materials. They were also able to put me in touch with another teacher in another school who was doing the same sort of work.

Supplementary materials included videos, a drama simulation booklet based on the pass laws, a booklet on notetaking, a discussion document which presented socio-economic questions about British society, media analysis questionnaires, plus introductory worksheets on the two socio-economic groups under apartheid, giving statistics comparing standards of living, but without stating the racial divisions or the name of the country.

When the source book and supplementary teaching materials were ready, the head of the English Department refused money to print them, hinting that the headteacher did not approve of the materials. The head of English's stated objection to using the materials in the Department was in case of complaints from parents, and also that the materials were too extensive and complex. I asked if I could invite the advisory teachers and the multicultural inspector to the next Department meeting so that the issue could be discussed more fully. They came. The work was discussed and further explicated by the advisory teachers. They presented the moral, political, pedagogical and educational case for the introduction of such materials into English teaching. All of them had previously been heads of English departments.

The fact that the work was now seen to have the support of advisory teachers and the multicultural inspector suppressed further present opposition re teaching about apartheid *per se* — although it did not win the larger argument for analytical teaching. Amongst all the points put by those supporting the use of the materials on apartheid, the one argument that seemed to hold sway was that none of the major political parties in the country condoned apartheid, and no newspaper in the country supported it. Therefore, few parents, or children, were likely to offer any strong objections to the classroom use of these materials. Anyone who did would have their objections met firstly on the grounds of the political parties' and media's general consensus on the unacceptability of apartheid. As far as the inspector for multicultural education was concerned, their objections would also be met on the more proper educational grounds of apartheid's fundamental contradiction to equal human rights, and on pupils' educational rights to greater political and moral understanding re not only apartheid, but generally. Further, the inspector declared that the development of such work was 'implicit in the school's view of itself as a multicultural institution'. Finally, one of the minority of teachers in favour of analytical education pointed out a fundamental educational need to state anti-racist perspectives — not to accommodate racism, either by censoring such work, or by other more liberal means of avoidance of it.

After this meeting, which the headteacher did not attend, it was stated that the headteacher had no objections to the materials being used, and had agreed that money for the printing of the materials would be found.

Analytic Education

Some Crucial Questions

The foregoing constitutes the political and moral circumstances in which the materials used in the one fifty-five minute lesson (to be described) were prepared and produced.

As stated previously, *all* lesson content, pedagogy, materials and interaction emanate from a political/moral complex. Analyses of lessons and their outcomes inevitably reveal the system's political and moral intentions towards pupils; and will also reveal the political knowledge and understandings (or, more likely under the present system, lack of political knowledge and understandings) construed by pupils from their 'learning' both within the educational system, and from elsewhere.

If this kind of work, trying via the mainstream curriculum to develop fragments of analytical mother tongue and English as a second language teaching which attempted to address political issues and political literacy, was unusual in the late 70s and early 80s, it was, nevertheless, possible. In 1989, with the advent of the central Conservative Party control of a 'national' curriculum, such work becomes less and less possible. Witness the exlusion of social studies from the National Curriculum, or the emphasis on British history rather than world history, or a national curriculum in English which pays next to no attention to the needs of bilingual learners. Furthermore, religion, as *per* the requirements of the new Education Act, is evidence of further attempts at indoctrination into the conservatist/liberal status quo.

It might be argued that not all teaching materials in other areas of teaching, science and maths for instance, need struggle to take on the moral and political issues of the contemporary human world in the way that humanities subjects do. At best, this presupposes that humanities subjects *do*, in fact, enter this struggle. The truth is that much of humanities teaching resists taking on contemporary issues in the world, whether local, national or international, preferring, instead, to 'historicize' and distance issues of exploitation, etc., and to 'universalize' moral and political concerns. Often, this is done in such a confusing 'balance of biases' fashion (equal time to both sides of patently unequal human rights arguments) that real intellectual analytical and philosophical thought is perverted, concepts of moral and political action based on equal human rights suppressed.

Moreover, to assign moral political and philosophically analytical thought to an alleged 'knowledge domain' of the humanities alone is yet another common educational subversion. No so-called 'domain' of knowledge, humanities, sciences, whatever, in constructed, developed or applied outside a socio-political context and, therefore, all must come under the same scrutiny.

For instance, have scientific and mathematical knowledge, concepts, and skills (or indeed even those of the arts and humanities) been developed and applied from a socio-political context *positive* to the support of human life and to *equal* human rights? Or from the contexts of sectionally vested interests — and, therefore, as far as hard pressed teachers delivering the curriculum are concerned, from contexts oppositional to the interests of working-class children, or pragmatically indifferent to or, oblique to, the issues of pupils' equal educational opportunities?

These are permanently crucial questions. As such they surely must form the humanly integrated bases from which future educational development of any 'domain' of the world's knowledge and education should spiral. If omission of these questions is embedded in science courses in schools, for example, then omission is as much an educationally political act as the inclusion of such questions would be — and such omissions diminish equal educational rights in any field of study.

Such questions relate not only to the content of lessons, but to the pedagogical methods used. Does the pedagogy promote intellectual development through the means of discussion, questioning and enquiry in an ethos of both exploration and intellectual rigour? Or are the pedagogic methods employed primarily behaviourist and authoritarian? Or merely pragmatically and politically liberal in both format and intent?

The Apartheid Materials

The materials produced were used by one or two teachers in the English Department with Third Years as intended. But it was not until four years later, when South Africa was daily in the news, that the materials were used more extensively within the Department. Yet, at that point, it appears they were more used in an emotionally and psychologically 'affective' manner with classes than in a true analytical mode of teaching.

A Consideration of Appropriate Learning Materials for Bilingual Students

The one lesson actually to be described did not take place in a mainstream English lesson, but with bilingual pupils learning in English as a second language in an English 'withdrawal' lesson. The students were Fourth Years, doing one or two O levels, but mainly following CSE courses, English being one of them. The 'Special English' option which these students followed as one of their Fourth Year options was designed to assist them with their English generally and with the English needed in the various other subjects they were following.

I was, at the time, also involved in a teachers' workshop at the local teachers' centre on strategies for teaching English as a second language, hopefully in mainstream lessons where such a policy of mainstreaming existed, or in withdrawal lessons where it did not. One of the matters under discussion in our workshop meetings was the question of appropriate learning materials for developing bilingual students in English lessons — materials which would allow them access to knowledge, and encourage oral work and discussion as well as writing. Since, in most English classrooms, the practices of comprehension, reading, vocabulary development, writing and discussion are predominantly based not on factual materials relating to their contemporary world, but on fictional texts (fictions produced by middle-class authors and publishers) the workshop teachers were mainly looking for ways of making these traditional practices accessible to the learners of English as a second language.

That certain alienations, miscomprehensions and lack of confidence can be engendered by this traditional 'fictional' approach to English teaching in indigenous pupils is sometimes recognized, if reluctantly. Less recognized is the fact that such teaching must also be a factor, *inter alia*, in producing no less than four million illiterates in this country.[2] Since it is working-class children, in particular, who are affected (and since it is also working-class children who, when literate, continue to fail or achieve only mediocre results in qualifications in English based on this system), then the politics of the content, materials and pedagogy of lessons, not just of the examination outcomes themselves, reflect a by no means insignificant dimension of working-class suppression.

What, indeed, are the 'educational' forces which might be said to almost compel you to 'fail' in your own language and thought processes? And now-adays, with a compulsory oral component to GCSE exam qualifications, if pupils choose not to 'talk', they've 'had it'.

If this primarily 'fictional' approach to English teaching is problematic for a considerable number of indigenous children, the problems of miscomprehension, alienation and lack of confidence are often compounded for pupils learning to use English as a second language, attempting, as they must, not only to engage with literature in a different language but also literature of a different culture.

Another crucial question that this teachers' workshop group of ESL and mainstream teachers at the teacher's centre were addressing was the racial antagonism, indeed racist abuse, that many pupils learning English as a second language suffer, along with other pupils from ethnic minorities whose first language is English.

Which pieces of literature are the least covertly racist, classist, sexist? Which can best be used in a multicultural classroom? What pedagogic strategies and teaching materials can be used to deal with both latent and not so latent racism? What language learning, comprehension, analytical and pedagogic strategies can best support *all* the children in their intellectual and skills development? If new factual materials are used and analytic teaching is employed in English teaching, what particular strategies need to be developed to support students in coordinating both language development and understanding of such materials? Further, if such materials are to be used in English, how are traditionally trained English and ESL teachers to be shown the value of including factually based and topically relevant materials in their teaching repertoire? Moreover, if factual materials and an analytical approach are to be used in English classrooms, not only as a complement to fiction, but in their own right, how do teachers decide *which* materials to use? How do they go about finding such materials, adjusting them for accessibility of language, layout, comprehension and analysis? On what bases do they assess their educational worth and pedagogic effectiveness? Our discussions were wide-ranging and daunting. The one thing that became obvious was the range of issues that needed to be *articulated* before they could even begin to be addressed.

Most of the teachers in this group were ESL teachers or traditionally trained English teachers. There were no teachers from other subject areas. Our discussions were certainly engaging, our conclusions disparate. However, the traditional premises ultimately prevailed. The final consensus was *against* using factually based materials and analytically based teaching in ESL or English lessons, on the gounds that the students, especially those learning to use English as a second language, would just not be capable of dealing with factually based materials. Exactly why or how they would be so incapable of dealing with complex factual materials in English, how was it they were supposed to deal with complex materials in science, geography, social studies or child development?

Since I dissented from the consensus, I was obliged to prove the case, which is how and why the factual worksheets (see Appendix 1) on the statistics of the standards of living under apartheid came to be used in this particular English as a second language support lesson.

Background to the Lesson Analyzed

The Class

The pupils were a small group of Fourth Years who have been in England from two to three years, except for Angelina, a beginner user of English who had been in the country for only a matter of months. The boys, Louis, Paul, Hammid, were classified as second stage learners of English, but at the top end of the scale, i.e., they were fairly fluent speakers of everyday English, but read slowly and hesitantly, and experienced grammatical, spelling and expressive difficulties in written English. They were all following the same mainstream Mode 3 CSE English course, each with different teachers using different materials. In these Special English lessons they did mainly traditional English work in terms of content, but with a focus on the actual language structures needed to produce the required assignments. They also got some help with the written and spoken work of other subject areas.

The ethos of the Special English lessons was friendly and relaxed, the classroom itself a much less anonymous place for bilingual students than was the mainstream classroom. There were four other students in this Special English group, another boy from Portugal, and three girls from Hong Kong.

For this particular lesson, which started late and haphazardly, the class was divided, equally haphazardly, into two groups, one to be led by a visiting lecturer interested in the learning of bilingual pupils and the other to be led by myself. The usual ESL teacher of this group was only temporarily in the transcript discussion group, spending most of her time with the other group and the visiting lecturer. The Chinese girls in the other group were particularly shy, and were a bit put off by the fact that the lecturer was a stranger to them, so their attempts at discussion were far more hesitant. Other factors in their reticence could well have been that this particular group of girls had less general knowledge with which to support their discussion, and that they were unused to expressing such knowledge, unused to their understandings being taken seriously. Certainly, they were less confident in attempting to evaluate and express political issues than was the transcript group of mainly boys.

I was a mainstream English teacher also trained in ESL teaching. Because of timetable logistics, I had this Special English option class one lesson a week out of their four lessons. I did not teach any of these pupils in their mainstream English lessons. I had previously taught Hammid and Paul in an ESL withdrawal session once a week when they first arrived, and had also taught Louis one lesson a week in the Third Year — under the auspices of the Remedial Department where he had been wrongly placed, partly with his own collusion, preferring a remedial Special Reading class of indigenous pupils as opposed to being seen as a 'foreigner' in an ESL withdrawal group. Another of his reasons was that the ESL group were more middle-class than the predominantly working-class composition of the Special Reading group with whom he felt more comfortable.

Indeed, and not incidentally, it will be seen from the pupils' discussion, the transcript of which appears in Appendix 2, that the politics of race, class and gender are by no means confined to the materials under discussion, but are very much present in the relationships of the pupils themselves. They permeate the whole event, rising explicitly to the surface from time to time and mainly expressed as disparagement and/or competitiveness. (For example, the passage between utterances 341 and 422).

The Group Members and the Group's Dynamics

Louis   Portuguese, in England for three years.

Hammid   Born in Iraq, mother tongue Kurdish, lived in Iran from 6 to 12 years of age, in England for two years, is also learning Arabic.

Angelina   Italian, in England a matter of months.

Paul   Mother tongue Hungarian, also lived in Greece for a short time, in England for two years, also learning Russian.

Paul does not contribute very much to this discussion, at least verbally. He has been the 'clown' of the ESL Fourth Year group. He is bright, but also over-confident, and not a little arrogant about his own abilities and personality. There are several reasons for his lack of contribution to this particular discussion. First, he is an 'embassy' child, i.e., his father works for the London embassy of his country, and as such he is well aware of the political nature of the worksheets. It would seem that embassy children are advised to be cautious when it comes to political issues. Paul is clearly middle-class in both his aspirations and his friendships.

Secondly, Louis and Hammid are taking the discussion work unusually seriously. Paul's jokey answer (deriving from the fact that there is a stick drawing of three people at the top of each column on the worksheet: utterance 13 in the transcript) of 'Three people', to the question pointing them to the information about population numbers of the country, is hardly acknowledged, whereas in other lessons such a comment from Paul could well herald the beginning of a lengthy distraction, with Paul the centre of attention.

Thirdly, although Paul is likely to regard his own political knowledge as superior to both Louis' and Hammid's, he seems to have decided not to jeopardize their concentration on a matter which he basically perceives worthy of their attention — despite his disdain for what he seems to regard as the inadequacy of their perceptions and interpretations (for example, in their first round of guessing on what country the information on the worksheet is based, utterances 70–81). Paul is also aware of Louis' defensiveness in terms of the class issue between himself and Hammid, and seems to be refraining from undermining Louis' confidence in this discussion lesson. It is a level of confidence and concentration not apparent in the more 'normal' support lessons based in writing and reading. A further reason for Paul's reticence is his disorientation over the out-of-the-ordinary nature of the work, both in terms of the content and the discussion method. He also seems suspicious of his teacher's motives. At the end of the lesson he asked why I had given them such work. I told him that it was to try to discover what they knew about the world they lived in, and about using discussion for learning and for learning English. Paul's response was that such work was not for children; that children should play and not have to consider such serious matters. A final reason for Paul's reticence could well be the presence of Angelina. She is new to the group, mature in appearance and attitude, and, for the moment, quiet. She seems to pose an as yet unspoken threat to Paul's more immature clowning and attention-seeking. As yet, Angelina is something of an unknown quantity to Paul. She is a working-class child, but there have been enough indications of her intellectual competence for Paul to have begun to modify his claims to knowledgeability and to suppress some of his assumptions of superiority. As for Paul's experiences of migration, they are more of diplomatic travel than migration — experiences which will enhance his scholastic and class aspirations, rather than experiences borne out of more fundamental life changes.

Louis is identifiably working-class *vis-à-vis* both Paul and Hammid in terms of his interests, aspirations and attitudes towards school. Although Louis has been in England longer, he and Hammid are at very similar levels in written English. Louis is familiar with conversations of a political nature and feels interested and confident about both the content and the discussion method of the lesson. He watches political debates on TV, *Weekend World*, for instance, and he has previously talked about having relatives who have been in the Portuguese Army in Angola. Louis is often absent from school and is following CSE courses only. Louis' family experience of migration is rooted in the questions of class, work and a desire to improve standards of living.

Hammid attends school regularly and is doing O levels in the sciences. Much more than Paul, the 'embassy' child, Hammid associates himself with the working-class boys in the school. However, despite the friendship between Hammid and Louis, Louis is well aware of Hammid's ultimate middle-class aspirations and loyalties. Hammid's experience of migration has been more that of a middle-class family seeking refuge from economic upheaval and war. I think all of this accounts for Louis' challenging banter with Hammid, and since Hammid is equally aware of all these elements in their relationship, I think that this awareness accounts for his relative patience with Louis — a patience bred from both real peer group friendship on the one hand and guilt and sympathy on the other. For example, Hammid puts up with quite a bit from Louis between utterances 343 and 370.

Angelina has not found it particularly easy to fit into the ESL group as a whole. She is a comparative newcomer. The other girls in the group are all from Hong Kong and are shy in comparison to her. The girls from Hong Kong are not as fluent as the boys in English, and they find security by sticking together quietly as a group. However, these girls and Angelina are building up relationships slowly, particularly she and 'Jenny', as one of the most outgoing of the other girls, in an attempt to assimilate herself into English culture, prefers to call herself. (She was absent on the day of the discussion). Angelina does not think the boys are as smart as they think they are. She is just beginning to express a certain disapproval of what she regards as their brash and immature behaviour and attitudes. It is disapproval expressed in a look, or a quietly overt statement that tends to evaluate behaviour and responses rather than being an outright personal attack on any particular boy. For example at utterance 455 she gets the boys back to the present point ('But maybe you don't understand the question. The question is "What are your *feelings*" '). The boys for their part are beginning to some extent to admire Angelina as well as be very wary of her (for the moment) quiet confidence and of her seeming lack of any need to conceal her intelligence.

The Teachers

Clearly the teachers, and how they are perceived by the pupils, have a role to play within group discussion dynamics. Comparatively speaking, ESL teachers are more or less approved of by the pupils learning to use English as a second language. Within a whole school ethos which marginalizes bilingual learners on the one hand, or is actually prejudiced against them on the other, bilingual pupils usually regard the Special English teachers as generally more supportive and sympathetic. Their regular ESL teacher joins the discussions at the beginning, then moves off to try to help the other group who are attempting, unsuccessfully, to do the same work with the visiting lecturer whom they do not know. I, as lead teacher for their discussion group, am seen as being 'all right', less traditional, more informal, more working-class and, paradoxically to them, more demanding. I expect sustained concentration and expect them to support their thoughts and opinions both in discussion and in writing.

As far as Paul is concerned I am not as worthy of respect as more traditionally oriented teachers, particularly his male teachers, since although he is from a socialist country, he is from the culturally conservative ruling elite of that country. To Paul I am, therefore, somewhat 'suspect' both in relation to the culture of his own elite and to the dominant culture of Britain. Also, in terms of my subject area, I am not as worthy of respect, since Paul rates the sciences and the more traditional approaches employed in those subjects more highly than the approaches of English and the humanities.

Hammid would be more reserved about expressing a similar attitude, but nevertheless be of quite a similar opinion, making use, at the same time, of his teacher's sympathetic attitude.

Louis regards many teachers as more or less supportive. But only up to a point. They are not entirely to be trusted because of their leftish and/or middle-class orientations, which he regards as generally unrealistic. On some issues he holds both covert and overt rightest perceptions, yet he also has what might be called underlying socialist feelings, but which again he doesn't trust as much more than wishful thinking. His real bases of thinking are those of an individual survivalist.

Angelina's spoken contributions early on in the discussion are minimal, but are structurally important. She is the one who answers the question as to how many more people there are in group A than B (utterance 21 in the transcript). The boys take up her answer. In terms of the politics of discussion, most modern educationists will recognize the familiar pattern revealed by gender research on discussion whereby the female gives the point and the males take it on as their own without acknowledgment, or after disparaging the female's contribution. It is not until well towards the end of the discussion that Angelina gets due recognition when Paul explicitly agrees with her (utterance 448). By this time her spoken contribution to the discussion has become substantial. She later said that she waited before entering more fully into the discussion because she wanted, as the newest member of the group and the most recent to start learning English, to get an impression of what was going on. She is the only girl in the group.

She begins to express her sympathetically moral opinions when the group are specifically asked by the teacher (at utterance 422) how they *feel* about apartheid rather than what they *think* about it. It is that line of enquiry which allows her to articulate her political thinking (begun at utterance 433). Although unspoken, her impressions and therefore her decision to enter the discussion in what amounts to an oppositionally independent political frame from the boys is probably based partly on her perception of her teacher as supportive of her position.

The Lesson Content

The pupils were given the sheet of statistics on South Africa, (see Appendix 1a) with the name of the country omitted. They were invited to examine these statistics, and then were given the second worksheet of basic questions to answer (Appendix 1b). They were then given the third worksheet called 'DISCUSSION QUESTIONS' (Appendix 1c). The questions here focused discussion on (a) what life might be like for human beings under a system which separates a population into an exploited and an exploitative group, and (b) how state institutions (economic, civil, military, legislative, social and cultural) function to support such a system. This sheet also had spaces for them to insert their own questions and comments about such 'A Place in the World'.

This group of pupils were not presented with the *Apartheid* source book, nor with any of the supplementary materials. They were given only these three introductory worksheets, worksheets designed to stimulate general political discussion, based on the factual information relating to the functioning of a particular political system. The strategy of omitting the name of the country and the racial identity of the groups was used to preclude pupils' possible racist attitudes. It was also used to make more possible a focus on the devices, civil and governmental, that states use to govern and control.

The Discussion Lesson

Comment on the Transcript

At this point it would be sensible to invite readers to read the transcript (Appendix 2). I have already noted some examples of the politics of interaction evident in this discussion, but would also point out the kinds of knowledge about the world that the pupils possess. To take a very small instance, when the subject of Italian films is raised by Hammid at utterance 90, Louis, at utterance 91, emphasizes their quality ('Yeah, *good* films'). This kind of knowledge, as well as political awarenesses such as are shown by all the participants, is not the knowledge taught in schools. They are examples of the understandings that very often go unrecognized, are often dismissed as irrelevant, seldom received as a contribution, or acknowledged as worthy of further development. If this is true of the life knowledge of indigenous children, in many ways it is even more true of bilingual children who are bringing different understandings of the world into a monocultural system.

Attention to the materials results in new realizations:

93. LOUIS   (*looking at the sheet*) Oh, my *gawd!* Group B's a bit . . . poor on doctors.
94. TEACHER How' you know that?
95. LOUIS   'Cause group A is . . . oh, no, it ain't . . . (*incredulously*) it's one for 44,000, and one for 400! Oh, my gawd!

Whatever else may be concluded about this discussion amongst developing bilingual pupils, what it unequivocably proves is that, contrary to the supposition that pupils learning English as a second language would be unable to deal with such factual statistics and a pedagogy based on the discursive methods of analytical teaching, they *can* and do sustain an *unusual* amount of concentration on these materials.

However, what also becomes evident about analytical teaching is that the *politics of discussion itself* must be made explicit. The context of the discussion plus the interaction of the participants themselves in relation to class, race, gender and dominant ideology need to become part of the educational enterprise.

The tape ran out before the discussion ended. I commented that the group knew quite a bit about the world they lived in. The boys commented that this was true because they came from different places in the world and therefore knew more, and were more interested in the world. Whereas, they said, their English classmates 'knew hardly anything'.

Louis and Hammid asked why I had given them this work and I told them it was both to see if they could deal with it, and in order to find out something about what they knew of the world. As previously mentioned, Paul pronounced this to be improper work for children.

Angelina asked if 'A Place in the World' was South Africa. When I said that it was, then, for the boys, the 'mystery' of the divisions between the main two groups under apartheid seemed to be resolved, even accepted. They seemed to return to an acceptance of racism as the matter-of-course reason for apartheid, rather than being able to maintain a focus on the economic and political foundations of racism and apartheid.

Follow-up

Given the logistics of withdrawal lessons for bilingual children, plus the marginalization, or non-existence, in mainstream English lessons of discursive, analytical work on contemporary issues, that one fifty-five minute lesson proved to be a one-off experience for these pupils, although we followed it up briefly in another support lesson with the whole group.

It is a pity that the group did not have the opportunity to engage with some of the literary, autobiographical and other material in the *Apartheid* source book. For, just as affective materials are not enough on their own, neither are statistical or factual materials enough in a learning and developmental complex. Neither is *uncritical dependence upon a pedagogy of discussion sufficient*. The very models for discussion have to become part of the analytic mode of education, especially in a culture where both the model and content of the discursive method is itself pervasively sexist, racist and classist.

Many months later in another ESL support lesson I presented the transcript of the fifty-five minutes to the ESL group, which that day also included two of the Chinese girls who had been in the 'silent' discussion group during the original lesson. The value of recording and transcribing is demonstrated by what followed. Certainly, whatever other functions they serve, transcripts not only acknowledge and celebrate pupils' achievements, they also illuminate further areas of potential learning development. They act not only as prompt to memory of a bygone fragment of learning, but as stimulus for further important recollections and reflections.

The group spent a good deal of time reading and exclaiming over the transcript. Although nearly a year had elapsed since the original discussion, it became apparent that the pupils recalled the occasion in remarkable detail. I asked them why they remembered *this* lesson, when if I asked them about a lesson which occurred only two days before they would recall next to nothing about it. They said the reason was that this lesson had been out of the ordinary — and that they had never had a similar discussion lesson since. Angelina said that she'd been in the school one year now and had never had a similar lesson. Louis said he'd been in the school five years and had never had a similar lesson. Angelina went on to say that in most of their lessons 'we talk nonsense', a sort of school knowledge that wasn't much use for thinking about the world outside school, about life. The others said this was true and that it was the teachers' fault.

I asked if the discussion itself had had any affect at all on their perceptions about South Africa, or about British politics, or about other places in the world. They said that although the discussion was vivid in their memory it wasn't enough. I took this to mean that although the discussion might be a useful sort of fragment, that it was just that, a fragment, and unsatisfactory as such. Jenny, one of the Chinese girls, having taken part in a follow-up lesson after the transcripted lesson, said that such discussion had had some effect, that she thought more often about people in the world who were poor.

Paul had left the school by this time. I asked the others why they thought Paul had been so uncharacteristically silent in the discussion. Louis said he was 'probably afraid of the Russians'. Hammid said it was probably because he belonged to the Embassy and had probably been told by his parents not to get into political discussions. None of this had been mentioned during the discussion, but it had been part of the silent sub-text of the group dynamic, tacitly accepted and forming part of what it was permissible to mention, or not, within the discussion.

Noting the arguments in the transcripts between Hammid and Louis, I asked whether they thought this competitiveness between them had anything to do with their class differences. They were unwilling to acknowledge this possibility, and said that although they often disagreed they were more friends than enemies. Jenny said that the jokes and banter in the discussion must have made it enjoyable to be in the discussion, and they also made it enjoyable to read the transcript afterwards. She thought that the opportunity to make asides like that in a discussion was important. It gave you a chance to think and also made the discussion more enjoyable. She also said that she hadn't realized before reading this transcript that Louis knew so much.

I asked what the sources of their knowledge about the world were. They said they picked up bits and pieces of information from TV, especially if they found the incident interesting, or if their country was involved, or if it was about sensational events, like the Falklands War. They also heard discussions between parents and other relatives, and they got some information from reading. Louis also said that he was born in the world, therefore he just picked up knowledge from being in the world, and from experience, and from the other bilingual pupils.

They said that they gained little 'live' knowledge about the world from school. In history, geography and humanities lessons they learned a bit about Africa, a bit about China and other bits, but not about how people lived there now. Jenny's final comment was: 'They don't really tell you about poor people'. And Hammid's: 'They don't talk about political matters'.

Jenny commented that she thought the guessing game aspect of the transcripted lesson was good, made you think and express your opinions. I said that perhaps it wasn't so good in that it might also have encouraged the competitiveness between Hammid and Louis. Her opinion was that you soon saw there wasn't really much point in being too competitive because you could be wrong, that the guessing just made you talk and learn things as you went along. I said that I wasn't so sure and that the guessing, plus the using of the TV debate models, especially since there had not been enough follow-up lessons, might have been negative in the long run.

Angelina intervened to tell Hammid and Louis in no uncertain terms that she thought they didn't really know how to think for themselves, that they just repeated what they'd heard on the TV, etc. Hammid retaliated, saying that yes, they did repeat what they had picked up from TV, etc., but that they also expressed what they knew from experience. They talked about what was in the world, not what might be, because they believed that very little could be done to change things from the way they really were. Angelina replied saying that if people expressed more of their feelings things could change. 'What you live every day is not what they say on TV,' she commented.

Hammid insisted that it was the case that the politicians on TV were usually right and that nothing could be done. Jenny said that things *were* done, that people saw things on TV and sent money and things to help people.

I asked them what they had learned about discussion itself. They said that they did learn bits from each other in the discussion. But they found it difficult to reflect upon discussion as such. Perhaps they also wanted to avoid making public any adjustments that they might have made to their own perceptions, about the topic, about each other — or making public the fact that they had had to make (or, indeed, had not made) any such adjustments.

Then Jenny said that it was a fact that most boys had to act tough, and that it showed in the transcript in the way that they couldn't talk about feelings. Angelina added that it was her opinion that men hid every single emotion they felt, that they pretended to 'forget about it' when they got upset. Hammid said that when boys got upset they *had* to forget about it, or things would get worse, because they had jobs to do. Louis added, 'It's like in a war when you shoot someone, you got to forget about it, 'cause you're going to shoot more.'

Perhaps unwisely, instead of pursuing the issue, I asked my next question — whether they preferred fiction in English lessons, factual information, or a combination. They said they would prefer more real information, that stories are not true. 'A story is a story', and as such you couldn't really argue with it.

Stories were more 'closed' in the sense that there wasn't a lot of real life point in discussing and writing about stories. There was more point in basing lessons on more real information. 'You know about the world because you know there is a world and it's true.' I asked them how often they thought they should have factually based lessons. Their answer was preferably three times a week, but once a week, at least.

On reading the transcript Angelina had exclaimed over her use of the world 'deprivation' (utterance 435). 'Where did I get that word!' she wondered. She then worked out that she had known the concept in Italian, and from the Italian had guessed at the form of the English word. I asked her if she often made that sort of cognate guess from Italian to English. 'No way,' she said. She had never done it before or since, because there had been no similar opportunity. In ordinary everyday talk situations, you didn't use that sort of language.

I asked them what sorts of effects the participation of teacher might have had on the discussion. They said that it might have some effect, but not a substantial one, that they would essentially say what they had to say.

Conclusions

This one lesson set out ostensibly to test whether or not bilingual pupils developing a use of English as a second language are capable of engaging with an analytical content and mode of teaching, using factually based materials. It is obvious from this evidence that they are. Equally obvious is that engagement with such materials promoted a considerable degree of oracy in English for them. And such oracy is a proper basis for the development of literacy in English.

*   *   *   *

But proving the capability of bilingual learners in engaging with this mode of teaching in English is the surface plot of this educational episode. The under-lying theme is the massive conservatist/liberal opposition to the development of the analytical modes of teaching.

There are plenty of curricular and pedagogical questions about *how* to make analytical modes of teaching *more* accessible to pupils, bilingual or not. These are important, ongoing questions of curriculum and pedagogical educational development. But such questions alone, about the accessibility of materials or pedagogical method, are inadequate, if not irresponsible, to the fundamental issue: the provision of an analytical education based upon the moral and political premises of equal human rights. What this does not mean is further cyclical, cosmetic tinkerings of a conservatist/liberal educational complex. What it means is stating that there needs to be, and working for, the restructuring of educational content, pedagogy and processes which will promote more equal, more individually satisfying, more economically and socially responsible, more intellectually rigorous outcomes for all pupils.

If that brings us slap bang up against the 'question' of whether society is to compensate for education, or education to compensate for society, the real issue is not endlessly to contemplate the 'question'. The issue is, at the very least, to promote that 'question' into active and productive dialectic, instead of allowing the political forces of the socio-economic powers that be to smother that dialectic.

The real obstacle to a holistic education is not any difficulty children have in engaging with a libertarian, analytical education, but the internalized conservatist-liberal, political opposition to it. That opposition consistently avoids positioning 'educational failure' within the intellectual, emotional and cultural contortions of the social and economic indecencies of the processes and outcomes of the state and of the state education system itself.

At the present political juncture of the late 80s the 'cure' for 'educational failure' consists of consolidating advantage for the few, and a further limiting, fragmenting and control of the majority through, for example, promoting a myth of more parental 'choice'; by schools opting out of the system; by businesses funding schools of 'excellence'; and for those not so 'excellent', the curriculum 'development' of 'personal and social education'; the presentation of more 'testing', profiling and tighter conservatist political control of the curriculum.

Traditionally, the individual advantage conferred by 'education' (certification) contributed to a pragmatic sort of consensus: the confidence of the middle classes and the future hopes of the working classes in 'education'. But both confidence and hope are reduced in the face of tighter divisions of labour: technologically skilled and management employment for the few on the one hand, service industry and under- and unemployment for the majority on the other hand. The 'educational' resource (acceptable certification) that the system conveys is going to be more tightly controlled and harder to come by — particularly for the working-class majority who will be more tightly contained by the 'key stages' and 'statement of attainment targets' of the 'national' curriculum.

In resurrecting 'education' as the scapegoat for socio-economic failures and oppressions, the conservatist/liberal establishment creates a culturally popular, 'commonsensical' and traditionally believable diversion. Indeed, all the more believable because of the recognizable failures of merely 'liberal', non-rigorous and unanalytical 'comprehensive' education to date.

Those who became teachers have benefited from their ability to cope with the contortions of the education system. Our continued employment is going to depend upon further contortions. Yet the value we place upon human educational rights; the value we place upon positive educational processes and outcomes which support both the socio-economic survival *and* the human integrity of our pupils — not to mention our own integrity — depends, in fact, upon exposing, articulating and analyzing those contortions and oppressions.

Without effective articulation of those educational contortions, and without the continued occupation of every small space left to the premises of analytical education, the perpetration of divisions between economically and 'educationally' advantaged pupils and an educationally disadvantaged under-class of young, working-class, politically ineffective people is more or less guaranteed.

Surely, we can do no less than challenge the so-called 'choice' and 'democratization' of education at its own game by requiring that the case for rigorous and analytical human rights education be put, presented and represented — not only at those junctures we happen to come across, but those we have the responsibility to create.

If ever those real educational rights begin to be established *then* we can talk more confidently about the 'language' for real and deep human 'learning', rather than using and abusing theories of 'language and learning' (or any other theory of education) for whatever it is expedient for those with control over education to allow pupils to learn.

Note

1. This refers to the first draft materials used and described by Susan Werner in ' "C'mon Shabir, Get Out All Your Ideas" or Recognizing the Limitations of Our Teaching', Chapter 11 of this volume.
2. According to the National Child Development Study, there are presently four million adults counted as illiterate in England.

Appendix 1a

Information Sheet

Source: Unesco Courier November 1977

GROUP A		GROUP B
19 MILLION	HOW MANY PEOPLE	4.5 MILLION
13 PER CENT	HOW MUCH LAND	87 PER CENT
LESS THAN 25 PER CENT OF TOTAL	HOW MUCH MONEY	75 PER CENT OF TOTAL
£15	WEEKLY WAGES	£210
£160	AMOUNT OF MONEY YOU CAN EARN BEFORE YOU HAVE TO PAY TAXES	£330
1 FOR 44,000	HOW MANY DOCTORS PER PERSON	1 FOR 400
200 PER 1000 CITIES 400 PER 1000 RURAL	NUMBER OF BABIES WHO DIE IN EARLY CHILDHOOD	27 PER 1000
£25	HOW MUCH MONEY IS SPENT PER YEAR ON EDUCATION PER PUPIL	£380
1 FOR 60	HOW MANY PUPILS PER TEACHER	1 FOR 22

Appendix 1b

a Place in the world

		A	B
1.	WHICH GROUP HAS THE MOST DOCTORS?		
2.	WHICH GROUP CAN EARN MORE MONEY BEFORE THEY HAVE TO PAY TAXES?		
3.	WHICH GROUP GETS THE MOST MONEY SPENT ON THEIR EDUCATION?		
4.	WHICH GROUP HAS TAKEN THE MOST LAND?		
5.	WHICH GROUP HAS THE MOST TEACHERS?		
6.	WHICH GROUP HAS THE HIGHEST WAGES?		
7.	WHICH GROUP'S BABIES SURVIVE PAST CHILDHOOD THE MOST?		
8.	WHICH GROUP HAS MOST OF THE COUNTRY'S MONEY?		
9.	HOW MANY PEOPLE ARE THERE IN THE COUNTRY?		
10.	WHICH GROUP HAS THE HIGHEST STANDARD OF LIVING?		
11.	WHICH GROUP IS IN THE MAJORITY?		

Appendix 1c

a Place the world

DISCUSSION QUESTIONS

1.	The information in the table "A Place in the World" is not invented. The figures are accurate and refer to a real country. Think carefully about the figures and the sorts of things they imply about life in that society. What are some of your first guesses about this society?
2.	You will have seen that in almost every way Group B appears to be better off than Group A. What are your feelings about this?
3.	What might the way of life and thinking be in a typical household in Group B. Do you think everybody classified as belonging to this group would think and act in the same way?
4.	What might the way of life and thinking be in a typical household in Group A? Do you think everybody classified as belonging to this group would think and act in the same way?
5.	Do you think friendships between any members of these groups would be possible? Under what circumstances? For what purposes?
6.	How do you think Group B gained control in the first place?
7.	How do you think Group B manages to maintain control and hang on to all its privileges? Through religion? Through control of education? Through control of jobs? Through control of government? Through control of money? Through force - use of police, prisons, the military? Through control of ideas through books, newspapers, comics magazines, T.V., films etc.? Through control of the legal system and the making of laws? Through control and ownership of land? Through economic support, technology, armaments and political support from other countries?
8.	All of these means of control can be put into 3 main categories. See if you can sort the list into 3 main categories.
9.	Powerful groups in many countries use these means, in varying degrees to keep power. List places in the world where you recognise such control happening. Make a comment about the types of control most used.

10.	Can you guess which country in the world "A Place in the World" refers to? Make a list of possible places, giving a brief comment of what you know about each place.
11.	Make a list of instances in the world where the control and power of the powerful groups are challenged by people. Mention the ways in which people challenge power?
12.	What sort of things do you think will happen in the future in the country "A Place in the World"?
13.	If you were a member of Group A what sorts of things would you do, either as an individual or with others, to change your situation.

Appendix 2

TRANSCRIPT		COMMENT

1. TEACHER — Tell me what languages you speak.

2. ANGELINA — Italian.

3. LOUIS — Portuguese and English and I'm learning French in school. I've been to Italy. But I've only been for a month and I only know a little bit.

4. TEACHER — It's still something though, isn't it?

5. LOUIS — Hmmm.

6. TEACHER — How about you, Hammid, what do you speak?

7. HAMMID — Kurdish, Persian, a little Arabic and English.

8. TEACHER — My goodness! What about you, Angelina?

9. ANGELINA — I speak Italian and little bit of English.

10. TEACHER — Paul?

11. PAUL — Russian, English, Greek, Hungarian.

12. TEACHER — Well, I don't speak anything *but* English. Terrible, isn't it? All right, can we have a look at this sheet, 'A Place in the World', then? Let's have a good look. TWO groups in this place in the world: group A and group B. OK? In group A how many people are there?

13. PAUL — (*clowning and pointing to the three stick drawings of people at the top of the statistics table*) Three?

14. TEACHER — From the drawing! Louis, would you say there are three people in this country?

	TRANSCRIPT	COMMENT

15. LOUIS	*No.*	
16. TEACHER	So how many people in group A?	
17. LOUIS	Nineteen million.	
18. TEACHER	OK. How many people in group B?	
19. LOUIS	Four point five million.	
20. TEACHER	OK. So how many more times people are there in group A than in group B?	
21. ANGELINA	(*quietly*) Five.	
22. LOUIS	That's a piece of *cake*.	
23. TEACHER	Piece of cake . . . tell me then . . . how many more times.	
24. LOUIS	Five.	
25. PAUL	Five.	
26. HAMMID	About five times.	
27. PAUL	Is this a maths lesson?	27. *Paul*, in asking 'Is this a maths lesson?', is challenging both the subject matter of the lesson and the breaking of the traditional subject boundaries.
28. TEACHER	Aha! How many more times?	
29. HAMMID	About five times.	
30. LOUIS	No, four, four.	30–36. The competitive banter between *Louis* and *Hammid* enters the discussion almost immediately. *Louis* is also anxious to take the opportunity of a discussion based lesson to dispel opinions of him as less academically able and to establish himself instead as a knowledgeable and skilful member of the group.
31. TEACHER	Four fours?	
32. LOUIS	No, four.	
33. TEACHER	Four times.	

TRANSCRIPT   COMMENT

34.	LOUIS	*Yes.*
35.	HAMMID	It's about five.
36.	LOUIS	Shut yer gob, you don't know what's about.
37.	TEACHER	Awright, awright. How much land do you think . . . does group A have?
38.	LOUIS	13 per cent.
39.	TEACHER	Uh huh. And group B?
40.	LOUIS	87 per cent.
41.	TEACHER	Look at the next question then. How much money?
42.	LOUIS	Less than 25 per cent. Of total. And group B 75 per cent of total.
43.	TEACHER	Awright, let's suppose that we are . . .
44.	LOUIS	So that means that that's Arabia.
45.	TEACHER	That's a what? Arabia?
46.	LOUIS	Yep. They're rich.
47.	TEACHER	How d'you figure it's Arabia?
48.	LOUIS	. . . They're rich. That's for sure. I'd bet my life on that [that it is Arabia].
49.	TEACHER	They're rich?
50.	LOUIS	Yep.
51.	TEACHER	OK (*pointing to sheet*). Who gets the most wages?
52.	LOUIS	(*pointing to group B on sheet*) Them.
53.	HAMMID	(*pointing to group A on sheet and speaking to himself*) Fifteen pounds.
54.	TEACHER	Hmm. Hmm.
55.	LOUIS	That's it. I know who it is.
56.	TEACHER	Who is it?
57.	HAMMID	Group A.
58.	LOUIS	Group B, £210.

TRANSCRIPT	COMMENT

59. TEACHER Hmm. Hmm. (*Pointing to sheet*) Amount of money you can earn before you have to pay taxes?
60. ANGELINA Group A. £160 pounds.
61. LOUIS And group B £300.
62. TEACHER Why do you think there's a difference there? There are all these people in the same country, yes?
63. HAMMID (*in surprise*) In the same country?

63. *Hammid* is surprised that the two groups live in the same country. This was a fact that Hammid and Louis had some trouble in assimilating, partly due to the way the worksheet was set out.

64. TEACHER Yes.
65. LOUIS That means they're *not* Arabians.

(*Laughter*)

66. TEACHER How do you know?
67. LOUIS Because if they're in the same country, how comes..., how comes some...some...oh yeah, yeah, they *could* be, you know.
68. TEACHER 'Cause why?
69. LOUIS 'Cause some could live in this poor village, and some in this rich thing.
70. TEACHER What country you thinking of then?
71. LOUIS I don't know.

71. *Louis* is willing to admit 'I don't know'.

72. PAUL England.

72. *Paul* indicates his knowledge of the politics of class by inserting the idea that the country could be England.

TRANSCRIPT	COMMENT
73. TEACHER England, yes?	
74. HAMMID (*quietly*) No.	74. *Hammid* dismissess Paul's comment, probably because he sees it as one of Paul's provocatives jokes rather than recognizing the political concept behind it. He also dismisses it because he recognizes that the actual statistics on the worksheet do not fit his statistical knowledge of Britain.
75. PAUL Kurdistan.	75. *Paul* persists in his provocation of Hammid in suggesting that the country is Kurdistan, perhaps as knowledgeable as Hammid about the nature of the war between the Kurds and the Iraqis.
76. TEACHER Kurdistan.	
77. HAMMID (*quietly*) Shurrup.	77. *Hammid* takes the suggestion that the country could be Kurdistan as an insult; and passes the insult to Angelina in suggesting that the country is Italy.
78. TEACHER Anybody else got any ideas?	
79. HAMMID Italy.	
80. TEACHER Italy.	
81. LOUIS (*in disbelief*) *Italy*? . . . Italy produces coal I think.	
82. TEACHER It's what?	
83. LOUIS Coal.	
84. TEACHER Coal?	
85. LOUIS Coal. I'm not sure.	
86. TEACHER (*to Angelina*) What do they produce in Italy?	
87. PAUL Wine.	

TRANSCRIPT   COMMENT

88. LOUIS   Yeah, they produce wine
                 a lot.
89. TEACHER   Hmm. Hm. What kind
                 of cars come from Italy?
90. HAMMID   Films. They make films.
91. LOUIS   Yeah, *good* films.
92. HAMMID   Hmm.
93. LOUIS   (*looking at sheet*) Oh
                 my *gawd*. Group B's a
                 bit . . . poor on doctors.
94. TEACHER   How'd you know that?
95. LOUIS   'Cause group A is . . .
                 oh no it aint . . .
                 (*incredulously*) it's one
                 for *forty-four thousand*?
                 And one for *four
                 hundred*? Oh my gawd.

(*Laughter at Louis*)

96. TEACHER   Hmm. So which is
                 poorer in doctors?
97. LOUIS   A.
98. HAMMID   Hmm.
99. TEACHER   Everybody agree with
                 that?
100. LOUIS   Yep.
101. HAMMID   Yep.

(*Laughter*)

102. TEACHER   (*to Angelina*) You don't
                 agree?
103. ANGELINA   I do, I do.
104. TEACHER   (*to Paul*) What d'you
                 think?
105. PAUL   (*shrugs shoulders*)   105. When *Paul* is asked
                                                     directly by the teacher
                                                     what he thinks, he
                                                     shrugs his shoulders,
                                                     declines comment and
                                                     withdraws from the
                                                     discussion temporarily.

106. TEACHER   Awright. (*pointing to
                 sheet*) Supposing you
                 were born into group A,
                 what sort of chance of
                 living . . .

TRANSCRIPT		COMMENT
107. LOUIS	But, I know where this country is now.	107–21. *Louis* is caught up in the puzzle of the question 'Which country?'
108. HAMMID	About fifty . . .	
109. LOUIS	It's that poor country, where is it called	
110. HAMMID	(*looking at sheet*) *Less* than fifty . . . about 25 per cent.	
111. LOUIS	Yeah it's . . . (*looking at Hammid's sheet*) . . . Cause of the diseases?	
112. HAMMID	Yeah . . . and there's no . . .	
113. LOUIS	Yeah, I know where it is . . .	
114. HAMMID	Uganda.	
115. LOUIS	No. It's that . . . country . . .	
116. PAUL	Zimbabwe.	
117. LOUIS	No, no, no, no.	
118. HAMMID	Where is it?	
119. LOUIS	I've forgot . . . I *know* it . . .	
120. HAMMID	(*insistent*) *Where* is it? Africa?	120. *Hammid* makes the mistake of naming Africa as a country rather than as a continent.
121. LOUIS	Yeah . . . I dunno.	
122. PAUL	(*smiling*) Asia.	122. *Paul* indicates Hammid's mistake by the mimicry of naming Asia also as a country.

(*Louis laughs*)

123. TEACHER	You think it [the country] is in Africa?	123. *Louis* understand the joke; it's not clear if Hammid does.
124. LOUIS	Probably. Or . . . El Salvador . . . or something like that.	
125. TEACHER	Hmm.	
126. LOUIS	I dunno . . .	
127. TEACHER	When you said they die from disease, d'you	

235

TRANSCRIPT	COMMENT
think its only disease they die from?	

128. LOUIS	Yeah, *and* hunger.	
129. TEACHER	How hunger? How d'you know its from hunger?	129–44 *Louis* supplies some general concepts about the working of the world, e.g. hunger, economic production, war, while *Hammid* demands that he be more precise. Louis attempts to do that and *Hammid* takes up some of the concepts he presents.
130. LOUIS	Starving.	
131. TEACHER	How do you know?	
132. LOUIS	Cause there's probably a war going on . . .	
133. HAMMID	There's less money, there's less money here, (*pointing to sheet*).	
134. TEACHER	There's less money?	
135. LOUIS	Yeah, and there's a war, I think.	
136. HAMMID	How d'you know?	
137. LOUIS	(*sarcastically*) What d'you think.	
138. HAMMID	It doesn't say it here.	
139. LOUIS	If they don't produce nothing, what d'you think? What's happening?	
140. TEACHER	You think they don't produce nothing. How d'you think . . .	
141. LOUIS	They might produce something, but, you know, sell it.	
142. HAMMID	They produce it for themselves.	
143. LOUIS	Hmm.	
144. HAMMID	Well . . .	

TRANSCRIPT		COMMENT
145. TEACHER	What about group B in the same country though? Where do they get the money if they don't produce nothing? Or anything.	145–66 The teachers use questions based on *Louis'* and *Hammid's* comments to try to get them to extend their understanding of their own comments.
146. HAMMID	Where do *they* get money?	
147. TEACHER	Hmm.	
148. LOUIS	They sell things...	
149. HAMMID	*Business*...	
150. LOUIS	...like cars.	
151. HAMMID	They make business.	
152. LOUIS	Hmm.	
153. TEACHER	But Louis has just said that they don't *produce* anything.	
154. HAMMID	What? Group B don't produce anything?	
155. LOUIS	No, I said group A.	
156. HAMMID	...A...	
157. LOUIS	...might produce something, but I don't they they *sell* it.	
158. HAMMID	Group A can't produce nothing, right because...they're poor...	
159. LOUIS	*They* [group B) must produce something. They got money for cars, I suppose...	
160. HAMMID	...they have to eat it themselves...	
161. ESL TEACHER	No, what you're saying that group A may grow things, but they don't sell it...	
162. LOUIS	They need if for themselves...	
163. HAMMID	Yeah, that's what I said. Group B is rich enough...	
164. LOUIS	Yeah.	
165. HAMMID	...to buy things.	
166. TEACHER	How do you get rich enough?	

TRANSCRIPT	COMMENT

167. LOUIS By cars. They have companies that build up cars; they sell it to other countries; that's how they get money.

168. PAUL How d'you know they build cars?

169. HAMMID Why?

170. TEACHER Hmm? How d'you know what . . .

171. LOUIS They must do *something*.

172. HAMMID How d'you know they produce cars, he said. They don't have to produce cars . . .

173. LOUIS They must produce something to be rich like this.

174. HAMMID They could be growing . . .

175. ESL TEACHER (*to Hammid*) But, you're saying that they produce *something* that produces money. You said business too.

176. HAMMID Hmm. No, it has to be something that you have to be *qualified* for. So this country . . .

177. ESL TEACHER What sort of qualifications d'you think they would need?

178. HAMMID Wide . . .

179. LOUIS Doctors.

180. HAMMID Engineering . . . to make computers.

181. LOUIS Yeah, right, especially doctors . . .

182. HAMMID . . . to make computers.

183. LOUIS And that lot too (*pointing to sheet*). There's more doctors here [group B] than in there [group A]. So that's money.

TRANSCRIPT		COMMENT

184. HAMMID (*pointing to group A on the sheet*) Yeah, they don't have any doctors here.

185. LOUIS (*pointing to sheet*) *They* [group A] have about one for forty-four thousand; and [group B] one for four hundred people.

186. ESL TEACHER How do people get into group A or group B?

187. LOUIS (*shaking his head to indicate he doesn't know*) Hmm. Hmm.

188. HAMMID Different countries.

189. ESL TEACHER Different countries; it's all the same country.

190. TEACHER (*pointing to education statistics on sheet*) What about this one? You said about qualifications. Let's look at that one now.

191. ESL TEACHER (*to Angelina*) Have you got any idea where it is?

192. LOUIS (*looking at sheet*) Only £25 spent on group A [for education] and £390 on . . .

193. HAMMID Well, that means that this part of the country can't go on no outings and things like, while this can . . .

194. LOUIS Yeah, its got more money, and it spends more than *that*.

195. HAMMID And like, they have gyms, swimming pool, and thing like that, big schools. This group . . .

196. LOUIS Like . . . like.

197. HAMMID . . . live in a village or something like that.

198. LOUIS Like here (*pointing to sheet*) one teacher for sixty people, and here

TRANSCRIPT	COMMENT

	are for twenty-two people.
199. HAMMID	Yeah, this must be a village . . .
200. LOUIS	So that one (*pointing to group B on sheet*) can afford more.
201. HAMMID	. . . this must be . . .
202. LOUIS	. . . It pays more teachers . . . than that one . . . can
203. HAMMID	Hm, Hmmmm.
204. TEACHER	So what d'you think the set up is in this country? There are *two* groups of people. And you say that one is very, very rich, and this . . .
205. HAMMID	(*pointing to sheet*) this is the employment . . . em . . . employers . . . and things . . .
206. TEACHER	Say that again, sorry, I didn't get you . . .
207. HAMMID	Nothing . . .
208. LOUIS	And there's more people . . .
209. ESL TEACHER	(*pointing to sheet*) You're talking about *these* [group B] being the employ*ers* and these [group A] being the employ*ees*.
210. TEACHER	Is that what you said?
211. HAMMID	Yeah.
212. TEACHER	Ah, I see.
213. HAMMID	So these . . . these have been divided, like.
214. TEACHER	Hmm. Hmm.
215. LOUIS	Yeah . . . and . . .
216. HAMMID	These have special private schools, and these . . .
217. LOUIS	Yeah . . . (*pointing to sheet*) and there's more people *here* [group A],

TRANSCRIPT		COMMENT
	so this country has to feed more people than *that* one could.	
218. TEACHER	It's the same country, though.	
219. ESL TEACHER	It's the same . . .	219–28. Again, the concept that such divisions exist in one country seems difficult to comprehend.
220. HAMMID	It's the same country, but . . .	
221. LOUIS	Yeah . . . but . . .	
222. HAMMID	. . . but they have private schools because . . .	
223. LOUIS	But they (*pointing to Group B on sheet*), but they feed . . . they have less people than that one can . . . that part . . .	
224. TEACHER	But to pick up Louis' point, if *these* people (*pointing to group B on sheet*) are the employers . . .	
225. ESL TEACHER	Employees.	
226. TEACHER	Employees, sorry, and these people are the employers, then . . .	
227. ESL TEACHER	You understand the difference, do you? It means that if you are an employ*er* . . .	
228. HAMMID	There's less rich people in this country than poor; so there's less . . . (*pointing to sheet*) . . . and this is more . . . Yeah, there *is*, there's less rich people than poor.	
229. TEACHER	What d'you think, Paul?	
230. ESL TEACHER	What would you say about the different parts of Africa . . . Which part	

TRANSCRIPT	COMMENT
	of Africa would it be if we've narrowed it down to Africa?	
231. TEACHER	But is it likely to *be* Africa? I mean, what about other countries in the world? What about this country? [Britain]	
232. HAMMID	Maybe the village . . .	
233. LOUIS	*This* country? This country can afford to feed its people.	233–5. The fact that the country in question could not be Britain (by implication other Western countries) is settled. *Louis* offers the concept about Britain: 'This country can afford to feed its people; and *Hammid* states that although there are differences between groups in Britain 'This country is more, like, the same . . . and that's right.'
234. TEACHER	Hmm. Hmm.	
235. HAMMID	*This* country is more, like, the same . . . and that's right.	
236. TEACHER	You wouldn't think there's a group A and a group B in this country?	
237. HAMMID	There *is* . . . but not much different, like this sheet.	
238. TEACHER	This is *too* much difference?	
239. HAMMID	Yeah.	
240. TEACHER	Hmm.	
241. LOUIS	Could be in South America.	
242. TEACHER	Hmm.	
243. ESL TEACHER	Could it be Hungary . . . for example?	
244. PAUL	(*Laughs*)	

TRANSCRIPT		COMMENT
245. LOUIS	They're always hungry . . . so?	245–6. *Louis* makes a joke about Hungary and hungry, *Paul* implies that Louis doesn't know what he's talking about, and is only good for making jokes.
246. PAUL	There for the joke.	
247. ESL TEACHER	No, but I mean, *could* it be? Hammid has said why it couldn't be Britain. *Could* it be Hungary?	
248. HAMMID	Yeah, it could . . .	248–51. *Hammid* reads a right answer implication into the ESL teacher's leading question about Hungary. But *Louis* resists being led by the teacher and makes a more independent judgment based on his own knowledge with 'that's a part of the world it couldn't be'.
249. LOUIS	Don't think it can, 'cause . . .	
250. ESL TEACHER	Got to count *out* places it can't be, and count in places it might be . . .	
251. LOUIS	. . . that's part of the world it couldn't be.	
252. TEACHER	*Why* not?	
253. LOUIS	Hungary can support itself.	253–5. Hungary can support itself, *Louis* possesses and uses basic political concepts, but also expands upon the ideas from the input of others into the discussion: 'It hasn't got differences between people . . . so much difference they're divided up into two parts', which is also picking up on

	TRANSCRIPT	COMMENT
		Hammid's earlier remark.
254. TEACHER	Does Hungary . . .	
255. LOUIS	It hasn't got differences between people . . . so much difference they're divided up . . . into two parts.	
256. ESL TEACHER	Could you say there's a group A and a group B in Hungary?	
257. PAUL	No. Because everybody would be even. Everybody has to work.	257–61. *Paul* offers his knowledge of Hungary as a different political system '. . . everybody would be even', that there's no unemployment there, 'or if you don't work they put you in jail'. And he also inserts into the discussion the point that 'There's three million unemployed in England now'.
258. TEACHER	You mean . . .	
259. PAUL	Everybody, everybody . . . get the money . . . and all that. So nobody's unemployed.	
260. TEACHER	Hmm. How would you compare it to here then . . . would you say . . .	
261. PAUL	There's three million unemployed in England now. And there's none in Hungary. Or if you don't work there, they put you in jail.	
262. TEACHER	Do they?	
263. PAUL	Hmm. So it just couldn't be, that's all.	
264. TEACHER	Hmm.	
265. ESL TEACHER	Right. (*to Angelina*) How about Hungary?	

TRANSCRIPT		COMMENT
266. HAMMID	Italy.	
267. ESL TEACHER	What about Italy, yes, could it be Italy?	
268. ANGELINA	Yes...	
269. ESL TEACHER	It *could* be. You think the difference is between rich and poor in that country...	
270. ANGELINA	Yes...	
(Pause)		
271. TEACHER	Would that be the difference between the countryside and the towns in Italy or is it just...	
272. ANGELINA	No... in the same ... even in the same city there are rich and poor.	272. *Angelina* speaks independently for the first time. She resists the teacher's open-ended question about the location of rich and poor in a country and presents her own observation that 'even in the same city there are rich and poor'.
273. HAMMID	Like rich parts of the city ... (*pointing to group B on the sheet*) there could be rich parts of the city and (pointing to group A on sheet) and poor like here...	273. *Hammid* uses her concept to try it out on the statistics on the worksheet, suggesting they refer to the rich and poor in a city, but he doesn't seem quite to believe it and is perhaps being polite and trying to welcome Angelina into the discussion.
274. LOUIS	I reckon its around Africa.	274–6 *Louis* opposes Hammid's contribution, which fits neither his perceptions of the world, nor much willingness on his part to give up his new position as a knowledgeable and

TRANSCRIPT	COMMENT
	confident contributer to serious discussion. He offers the concept that the country is likely to be a third world country.
275. TEACHER You think its in Africa?	
276. LOUIS It's a third world country probably.	
277. TEACHER You think so?	
278. PAUL But there are many . . . ehm . . . rich people in Africa . . . to put up the 4 million, the 4.5 million . . .	278–280. *Paul* objects to this generalization of 'third world' / Africa applied to what he probably already knows is South Africa, and he offers strong hints about raw materials, diamonds, in Africa and the exploitation of the country by the 4.5 million members of the rich group.
279 ESL TEACHER So where do those rich people come from? . . . so they just couldn't come from Africa, because there is only . . . there is diamonds in Africa, you know that.	
280. HAMMID They come from Europe. They come from Europe. Out to Africa.	
281. TEACHER There's diamonds in Africa? Where?	281. This leads *Hammid* to suggest that these rich people come from Europe out to Africa.
282. LOUIS Yeah, in the mines, diamond mines. I know that there *is* diamonds in Africa. I am sure.	
283. TEACHER Hmm. Hmm. So what do you say about that?	283. *Louis* confirms that there are diamond mines in Africa, of that he is sure. But he presents it so far as a fact without any particular economic or political significance.

TRANSCRIPT	COMMENT

284. LOUIS — I dunno. There is.

285. HAMMID — The Europeans take the machinery and everything, and they dig it out.

286. LOUIS — Yeah. Diamonds.

286. *Hammid* picks up on Paul's point and presents the concept of Europeans' exploitation of Africa and Africans.

287. TEACHER — Hmm. Do *they* do the digging ... or what?

288. LOUIS — The people ...

289. HAMMID — No, they make the people work ...

290. LOUIS — The citizens.

291. HAMMID — ... and *they* just do all the office work and things like that.

292. LOUIS — Yeah, *good*, eh?

293. HAMMID — Bring the machinery ...

293. *Louis'* comment of 'Yeah, good, eh?' in response to *Hammid's* '... and they just do all the office work and things like that,' is at one and the same time sarcastic, oppressive, resigned and pragmatic, and a firm indication that, since that's the way things are (to the advantage of the rich, and, indeed, of middle-class people like Hammid and his family), he does not intend to belong to the class of people who 'do the digging'.

294. LOUIS — 'Cause Africa *is* rich in a way. It soil and that lot.

295. TEACHER — Hm. Hm. All of Africa, or just bits of Africa.

294–304. More ideas about Africa are presented by *Louis* and *Hammid*. Some of that knowledge comes from their friendship with *Asmerom*, who is another member of the

TRANSCRIPT	COMMENT
	ESL group, not present that day, who comes from Eritrea. Their knowledge of war is considerable. *Hammid's* family comes from a war-torn country. *Louis* uncles were Portuguese soldiers in the war in Angola. *Asmerom* from Eritrea, a nation in conflict with Ethiopia, suffers serious injury from the instruments of war. *Asmerom* and his school friends in Eritrea once found a grenade which they tried to open. It exploded and killed one of *Asmerom's* friends. It also blew *Asmerom's* hand off and injured his face and eyes.

296. LOUIS   *All*. If you were to dig everything you'd find lots of things.

297. ESL TEACHER   Well, what about where, say, where *Asmerom* comes from. Is that rich?

298. LOUIS   No, that's poor.

299. HAMMID   Could be.

300. LOUIS   It *is* rich under the soil . . . and if they had the money to plant food and that lot, it would become rich. But it's poor *now* because they've been at *war* with Ethiopia.

301. HAMMID   There could be oil.

302. LOUIS   *Easily* there's oil.

303. HAMMID   'Cause it's hot and dry.

304. LOUIS   Hm.

(*Pause*)

TRANSCRIPT	COMMENT
305. TEACHER OK. Why don't you ... (*passing out sheet 2 of study unit*). This'll be easy to fill in now because you've actually looked at that (*sheet 1*) very carefully and you know ... you know the answers to these questions. Fill that in, and I've got another sheet for you that you can look at. I think you can do that (*sheet 2*) *very* quickly. OK?	305–13. Having been presented with worksheet 2, which they are filling in, they are also asked to speculate on what sort of governmental system might hold power in such a situation.
306. LOUIS A piece ... of ... cake ...	
307. TEACHER A piece of cake. Yes.	
308. LOUIS So do I just tick?	
309. TEACHER Yes.	
310. ESL TEACHER Whichever you think. OK? Some of these are just straightforward answers, I think.	

(*Pause while group fills in sheet*)

311. TEACHER Group B has all the good things. *But* group A is in the majority.	
312. HAMMID Yeah.	
313. TEACHER OK. What does that tell you about the kind of ... ah ... government, or voting system that that country might have?	

(*Pause*)

| 314. LOUIS   Let me see. So they both have governments. They're in the same country, but ... | 314. *Louis* accepts the premise at this point that the two groups live in the same country. He repeats that fact to himself as if to confirm |

TRANSCRIPT	COMMENT
	it. But he still does not conceive that the two disparate groups operate under the same government; he thinks they have different governments.
315. TEACHER They're in the same country and there's one government. What kind of government do you think it might be?	
316. LOUIS Communist. *Could* be.	316. And if it's bad, probably it's communist.
317. HAMMID No, it *can't* be ...	317–28. *Hamid* and *Paul* object to *Louis'* suggestion that the country might be a communist one, because there are 'no two groups in communist countries'.
318. TEACHER Paul is laughing ... Tell them why.	
319. LOUIS He *is* a communist.	
320. HAMMID It can't be a communist government ...	
321. TEACHER Go on.	
322. LOUIS I know what a communist is, you know. We got communists in our country ...	
323. HAMMID There's no ... there's no *two groups* in communist countries.	
324. PAUL No, there isn't. Because everybody's equal.	
325. HAMMID 'Cause everybody's equal.	
326. PAUL So it can't be a communist government.	
327. HAMMID So it can't be communist (*points to sheet*) because there's two groups here.	

TRANSCRIPT	COMMENT
328. LOUIS Tell him Paul and then he starts saying. He starts copying.	328. *Louis* objects to *Hammid's* collaboration with *Paul*: 'Tell Paul and then he starts saying. He starts copying.'
329. HAMMID Shurrup.	
330. TEACHER (*to Louis*) What d'you think then?	
(Pause)	
331. TEACHER (*passing out sheet 3*) All right. Let's ... has everybody got a sheet of these questions, then? You got one? Let's just look at these questions. Read number one somebody. 'A Place in the World: Discussion Questions.'	
332. LOUIS 'The information in the Table 'A Place in the World' is not invented. The figures are ac ...'	
333. TEACHER Accurate.	
334. LOUIS '... accurate and refer to a real country. Think carefully about the figures and the short of things ...'	
335. TEACHER The what things?	
336. LOUIS '... the *sort* of things they imply about life in that society. What are some of your first guesses about this society?'	
337. TEACHER All right, you've already had quite a few guesses about that. Question number two. (*To Angelina*) Can you read that one?	337. The *teacher* attempts to bring *Angelina* back into the discussion by asking her to read.
338. ANGELINA 'You will have seen that	

TRANSCRIPT	COMMENT

in almost every way group B appears to be better off than group A. What are your feelings about this?'

339. TEACHER — Hmm.

340. LOUIS — Group B is simply more *richer*.

340–348. *Louis* reaction to the question asking what pupils feel about such unfairness between people is to ignore it, and to reiterate the fact that 'Group B, is simply more richer'. He goes on to make sense of the situation by comparing it with his knowledge about East and West Germany. Louis' knowledge/myth about East and West Germany has the flavour of popular media anti-communism.

341. TEACHER — You said group B is simply more richer. What are your feelings about it? Hammid?

342. LOUIS — Oh. I get it, it's like West Germany, ennit. East and West Germany when they broke out. So one was communist and the other one . . . thingy . . . but they have different governments.

343. TEACHER — Yeah, but this is . . .

344. LOUIS — Yeah, and there's a wall breaking their city, their country. Germany used to be one country once. Until this, eh, thing broke out. And some of the, eh, East Germany wants to break to the West, so they can have freedom. It's like that.

TRANSCRIPT		COMMENT
345. TEACHER	You think it's like that? But East and West Germany are in fact two different countries now, aren't they?	
346. LOUIS	Yeah.	
347. TEACHER	So you think...	
348. LOUIS	One the Russian's side, communist, and the other one's in America, and the Europe.	
349. TEACHER	Hmm. Hmm. So you think it's like that. Or it's not like that now, it might...	
350. HAMMID	It can't be like that.	
351. TEACHER	...eventually be like that.	
352. HAMMID	It can't be like that.	
353. TEACHER	Hmm?	353. Again, *Hammid* objects to Louis' lack of rigour, repeating 'It can't be like that'.
354. LOUIS	Shut yer face! Look at him! Politics, Hammid!	354. Louis doesn't accept Hammid's statement as legitimate, but as a challenge to Louis' supposedly superior political knowledge, an attack on Louis' credibility and self esteem.
355. HAMMID	It can't be like that, Louis.	
356. TEACHER	All right, tell us why.	
357. LOUIS	C'mon, *tell* us why.	
(Pause)		
358. TEACHER	He has an idea, you got to let him give it, don't you?	
359. LOUIS	(*teasing*) Hammid's gonna be Prime Minister.	
360. HAMMID	Shuttup.	

TRANSCRIPT	COMMENT

361. LOUIS Come on, Hammid,
we're waiting.

(*Pause*)

362. TEACHER C'mon, Hammid. You
said it can't be like that.
Why?

363. HAMMID I dunno.

364. LOUIS D'you wanna go to the
House of Commons?

365. TEACHER You're not giving him a
chance, Louis. Just
because he disagrees
with you.

366. LOUIS All right. C'mon.

367. HAMMID 'Cause . . .

368. LOUIS I'll give you five
seconds.

369. HAMMID . . . This is . . . this is *one*
country we're talking
about, right?

370. TEACHER Yes.

371. HAMMID And the parts of one
country, but West
Germany and East
Germany's different
countries, and they're
different governments.

372. LOUIS But they used to be the
same . . .

373. HAMMID *Used* to be . . . but . . .

374. LOUIS . . . country.

375. HAMMID . . . used to be . . . it's
not . . . the

376. LOUIS *Shut* yer gob, they're
still trying to
escape . . . the other side.

376. . . . The argument
between Louis and
Hammid which follows
could almost stand as a
paradigm for the
Western popular culture
state of debate about
capitalism vs
communism. Louis
presents information
about East and West
Germany and the

TRANSCRIPT COMMENT

concept of freedom,
which he has probably
gained from TV and
from discussions at
home.

377. HAMMID	I swear!	
378. LOUIS	They're *still* trying to escape, you know.	
379. HAMMID	Yeah, but its not...	
380. LOUIS	For freedom.	
381. HAMMID	...It's a different *country* though...	
382. LOUIS	'Cause they're under Russian control.	
383. HAMMID	It's a different country.	
384. LOUIS	So? Which is richer, Russia or West Germany? (*Pause*) I mean East Germany or Russia?	

(*Laughter*)

385. HAMMID	West Germ...	
386. LOUIS	(*laughing*) East Germany or West Germany.	
387. HAMMID	We're not talking about West Germany or East Germany.	
388. LOUIS	No? We *are*, we are... we're...	
389. HAMMID	We're talking about the same country, one country divided in two parts, right? The rich and poor...	
390. LOUIS	This was the *same* country...	
391. HAMMID	Rich or poor. You don't know which one is richer, West Germany or East Germany.	
392. LOUIS	Yes I do.	
393. HAMMID	Which one?	
394. LOUIS	West Germany.	
395. HAMMID	How richer?	
396. LOUIS	Cause they're...right?	

	TRANSCRIPT	COMMENT

If you look at East
Germany's buildings
what d'you see, writing
on the wall?

397. HAMMID   What?

398. LOUIS   And that lot?

399. HAMMID   What?

400. LOUIS   You see things writing
on the wall, 'cause I saw
the programme about
East and West Germany.

401. HAMMID   *I* saw it.

402. LOUIS   *So?*

403. HAMMID   *I* saw it.

404. LOUIS   Which is cleaner? East
Germany or West?

405. HAMMID   *So? So...so...*

406. LOUIS   So, *shut* yer gob. You
don't know what you're
talking about!

(*Laughter*)

407. LOUIS   So, I think West
Germany's richer...

408. HAMMID   ...Not as much,
not...

409. LOUIS   ...They keep their
streets clean and
neat...

410. HAMMID   ...Not as much as this.
There's no different ...
The difference's not as
big as this one.
Anyhow, Louis ...

411. LOUIS   Could be, could be.

412. HAMMID   Can't be.

413. LOUIS   Well, it won't be about
£25 [monthly wage for
group A]. Well that's
something, the place,
... yeah, but not
Africa, Africa can't get
about £390 [average
wages of group B for
month]. Anyway, they
don't *have* pounds.

TRANSCRIPT	COMMENT
414. HAMMID It's not Africa.	
415. TEACHER OK. Well, I don't know if we could solve that at the moment. But anyway let's look at . . . ahm . . . You haven't really said what your feelings are, Paul. What are your feelings about question number 2? It says here 'You will have seen that in almost every way group B appears to be better o then group A. What are your feelings about this?'	415. The *teacher* attempts to bring the discussion back to the question on the worksheet: 'What are your feelings about this?'
416. PAUL Same as Hammid's.	416. *Paul* enters the discussion, using the question as an opportunity to underline his agreement with *Hammid's* political understandings, as opposed to *Louis'*, which prompts Louis' self protective, bantering sarcasm.
417. TEACHER Which is what?	
418. LOUIS Hammid, *(to Paul)*. You going with him. This is an idiot over here! *(Referring to Hammid)*	
419. TEACHER Louis has said 'Well, Group B is simply richer.' Hammid is saying what? What are your feelings about it?	
420. HAMMID About what?	
421. TEACHER That group A is so much richer than group B. What do you *feel* about it?	421. The *teacher* intervenes again, focusing on the question about what they feel about the situation.

(Pause)

	TRANSCRIPT	COMMENT

422. HAMMID   It's the government, innit?

Hammid returns to the general concept of government, rather than to the question of feelings, and the argument about types of government breaks out again.

423. LOUIS   What, group A is much richer than group B?

424. TEACHER   The other way around, sorry, sorry. . . .

425. LOUIS   They're richer in *one* thing. *Probably.* Probably one thing.

426. HAMMID   It's the government. Because of the government, innit?

427. LOUIS   So, if it's one country it must have one government, right?

428. HAMMID   Yeah, and if it's like a communist country they can't be different.

429. LOUIS   Yeah . . . and some ain't communist . . . if it's a communist government, right . . .

430. TEACHER   But . . . you're arguing on . . . ah . . . governments and 'well it's simply richer', but the question really *asks* you 'what are your *feelings* about it?' How do you feel about these two different groups? what d'you think?

430. The *teacher* refocuses on the question about feelings, judging that in the short time left the likely presentations of 'received opinions' on types of goverment are likely to frustrate rather than further discussion. It is possibly this intervention that allows *Angelina* to enter the discussion.

431. PAUL   (*clowning*) Bad! Bad!

431. *Paul* by using his characteristic clowning, gives a sort of detached political hint about what people's feelings about

TRANSCRIPT		COMMENT
		exploitative inequality should be.
432. ANGELINA	(*speaking slowly*) But group A has got, have got, have got a lot of problems because they are not rich as group B.	432–9. *Angelina* approaches the question, using information from the worksheets and from the discussion, to make a summary about the sort of life lived by people in Group A, concluding that she thinks 'someone must help group A'.
433. TEACHER	Hmm. Hmm.	
434. ANGELINA	And they are *very* poor . . . and a lot . . . with a lot of deprivation.	
435. TEACHER	Hmm.	
436. ANGELINA	So they . . . they haven't got a . . . nice kind of life.	
437. TEACHER	Hm. Hm. And how d'you feel about that?	
438. PAUL	(*clowning*) Bad! (*Shrugging off his clowning*) It's all right.	438. The boys are both impressed and not a little intimidated by *Angelina's* quiet seriousness, with her ability to make a neat summing up, to legitimately shift the direction of the discussion — and to use the word 'deprivation'!
439. ANGELINA	I don't know, but I think that someone must *help* group A.	
440. TEACHER	Hmm. Hmm.	
441. HAMMID	*How?*	441. *Hammid* responds by offering the polite challenge as to how the people in Group A can possibly be helped. Both the shift in the discussion towards the unfamiliar ground of feelings and the

TRANSCRIPT	COMMENT
	presence of *Angelina*, now proven to be not just attractive but intellectually mature and a new threat to *Louis'* position in the discussion, all combine to make *Louis* admit that the entire situation is making him 'nervous'.
442. TEACHER What d'you think then, Paul?	
443. LOUIS I'm nervous.	
444. TEACHER (*to Paul*) You said you agreed with Hammid a minute ago and now you say you agree with . . . I'm sorry I don't know your name . . .	
445. ANGELINA Angelina.	
446. TEACHER Angelina.	
447. PAUL Yeah, I agree with *Angelina*. Yeah.	447. Challenged out of his devil's advocacy, *Paul* admits that he agrees with *Angelina's* conclusions and responses.
448. TEACHER You're saying that for a peaceful life, or d'you mean it?	
449. PAUL I *mean* it!	
450. LOUIS All right, let me see, miss (*picking up sheet*), Right *this* . . . like . . . let me give you an *example* . . . (*smiles from all round*) you better shut up, right.	450–6. *Louis* makes a bid to recapture his position in the discussion by trying out an 'adult' mode of discursive behaviour, 'let me give you an example' and relevant new information about the situation in Brazil, privileged ethnic knowledge via his Portuguese connections, which he knows the others won't have. But

TRANSCRIPT	COMMENT
	his knowledge only reiterates the structure of inequality. And *Hammid's* unproductive responses to Louis' knowledge threaten to reduce the discussion again to argument. *Angelina* intervenes, insisting on a return to the question of feelings. she is probably partly using the teacher as model; partly using the teacher's focus on this question as support for her own responses; partly as unwilling as *Hammid* to accept *Louis'* attempt at 'expertise'.

(*Laughter*)

451. LOUIS   This is like, ah, Brazil. Right, Brazil is rich in one part, and Indians live in the other. (*To Hammid who is smiling*) You better shurrup. So . . . ah, the one's that live in the city get more than the ones that live in the other part. Like *that* ain't it. (*To Hammid*) Shame! You got sussed there. Now . . . eh . . . ?

452. HAMMID   Who you *talking* about?

453. LOUIS   But you don't know what Brazil is . . .

454. ANGELINA   But maybe you don't understand the question the question is 'What are your *feelings?*'

455. LOUIS   Oh, oh, we're on these is it now I see.

TRANSCRIPT	COMMENT

(*Laughter*)

456. ANGELINA   What you *feel* about this?

(*Pause*)

457. LOUIS   Eh ... I'm in trouble ...

> 457. *Louis* makes the good-natured admission that he's 'in trouble' when it comes to considering feelings. It would seem that Louis, unlike his means of relating to the 'political' aspect of life, has no significant debate, discussion, media or personal role models for dealing with questions of feelings or the development of feelings towards oppressed people.

(*Laughter*)

458. LOUIS   (*also laughing*) I don't know what to say.

459. TEACHER   You're in trouble ... What d'you mean.

(*Laughter*)

460. LOUIS   Next. Next. I'm leaving that to you.

461. HAMMID   I've said my piece already.

> 461. *Hammid* with his 'I've said my piece already' seems to be more or less in the same position.

(*Pause*)

462. TEACHER   Isn't it interesting though, that it's Angelina who says that it's people should help these people ...

TRANSCRIPT		COMMENT
463. LOUIS	Other countries.	463. *Louis* ignores the *teacher's* observations about the difference between male and female reactions in the discussion. He picks up the cue that people should be helped — by other countries. He is more intrigued as to where this particular country might be and guesses at Cambodia.
464. TEACHER	But the boys. Ah, Paul agrees, but he's not saying much here, but the boys are really getting into arguments about . . .	
465. LOUIS	It's probably Cambodia . . .	
466. HAMMID	No, But who can help? No one can help . . .	
467. LOUIS	Yes, you *can*.	
468. ANGELINA	Yes.	
469. LOUIS	The Arabs is the nearest.	469. *Louis* disagrees with *Hammid* and hands the responsibility over to the Arabs on the grounds that they're the nearest.
470. ANGELINA	Yes. *Group B.*	470. *Angelina* presents the solution that it is the people in Group B who should help the people in Group A.
471. HAMMID	Yes. Group B?	471. *Angelina* presents the solution that it is the people in Group B who should help the people in Group A.
472. ANGELINA	Yes.	
473. HAMMID	Could help Group A?	
474. ANGELINA	Yes.	
475. HAMMID	But . . .	
476. ANGELINA	Because they are in your *same* country.	

TRANSCRIPT	COMMENT
477. HAMMID But *why* don't they *help* them?	477. *Hammid* challenges her with the obvious — they don't.
478. LOUIS What?	
479. PAUL Let's put together some money.	479-82. *Paul*, probably understanding the economic and political structures of exploitative poverty, plays devil's advocate again by suggesting charity as a solution, double devilling since he also probably has a good idea of what *Louis'* and *Hammid's* responses are likely to be.
480. LOUIS What?	
481. PAUL Right? Let's put together some money, and give to to group A.	
482. LOUIS Yeah, twenty 'p'. That'll do.	
483. TEACHER Angelina, if they're in the same country...	
484. LOUIS Yeah, but...	
485. ANGELINA If there is group, a rich group and poor group of people, but they live in the *same* country, the *same* city, I think rich people must *help* the poor people.	485. *Angelina* insists that the rich have a moral obligation to the poor, while *Louis* and *Hammid* point out that the rich do not operate in this fashion.
486. HAMMID You mean if you were rich...	
487. LOUIS Yeah but one thing... one thing, most rich people don't like helping.	
488. HAMMID Yeah.	
489. LOUIS That' the thing.	
490. HAMMID They don't want to divide the... money	
491. ANGELINA Why... they're rich aren't they?	
492. HAMMID ...They...don't want to divide the money.	

TRANSCRIPT	COMMENT
493. LOUIS — Like you, Hammid.	493. From his working-class perspective, *Louis* points out that neither does better off *Hammid* like to 'divide' his money.
(Pause)	
494. TEACHER — So you take it that that's the way it is: The rich people don't like helping poor people — that's the way it is.	494. The *teacher* asks them if they accept this status quo.
495. HAMMID — If they were poor, if they were poor, they would have liked some help, right.	495–6 *Basically they do.*
496. LOUIS — Yeah, but now that they're rich, they find themselves rich, why should they help?	
497. TEACHER — Why *should* they?	
498. LOUIS — So *they* leave it to the *other* countries.	
499. TEACHER — And you're quite happy about that?	
500. LOUIS — Well, no they should . . .	
501. HAMMID — Not happy about that.	
502. LOUIS — . . . but most people don't like to help, like if they're rich they say 'Why should I help, it's *my* money'. So they leave it to other countries.	
503. TEACHER — What about *you*, if you were rich?	503. She asks them what they would do about people's poverty if they were rich.
504. LOUIS — Me?	
505. HAMMID — If I was rich?	
506. LOUIS — I'm not over *there* (meaning 'A Place in the World).	
507. HAMMID — Oh, I don't know, if I was rich, because I've	495–509. Neither of them can actually conceive of the

TRANSCRIPT COMMENT

never *been* rich. Don't
know how it feels like.
But I know . . .

possibility of having
significant wealth or
power to make a
difference, although
again Louis takes the
opportunity to tease
Hammid about his
relative middle class
advantages.

508. LOUIS   OK what's that Rolls
Royce parked
out . . . parked outside
you house?

(*Laughter*)

509. HAMMID   But I know most of the
rich people are greedy
and they don't give
away no money.

510. HAMMID   . . . but if the boss is rich
and he's greedy
(*laughing*) how can he
pay them more money?

510–22. The status quo and
status quo reforms are
reiterated authoritatively
by *Hammid* and *Louis*.

510. Bosses are by nature
greedy. Poor people
must work hard. More
jobs should be created.
More money should be
given to educate people
to get better
qualifications for better
jobs.

511. LOUIS   Yeah, they'll have to
work anyway . . .

512. HAMMID   Yeah . . .

513. LOUIS   . . . 'cause if they don't
work it's not good for
their children.

514. HAMMID   Yeah, they have to
work, they can't just say
I give up, I'm not
working any more . . .

515. LOUIS   And anyway they should
make more jobs in
group A. 'Cause group
B, is alright for jobs an'

TRANSCRIPT	COMMENT
	that lot, and they've got less population than group A so they should make more jobs here.	

516. TEACHER — Hmm.

517. HAMMID — And...and they have to give more money for the schools so they, so they could educate...

518. LOUIS — It's like *here*, some jobs are closing down, around the country, and some are opening, for those who lost *their* jobs. So, that's what they should do there. (*Pause*) Correct. *Who* votes? (*Pointing to Hammid*) He votes.

518–21. As in Britain re unemployment more jobs have to be created for people who lose their jobs because, inevitably, some jobs have to close down, yet in a mix of strange logic, the jobs opening up are more or less equal to those closing down. If that isn't the case then 'the country will get poorer and poorer until they'll have to eat sand'.

519. TEACHER — If they won't do that, what happens?

520. HAMMID — If they *won't* do that...

521. LOUIS — More job losses. Like, 'cause some day something *has* to close down, so that'll be more jobs gone and the country will get poorer, and poorer, until they'll have to eat sand.

522. HAMMID — And the rich gets richer and the poor gets poorer.

522. *Hammid* is able to employ the proverb in English: 'And the rich gets richer and the poor gets poorer'.

523. LOUIS — Yeah, cause the rich has enough jobs for their population.

524. HAMMID — The rich works...

524–6. *Hammid* starts out with the concept that it's the rich who work then

TRANSCRIPT	COMMENT
	modifies that to 'doesn't work a lot anyway, they just have their offices', while 'the poor have to use muscles'.
525. LOUIS Yeah.	
526. HAMMID ... doesn't work a lot anyway, they just have their offices ...	
527. LOUIS I *know*, they just have their business an' that.	527–31. *Louis* agrees: the rich have these shops, etc., and the money come to them — and accuses Hammid of being one of the rich.
528. HAMMID ... office and they just write ... but the poor ...	
529. LOUIS And they have these shops, what they sell, and money comes to *them*.	
530. HAMMID ... the poor have to use muscles ...	
531. LOUIS And Hammid sitting at his desk.	
532. TEACHER All right, let's look at ... ahm ... well, no let's follow that up. If you say that the poor are going to get poorer and poorer and poorer, then what do you do if you're in group A? You're still, you're in the majority of the population, remember. What would you do?	
533. HAMMID You try to get a *job*, *any*, *any* job, *any* money ...	533. *Hammid's* solution to poverty of the majority is that they 'try to get a job, any job, any money'. The implicit assumption is that the poor are not always moved to do so. The further implication is

TRANSCRIPT	COMMENT
	that Hammid does not understand the nature and function of structured unemployment.
534. LOUIS Miss, why can't we do this on TV?	534. 'Miss, why can't we do this on TV' indicates not only a model of debate he has seen using, but a significant complementary source of his political, economic and moral concepts. Also, because such media models present political/moral/econo-mic debates in con-ceptually fragmented 'balance of biases' modes reflecting positively, more or less, on the status quo, little wonder that the same sort of media, politi-cal/moral perceptions should be reiterated as 'knowledge' by adolescents looking for ways to understand the world. Particularly so when another potentially significant complementary source of political/moral/econo-mic understanding — education — offers them next to nothing in the way of intellectually rigorous analytical alternatives.
. 535. TEACHER Ah well, you mean you'd rather have discussion on TV?	
536. LOUIS Yeah, yeah, they could put this on TV. Went to the TV place yesterday, you know. And I was	536. Novel, interesting and exciting as the visit to the TV studio was for *Louis*, it seems not to

TRANSCRIPT — COMMENT

the cameraman. It was *really nice*. I'd like to be on TV talking about this. I'm gonna go to *Weekend World*.

have combined these qualities with very much in the way of critical analysis of how news is selected, by whom and for what purposes.

(*Laughter*)

537. TEACHER — You could do. Why couldn't you?

538. PAUL — (*to Louis*) You can invite Mrs Thatcher next week.

538. *Paul* is moved to sarcasm at what he regards not so much as Louis' joke or fantasy about appearing on *Weekend World*, but his delusions of grandeur and lack of understanding of the politics of the media.

539. LOUIS — I'd like to go the House of Commons.

540. TEACHER — You could trip her up on the stairs, couldn't you?

540–6. *Louis* ignores the *teacher's* imagined bringing down to earth of the Prime Minister, voicing his approval of Mrs Thatcher instead: 'She's my mate, miss,' etc. Which draws expressions of sarcasm from *Paul* at what he regards as *Louis'* political ignorance.

541. LOUIS — She's my mate.
542. TEACHER — She's your mate?
543. LOUIS — Hm. Hmm.
544. TEACHER — You like her?
545. LOUIS — Yeah. She's *all right*, Miss. She's not bad.
546. PAUL — (*tapping on tape recorder; imitating, sarcastically*) Yeah. Yeah.
547. TEACHER — What was that? All right, so, OK, let's go to the next . . . ' How

547. The *teacher* focuses the discussion back to the worksheet and the

TRANSCRIPT	COMMENT
	d'you . . . let's go to this question number 6. 'How do you think group B gained control in the first place?'
548. LOUIS	'Cause they had more war things, and if a war broke out they'd *easily* win. 'Cause they have the most money, ennit. It's like guerillas . . . like guerillas . . . (*to Hammid*) you dunno what guerrillas are.
549. HAMMID	Yeah, it's like civil war . . .
550. LOUIS	Yeah.
551. HAMMID	. . . civil war they . . .
552. LOUIS	And the other side has more money, they can buy more material, like tanks and that lot, and what has the other one's got, bricks. Sometimes. That ain't gonna do nothing.
553. PAUL	(*quietly*) Northern Ireland.

COMMENT column:

question of how the dominant minority group in 'A Place in the World' gained control in the first place.

548. *Louis* equates control with military force. He then introduces the concept of guerrilla warfare, but is vaguely aware that this doesn't square with the concept of dominant military force, and fashions a challenge out of error, claiming that it's *Hammid* who doesn't know what guerilla warfare is.

549. *Hammid* introduces the concept of civil war, which allows *Louis* to pick up on what he does know about the concept of guerrilla warfare — the guerrillas are the ones with inferior weapons, sometimes little more than bricks and 'That ain't gonna do nothing'.

553. *Paul* quietly inserts the British equivalent of civil war — Northern Ireland.

TRANSCRIPT	COMMENT

554. HAMMID   They get like Eritrea and Ethiopia.

554–5   But *Hammid* and *Louis* are not as informed about that civil war as they are about the Eritrean/Ethiopian Civil War, because of their friendship with Asmerom, the Eritrean member of the ESL group, who is absent today. What they seem to understand of that conflict is not the political basis of it, but the question of who has the most arms, who has the least.

555. LOUIS   Ethiopia, right, cause they had most of the things. They had their jets, the Eritreans, they didn't have quite nothing. All they had was these arms.

556. TEACHER   Hm. All right, let's look at, look at five, question five, 'Do you think that friendships between any members of these groups would be possible?'

556. The *teacher* refocuses them on the worksheet question as to whether or not friendship between dominant and oppressed groups is possible, under what circumstances and for what purposes.

557. ANGELINA   Could be, but theres no . . .

558. HAMMID   Yeah.

559. ANGELINA   But not very good, because rich people . . . will . . . would be snobby with the poor people.

559. *Angelina* proposes the slight possibility that there might be. 'But not very good because rich people . . . will . . . could be snobby with the poor people.'

560. LOUIS   Miss, d'you know what country this is?

TRANSCRIPT		COMMENT
561. TEACHER	Let's look at this one, 'Under what circumstances would friendship be possible?' For what purposes . . .	
562. LOUIS	If it was a war, if there was a war, the only thing that would make them friends again would be to make up for their losses an' that lot.	562–8. The *boys* conclude that there could be no friendship 'in real', not 'in heart', but only in economic terms 'to make up for the losses an' that lot,' or when the poor act as bodyguards for the rich because they need the money.
563. TEACHER	No, I just mean in terms of ordinary friendship, never mind the war.	
564. HAMMID	Yeah, there would be friendship but no . . .	
565. LOUIS	Not in real.	
566. HAMMID	Not real, it's not in heart, right, it's like you have to pay money, the rich pays money like to get a bodyguard. The bodyguard's most probably the poor because they're strong, they work, and the muscles . . . and the rich doesn't need money . . . to be a bodyguard.	
567. LOUIS	Yeah, Hammid.	
568. HAMMID	So they pay the poor to be their bodyguard, right, and so that's the kind of friendship; it's not real.	568. The possibility of friendship between rich and poor is discounted for any other purposes that they can conceive.
569. TEACHER	Hm. Hmm. What . . . d'you think . . . all right. Do you think all the poeople in group B are happy with the situation of *being* in group B.	569. The *teacher* proposes the question as to whether all the people in the rich group are happy with being in that group.

TRANSCRIPT		COMMENT
570. LOUIS	Yeah.	
571. TEACHER	You think so?	
572. LOUIS	Hammid looks a bit too much, you know. If he was...if he was to be Prime Minister. Miss, you wouldn't get your wages, right?	572. *Louis* is sure they would be. He indicates that if the teacher belonged to the rich group and *Hammid* were to be Prime Minister of the poor group that the *teacher* would not get her wages.
573. HAMMID	(*tape unclear*)	
574. LOUIS	Because they're rich...	
575. TEACHER	If you were born into group B, the rich are...	
576. LOUIS	Hm?	
577. TEACHER	If you were born into group B...	
578. ANGELINA	I wouldn't like to be born in it.	578. Presented with the question of which group they'd prefer to belong to, *Angelina* claims she wouldn't like to belong to the rich group.
579. TEACHER	Why's that?	
580. HAMMID	'Cause you get greedy, innit?	580. *Hammid* understands that being born in the rich group tends to make you greedy.
581. ANGELINA	Yeah.	
582. LOUIS	Greedy? Who gets the most computer heads?	582. *Louis* makes a pointed joke about who gets the most technology and education as a substitute for stating his preference for being a member of the rich group.
583. ANGELINA	I prefer to be in group B...	

Part Three
Bilingual Learners and
Mainstream Curriculum

13
Concerns and Entitlement

Josie Levine

We have seen from the foregoing chapters why it is so vital that provision for bilingual learners developing a use of English should be embedded within mainstream school organization, within appropriate curriculum content and within a socially based, interactive, discursive pedagogy. We have also seen how such provision, if it is to be consonant with equality of opportunity, and contribute to the enhancement of achievement and greater equality of educational outcomes, must be intent upon:

— integrating learning and language-learning,
— engendering self-confidence, and self and inter-group respect,
— being positive to pupils' identities and cultures,
— not 'selling short' any of the students: either by a failure in intellectual rigour and analysis in the stance taken towards them, or by failing to provide the means through which they may develop their own intellectual rigour and ability to make critical analyses.

The advent of a National Curriculum with its programmes of study, attainment targets, levels of achievement, and assessment procedures in no way diminishes the responsibilities of LEAs, advisory and inspectorial staff, school management teams and teachers towards ensuring such positive provision. On the contrary, there is considerable danger that the practices so far developed by teachers themselves for an interactive education which includes bilingual learners might be neglected, even lost. For example, it is cause for some concern that some discussions of the proposals for the core subjects have revealed more than a few who suggest the impossibility of fulfilling National Curriculum requirements from within mixed ability practices.

Although the National Curriculum documents can lend themselves to such interpretation, we do not believe that a return to streaming is an inevitable consequence of the introduction of the National Curriculum; as with all such global statements, there are other readings to be made of them.

Perhaps the most intersting and useful observation on the National Curriculum documents to emerge is the focus on process within the expression of attainment targets in all three core subjects, Maths, Science and English.[1] That it took so long for a recognition of the presence of process elements in the National Curriculum to be observed suggests that there was far too tenuous a grasp in the education system as a whole — inclusive of the curriculum proposal makers — of the importance of *real* attention to process in learning. Certainly, a firmer grasp is needed if education is to play its constituted role of enhancing the school achievement of all pupils.

For bilingual learners, an understanding of process in learning — especially as it relates to first and second language development — is crucial. Without such understandings to counter the potential negative side of the effects of the National Curriculum proposals, bilingual pupils would undoubtedly be trapped in a spiral of perceived downward achievement. In this chapter our concern is about such 'lurking dangers' within the National Curriculum as well as being about redressing the lack of general awareness about the nature of process and of the key role such knowledge plays in the development of a holistic view of learning, progress and achievement.

The entitlement we speak of belongs to teachers as well as pupils. For pupils, entitlement is a set of necessary conditions for fostering egalitarian educational practices. For teachers, entitlement must be about resourcing and the in-service support from which to develop appropriate school organizations, classroom practices, materials and forms of assessment. It must also, fundamentally, embrace the right to a sound knowledge base from which to generate these things. We take the view that understanding about process and its positioning within developmental theories of learning is an essential part of this knowledge base and is a further reason why we concentrate on it here.

Lurking dangers[2]

We have used the *National Curriculum Proposals for English for Ages 5 to 16* (DES, 1989) as our vehicle for spelling out some of the dangers of the National Curriculum, not because we think it unique in being able to lend itself to such analysis — it is certainly not so, either in respect of its patchy levels of attainment, or in its not unexpected ambivalent attitude to this country's bilingual school population. It shares with all the other National Curriculum subject proposals the enforced compliance with unrealistic arrangements for assessment. In one respect only is English unique in that it is both a subject of study in the curriculum, as well as the principal means through which it and all other subjects are delivered. What the English proposals are, and how they are couched, does, therefore, have enormous effect.

The Effects of Assessment

The demand that pupils be graded according to levels on a scale of one to ten for each attainment target has grave implications for all pupils. There are the dangers of pupils being labelled as low achievers, then of pupils being given limited language and conceptual experiences because of this view. Then comes the possibility of a return to over-use of withdrawal teaching, and teaching unconnected with mainstream education. The assessment procedures make it very difficult for the early stages of progress in developing a use of a second language to be recognized and formally acknowledged as successful learning. To conceive of pupils having made such progress as underachievers after, say, only two years of experience in English education because they are not at similar levels of measured achievement as those of the same age who have received all their education in their mother tongue of English, seems almost wilfully damaging. It certainly ignores developmental facts which contribute to bilingual learners' achievement. Secondly, the attitudes which contributed to the formation of linear stages of language development and linear assessment of language attainment are those which make it very difficult for teachers to see bilingual learners in particular in terms of their overall language abilities.

Assessment and the Building of Low Expectations

For bi/multilingual learners in particular there is always such a great deal that resides within the realms of the potential. It may be that in the production of written work in English, a 12-year-old may be adjudged to be performing poorly and leave a teacher with little option under the statutory orders but to assess that pupil as achieving little more than Level 3 in writing. Yet, at the same time, that child may be able to write very proficiently in another language, for which, of course, there is no acknowledgment in National Curriculum terms.

Consider also the following extracts from a transcript of a taped discussion[3] between a teacher and a 12-year-old boy, an Egyptian national, who had been born in England but who had lived in Egypt for the past nine years. At the time the discussion took place, he was generally perceived by teachers — including the teacher in the recorded conversation — as 'struggling' and certainly having difficulties in writing in English.

35. TEACHER   Are there different kinds of Arabic . . . er . . . is different . . . er . . . is the Arabic spoken in Egypt, for example, different to the Arabic spoken . . . elsewhere, in the Middle East?

36. HASSAN   Er . . . yes, there is, Libya there is four different and . . . er . . . Sudan and Libyans and Algeria, Morocco, but Syrians speak the same like Egypt.

37. TEACHER   Syrians . . . er . . .

38.	HASSAN	Yes, the same.
39.	TEACHER	And what are the differences between Libya and Morocco? Er . . . the differences between Libya . . . ?
40.	HASSAN	Yes, and Egypt. Libya?
41.	TEACHER	Yes, what are the differences?
42.	HASSAN	Er . . . there's no difference . . . er . . . but . . . er . . . the language . . . the . . . er . . . Libyan, the language they speak, they spoken at home is different than the . . . than the language Egyptian spoke at home. (*Longish pause*) It's different.

One of the critical points that needs to be made, which is unlikely to be obvious from just the printed words on the page, is the confidence shown by Hassan when he is discussing both where Arabic is spoken and the extent of the similarities in the Arabic spoken in each of the countries he mentions. This confidence has much to do with the social and cultural context of the discussion. He is aware that in this situation it is the teacher who is the learner and he the expert. The subject under discussion is one that is within his territory. He has Arabic lessons outside school, and he is happy to offer what he has learned from his Arabic teacher: 'The teacher say Arabic the hardest language in the history . . . er . . . teacher told us . . . er . . . that Arabic is the hardest language'. His confidence increases even further as he realizes that the teacher's interest is not feigned, that it is a genuine conversation that is taking place.

69.	TEACHER	So let's return to the language spoken in the home. Now, that's different than the language written down?
70	HASSAN	Yes, it's different.
71.	TEACHER	In what ways is it different?
72.	HASSAN	Er . . . like when you write something to your . . . when you write to him a letter to a friend in Libya, he will read it . . . er . . . it's not difficult to read, but . . . er . . . but if he write it . . . er . . . from his language, Arabic, other Arabic language, he don't understand. It sounds OK, but . . .
73.	TEACHER	I'm not sure what you're saying. Can you repeat? Can you explain that again?
74.	HASSAN	Er . . . d'you know when the . . . when the . . . some . . . er . . . some of my people write a letter to his friend . . .
75.	TEACHER	Um . . . um.
76.	HASSAN	. . . and they sound different. You will read it and understand because there is . . . er . . . it . . . it . . . the Middle East can read Arabic, all of them, and they understand, but the other Arabic they don't understand.
77.	TEACHER	Are what you are saying . . . is what you are saying is that they can understand the written Arabic . . .

78. HASSAN   Yes.
79. TEACHER   . . . but not the spoken?
80. HASSAN   Yes. They can . . . er . . . understand the spoken, but it's difficult to understand.

Now, Hassan's utterances have become more sustained as he struggles to clarify his meaning to the teacher. Notice, too, how, at utterance 78, he supports his teacher's attempt to understand.

But what of this in terms of levels of attainment? At first glance, Level 4 (ii) of Speaking and Listening seems appropriate:

Ask and respond to questions with increased confidence in a range of situations.

Could Hassan be said to have achieved this strand of Level 4 even though he was responding only? Would teachers make a note, be satisfied at this point, or would they cast an eye over Level 5 (v)?

Talk about variations in vocabulary between different regional and social groups, e.g., dialect vocabulary, specialist terms.

Would this include the talk about the Arabic of different countries? Perhaps. But what about this reference to the use of transactional language at Level 5 (iii)?

Use transactional language effectively in a straightforward situation, e.g., an eyewitness account of an event or an incident; reclaiming an article which has been lost.

Or is Hassan engaged in something qualitatively different; something more difficult? Maybe Level 6 (ii) ought to be considered:

Understand and use transactional language effectively in a variety of relatively straightforward situations where the subject is familiar both to the pupils and to the audience and other participants.

Was Hassan effective in his use of transactional language? The teacher certainly knew much more about Arabic at the end of the discussion than he had before. And given that the teacher was not too familiar with the subject, does that mean that Hassan was achieving something further in Level 6? Perhaps 6 (iv) which reads:

Talk about some grammatical differences between spoken and standard English.

Hassan has yet to show himself able to do that. On the other hand, he can certainly talk about grammatical differences between varieties of Arabic, and did so during other parts of the discussion. However, we know that this does not count within the terms of 6 (iv), though the particular ability or knowledge required appears to be comparable. Furthermore, Hassan has yet to achieve many of the other strands of Level 5, let alone Level 6. So since pupils have to achieve all aspects of any one level before they can be said to have attained it, Hassan would certainly not be assessed, at the most, at more than Level 4 — perhaps even lower — despite his considerable language ability and knowledge about language.

It is very worrying that under the process of assessment in the National Curriculum children can be perceived as being of a particular level. The danger of discrimination is obvious, and this is simply because the chosen system does not recognize the fact of differential achievement either in relation to targets at different levels or in relation to abilities beyond English. This has to be a matter of grave concern.

Standard Assessment Tasks and Teachers' Internal Assessments

We are told that Standard Assessment Tasks are likely to be embedded in good teaching practice, but, of course, that does not help much those bilingual learners who are as yet inexperienced in using English. As external assessments, there must remain an overwhelming connection between age and level of attainment in the valuations they provide, with all the ensuing reinforcement of negative beliefs and low expectations concerning bilingual pupils' abilities.

Teachers' internal assessment provides more helpful conditions, however, and here we are in agreement with the authors of the National Curriculum Proposals for English (DES, 1989) when they recommend the approach exemplified in *The Primary Language Record Handbook for Teachers* (Barrs *et al.*, 1988; see also Barrs *et al.*, 1990). The philosophy underpinning this particular record of achievement is supportive of bilingual learners. It provides a structure for teachers to observe children in a variety of contexts. The focus is on the processes of language development and learning skills, and is a record of what they can already do and are moving into being able to do. It involves child conferencing, discussions with parents and, significantly, it expects and helps teachers to be aware of and note children's bi/multilingual linguistic abilities. It encourages teachers to see children in terms of *language* users rather than solely as users of English. It encourages teachers to engage in discussion with children about the languages they use in all parts of their lives, and gives languages spoken in the community and the speakers of those languages a place in the classrooms. Within this kind of much needed approach, Hassan's ability in Arabic, and his linguistic understandings, would become part of his record and contribute to his overall assessment.

looking at how we come to learn our first languages, and can be recognized afresh when the processes and contexts for successful learning of additional languages are looked at.

Knowledge about process learning stems overwhelmingly from studies of child language acquisition (e.g., Wells, 1981; Bruner, 1975), from sociological and cultural accounts of the development of language functions (e.g., Halliday, 1978), from socially based theories about learning development (e.g., Vygotsky 1962 and 1978), and those recent studies of classroom interaction (e.g., Edwards and Mercer, 1987) which focus on education as 'situated discourse' for the purpose of understanding how and what kinds of meanings get generated in classrooms.

From a standpoint of concern for the educational entitlement of bilingual learners, we will first turn to an informal account of first and additional language development — in order to see how closely matched are their processes — and then to the Vygotskian psychological theory that gives primacy to culture and communication in cognitive development, over against those forms of schooling which see interaction, at best, as an added extra — something to do when the serious work is done — and, at worst, as a form of 'cheating' — if you help each other, it isn't your own work — or disobedience — talking instead of working.

The Spectacular Feat of Learning to Talk

Whatever the nature of the linguistic environment to which we happen to have access, learning to talk is possibly the most spectacular, speedy and all embracing learning that we ever do — and we do not learn to do it *except* by being inside communicative situations. It is in communicative situations that we hear the utterances that comprise the language(s) into which we are being inducted. We then progressively construe what talk is for and the variety of functions it performs. We accept guidance, deduce meanings, attempt expression of our own, take and give responses to those meanings. We achieve our places in our families — or other form of primary group — and in the larger world partly, and significantly, by the way in which language acts as our means of knowing and being known. Our knowledge of the world, of things, events, ideas, and our increasing linguistic repertoire is centrally effected by communicative exchanges of one kind or another. How we grow to see the world is affected by the nature and content of those exchanges. Young children learning to speak the language(s) of their speech communities are listened to, have their meanings interpreted; are deeply involved in cognitive learning. Importantly, children do not use the forms of the more mature speech around them, yet everyone knows their learning will progress *but* that it is a *process* which will take time.

The secret of our success seems to lie in the fact that we are included in the communicative framework and are encouraged to be active in it. It is a joint, holistic enterprise clearly demonstrating a social base for learning. It must make sense to form a theory about teaching and learning based on these observations. Such a theory would read: the closer teaching permits learning to follow natural learning processes, the deeper the learning will be.

Perhaps this simple analysis can help us to get our expectations of all learners right.

— Learning is a developmental process.
— It takes time.
— It is socially enhanced.
— Students need to be actively engaged to do it well, be in situations where they can be tentative when trying out new things, ideas or language forms.
— They need to be able to build on what they already know, and be free to express themselves in the language which is closest to them.
— They need teachers who attend to their *meanings* — not just to the surface expression of meanings.

When we do encourage active learning, with students negotiating social and working relationships with each other, classrooms are then akin to other active, natural language learning situations, and we can expect pupils to move forward both in increased knowledge (e.g., school subject matter) and also in linguistic repertoire and the language related skills (both used and developed by use across the whole curriculum).

Process, Interaction and the Developmental Learning of Additional Languages

It is, however, a fact that many people (especially those who have experienced minimal interactional learning in their own formal education or have practised it only minimally in their teaching) have difficulty in believing that an additional language can be learned through curriculum activities. To understand how it can be so and to see how contrarily we have been behaving in relation to bilingual pupils' learning of English, let us consider our own additional language learning, however small that may be in scope.

In any general talk about additional language learning it is no accident that the circumstances chosen as the most favourable to developing another language are those where we have the opportunity of acquiring it *in situ*. People recognize that the extent to which we acquire another language depends on the range of situations to which we have access, on the encouragement (including teaching) given us, and on the demand for its regular use in interaction. It will be taken for granted that we need time to learn and that the greater the frequency of opportunity to use the target language the better enabled will be the internalization process. Consciously or unconsciously, it will be acknowledged that learning an additional language is a process and that it is one that does not necessarily go forward by linear progression. But not only that. We also know that such natural learning takes place alongside a continuing use of our first language and that this use is important to a sense of wholeness in our lives. It is not simply that to be deprived of the use of our first language makes us feel seriously inadequate as language users, it is also that the act of being deprived can signal both to ourselves and others that our first languages, and our developing bilingual skills, are of no particular consequence in the world.

It is, therefore, in people's experience to know that as long as we have access to and constructive pressure to learn, we will develop skills and a repertoire in a new language to the degree that circumstances require or allow us to learn. We should, therefore, surely be making use of, not denying, this knowledge about learning additional languages *in situ*.

The fact is that as subject, class and 'special' English teachers, we are in a position to share a natural language learning environment with our pupils, i.e., the curriculum and the interactive classroom cultures that we establish for working with our pupils. It is encouraging to note that the best of Modern Languages teaching is now turning to more communicative, interactive methods. We also should be putting our energies into trying to make our classrooms comprehensible places for natural language learning and development *through* our curriculum work and pedagogy, rather than continuing with our historical response to bilingualism and multilingualism — indeed, to curricular considerations of pupils' class and gender identities — and turning them into a situation of learning difficulty for our pupils. The potential for the acquisition of additional languages is high and almost as spectacular as first language learning, when the features of natural interactive learning contexts prevail.

Vygotsky and the Social Origins of Learning

The theory of development which underlies all these observations about the need and value of interactive learning — whether to do with concepts and knowledge and language development in general or additional language learning in particular — is best articulated in the work of Lev Vygotsky (1896–1934).

It would be difficult to overestimate the importance of Vygotskian theory to our concerns. Vygotsky offers a theory of intellectual development which accounts for children's progress in terms of their interaction — joint activity and conversation — with other people, the adults and peers with whom they have contact. The structures of these encounters, the medium in which they take place, the culture(s) in which they are embedded, the meanings with which they are imbued are taken inwards, internalized, through the process of interaction. Being complex sets of interrelated features, taking their meanings from their relatedness as much, if not more, than from the individual components, interaction provides multilayered, connected material from which participants with a wide range of experience can extract different kinds of knowledge and skills according to their needs. At the same time, they come into contact with, and therefore preparation for, the next and successive phases of their development. Finally, being developmental, such learning is incremental in the sense that learners, young and old, are also always in states of approximation towards the thing or things which are being learned and/or developed.

Vygotskian theory is theory which gives an active and structuring role to teachers and more experienced peers in the learning development of other less experienced individuals; indeed, their active participation is central to successful progress since it is the interaction that both represents the forms and the meanings of particular cultural and intellectual activities — including language development — to the learner, and also is the means by which these forms and meanings come to be negotiated by learners and enter into learners' use.

Furthermore, the differing experience of participants, as well as the complex nature and features of interactions themselves, means that everyone is potentially positioned for further development when they participate. For example, a teacher may learn from an interaction with pupils how such a learning event may be more usefully structured; a peer (or a teacher, for that matter) may arrive at deeper understanding of an idea or concept through being in discussion with other people more, less, or as experienced; linguistic repertoire may be broadened. In natural learning, all these things, and more, can happen at once in different people, and at different speeds for different people in the same group. They can also be taking place simultaneously within one individual. An important property of interactive learning is that it enables internalization of complex, interrelated wholes, but also internalization of smaller units of the whole, through the opportunity participants get to perceive the relationship of parts to the whole.

For a teacher-participant and for pupil-participants, in this Vygotskian, socio-cultural theory of intellectual development, the place of structure is within the interaction. The form it takes as interactive pedagogy derives from understanding the features of the whole, and the nature of those features' relationship to meaning, together with perceptions of where children are at in the various aspects of their development. Interaction, therefore, offers teachers a means of constructing a rigorous, supportive pedagogy which can follow natural learning patterns and which is productive for pupils' learning.

In this theory of interactive learning, language, as well as other environmental experiences, is seen as an important medium for learning and thinking. Language is understood as being the chief material from which people build ways of thinking. Importantly for bilingual learners, the 'mysterious' nature of language learning and development is explained: the processes of interaction foster, through the joint, active attention and participation of learners, internalization of the material to be learned.

In classrooms organized for interactive pedagogy teacher–pupil talk changes role relationships. Instead of seeing the classroom only as two sets of people, students and teachers, there is the potential for teachers to see themselves as part of one single educational complex of teacher(s) and students, all having better access to each others' ideas, thoughts, purposes and intentions. Debate and questioning go on, experiences surface, ideas are wrestled with, mutual support and understanding become more possible. We get to know better what is inside each others' heads, to 'know where the other is at'. Shared knowledge is increased, as are the further possibilities of students helping each other to learn (not merely waiting upon the teacher), and of pupils in their peer groups as well as teachers responding to individual needs and starting points of others.

In this consultative mode, teachers do not abrogate their role as teachers, but being on the inside some of the time changes their vision, and makes possible a whole range of reciprocities between teacher and pupils, pupils and pupils and teachers and teachers. Furthermore, when teachers have begun to work within the consultative mode, some of their fears relating to the fragmentation of traditional organization and control recede. They learn new and more appropriate ways of organizing and intervening in order to support their students' learning. What also recedes is the misplaced notion that mixed ability teaching must necessarily and constantly involve what we all recognize as an impossibly daunting task, that of preparing different material for every student in the class.

In an interactive learning environment, multilingual to the extent the class is, with active participation and all students' language resources admitted, students' confidence to act, and their power to make choices can grow; analyses can be formed and expressed, and social and language related skills can develop alongside knowledge.

Finally, through his concept of 'the zone of proximal development', Vygotsky also makes a constructive contribution to the relationship between teaching and assessment. He describes the 'zone of proximal development' as: 'the distance between the actual development level as determined by independent problem solving and the level of potential development as determined through problem solving under adult guidance or in collaboration with more capable peers' (Vygotsky, 1978, p. 89). With this idea comes a clear underlining of the importance of interaction in mixed experienced groups — adult to child, pupil to pupil — for the enhancement of learning through shared experience. Learning is seen as developmental, socially enhanced and with a role for others. But as important, it suggests an encouraging view of the monitoring of progress as well as a dynamic view of what counts as achievement. In this scheme of things, which reflects the way we are all positioned — pupils and teachers — in relation to the development of skills, understanding and knowledge, it is progressive approximations towards goals which we have as much to count as achievement as any final attaining of mastery. In this scheme of things, an individual's progress is assessed in relation to past achievements, and importantly, in relation to the contexts for and in which learning is undertaken.

Why Interactive Pedagogies are Not Just an Option Among Others

The statements we have made throughout this book for the need for interactive pedagogies as means to equality of opportunity and greater equality of outcome in education for all learners, including bilingual learners, are made out of developing practice. They are no longer theoretical idealizations even though the practice as a whole, in terms of necessary improvements in organization and in pedagogic strategies, is, naturally, still in the process of development.

In the overall context of educational practice, arriving last on the scene, interactive education is likely to be regarded as just another fad, or, somewhat more positively, as an optional strategy among others of equal value. These two views leave unrecognized the distinctive contributions this mode of teaching and learning can make through its processes: directly to education, through the raising of achievement among individuals across the full range of society; and via education, indirectly, to the establishment of a society capable of constructive interaction undertaken by individuals capable of independent judgments. They leave absolutely unacknowledged that the more deeply embedded practices that constitute the culture of schooling at this point in time and which may or may not be counted as good practice by one group or another have produced a society in which more than half the population are regarded as educational underachievers.

Perhaps the most deeply embedded notion across the whole of society as to what counts as 'commonsense' teaching practice are those didactic methods that thrive on behaviourist psychology. Generally speaking, these hold sway as good practice only amongst the 'back to basics' lobby. Their voice is, however, a powerful one at this moment. Such methods are seen as being effective in increasing 'discipline' and of defeating low levels of literacy. Such calls do not take into account the fact that one of the chief consequences of highly teacher controlled, didactic pedagogy was the considerable problem of engaging learners' interest. Thus discipline was forced and enforced, and pupils were seen as failing to learn because they lacked motivation.

The practice currently more widely accepted in educational circles as good practice is that founded on the Piagetian notion of individual and individualistic development of cognition and learning. Historically, the Piagetian 'good' practice was established in opposition to the stultifying effects of the didactic tradition. Talk and pupil interaction within the latter mode were clearly regarded as reprehensible. Thus the chief medium by which people develop their thinking and analytic abilities was formally withheld from the classroom. In the discovery learning of what came to be regarded as the progressive classroom, children, of course, played and talked with each other, but talk, itself, had a peripheral role in learning — peripheral, that is, in the analytic sense of reflecting on what is being done or has been done, and also in the structuring sense of inducting pupils into ideas or helping them with how to reflect upon, analyze and express meanings. Indeed, direct structuring of thinking was often seen as harmful to pupils' individuality. The need to cue pupils into the purposes of lessons in order to help them get a better purchase on the purpose of a particular bit of learning also seems not to have been perceived by teachers — or, if it was, they were made to feel guilty in practice for being too directive. Discovery learning seems often to have meant 'guess what this is all about'. Thus teachers remained in control, but masked that control behind a pedagogy that appeared to let pupils learn at their own pace, and make their individual progress however slow or fast. It is an implicit form of education, which advantages those who already know how to do it, and leaves floundering those who have to keep guessing. It is ultimately un-rigorous, since it treats everyone as having the same need for open-endedness and everything as being in need of discovery. A deeply unfortunate conse-quence of viewing cognitive development as an engagement with concrete ex-perience and also individually achieved is that failure, as perceived in an indivi-dual, is construed as a failure of that individual. There is no possibility, theore-tically, of perceiving failure as residing in the context. In this theory of cogni-tive development, talk is permitted, but it is not used for learning, or seen as a way of helping learners, in ways appropriate to their needs, to organize their own thinking. And in practice, coexistent with the discovery method, when it is time for 'serious' work, children are told to settle down, stop talking and get on with their work.

Because the practices which derive from both Piaget's and Vygotsky's theories of learning development can both be perceived as child centred pedagogies, the contrasting force of the two different theories is often lost — even to the extent that people construe the methodologies as the same. This is not, however, the case. The individualistic orientation of Paiget's theory has produced practices whose outcomes are utterly in contrast with the actual and potential outcomes of Vygotsy's cultural interactional theory of cognitive development.

For Piaget, cognition grows out of an individual's engagement with experiences, and development is governed by possibilities within the structure of the mind that relate to chronological age. Hence the educational promotion of discovery learning — and the willingness of teachers to await learning readiness. The teacher's role is seen as centrally useful as the provider of the right kind of experience from which a child on her or his own is to creatively discover meanings. However, this positioning leaves teachers with fundamental dilemmas. Is it incorrect to help children directly? Does it smack too much of didactiveness? How may one help children directly without being harmful to the singular growth of their particular individuality?

Such dilemmas are resolved in the cultural theory of cognition advanced by Vygotsky. Teachers are seen as more experienced adults who through their interaction are in partnership with their pupils and the learning. They act with their pupils in the learning process, can see how, when and what structuring is needed, and negotiate decisions about learning with their pupils. The practicalities and outcomes of an education which incorporates the zone of proximal development are very different from discovery learning, simply, but essentially, because there is this central, interacting role for teachers in achieving learning.

Of course, people have learned by the didactic method. They have also learned in the 'busy-ness' of the classic progressive styles of teaching, but great swathes of the population have not done so. This is not because the majority of the population is stupid or uninterested in knowledge, or incapable of analysis, but because the methods employed in education have not been culturally responsive to their needs in learning and cognition. The distinctive contribution to education of making talk and interaction central modes of learning is that it lets more people in. The reason that communicative, developmental interaction is vital is that it lets people learn by doing what they know how to do. Through that and the careful structuring that teachers provide, as it is needed, learners develop interests, knowledge, understanding and skill. And they learn how to be confident, to develop critical awareness as individuals and as members of groups, and to see achievement as natural, not as something out of their reach.

Interactive methods of teaching and learning are not just an option. None of the other methods are capable of making such a critically distinctive contribution to society.

Notes

1. The proposals for English almost exclusively express attainment targets in process terms.

   Attainment TARGET 1: Speaking and Listening.

   > The development of pupils' understanding of the spoken word and the capacity to express themselves effectively in a variety of speaking and listening activities, matching style and reponse to audience and purpose . . .

   Attainment Target 2: Reading.

   > The development of the ability to read, understand and respond to all the types of writing, as well as the development of information-retrieval strategies for the purpose of study.

   Attainment Target 3: Writing.

   > A growing ability to construct and convey meaning in written language matching style to audience and purpose.

Spelling and Handwriting are ATs 4 nd 5. After Attainment Level 4 they combine to become AT, 'Presentation'.

In the Mathematics curriculum, Attainment Targets 1 and 9 are both called 'Using and Applying Mathematics'. AT 1 states that 'pupils should be able to use number, algebra and measures in practical tasks, in real-life problems, and to investigate within mathematics itself'. AT 9 requires that 'pupils should use shape and space and handle data' in the same situations.

Attainment Target 1 of the Science curriculum, 'Exploration of Science', is the process aspect of the other ATs.

> Pupils should develop the intellectual and practical skills that allow them to explore the world of science and to develop a fuller understanding of scientific phenomena and the procedures of scientific exploration and investigation. This work would take place in the context of activities that require a progressively more systematic and quantified approach, which draws upon an increasing knowledge and understanding of science. The activities should encourage the ability to:
> i plan, hypothesise and predict
> ii design and carry out investigations
> iii interpret results and findings
> iv draw inferences
> v communicate exploratory tasks and experiments.

2. My thanks to Leon Gore who generously contributed the section, 'Lurking Dangers', of this chapter.
3. The numbering of the utterances in the two extracts from the taped discussion indicate their position in the whole transcript.
4. In the proposals for English, Attainment Target 1: Listening and Speaking tells us that 'from level 7 pupils should be using Standard English wherever appropriate to meet the statements of attainment'; no other chapter in the proposals is as long as Chapter 4, the chapter on Standard English; and about one-fifth of that is devoted to exhorting the teaching of Standard English, e.g., paras, 4.4, 4.5, 4.7, 4.8, 4.9, 4.34, 4.35, 4.36, 4.38, 4.48, 4.49.

Bibliography

BARNES, D. (1976) *From Communication to Curriculum*, Harmondsworth, Penguin.

BARNES, D., BRITTON, J. and TORBE, M. (1986, 2nd ed.) *Language, the Learner and the School*, Harmondsworth, Penguin. (NB The first edition of this book by Barnes, Britton and Rosen, published in 1971, is the version which will have first influenced teachers in respect of language and learning.)

BARNES, D. and TODD, F. (1977) *Communication and Learning in Small Groups*, London, Routledge and Kegan Paul.

BARRS, M., ELLIS, S. HESTER, H. and THOMAS. A. (1988) *The Primary Language Record Handbook for Teachers*, London, ILEA, Centre for Language and Primary Education (CLPE).

BARRS, M., ELLIS, S. HESTER, H. and THOMAS, A. (1990) *Patterns of Learning: The Primary Language Record and the National Curriculum*, London, ILEA, Centre for Language in Primary Education (CLPE).

BARTHES, R. (1976) *The Pleasure of the Text*, London, Jonathan Cape.

BEGUM, S. and H. *Halima's Story*, (limited circulation) London, Thomas Buxton Infant School.

BIRO, V. (1983) *The Boy who Cried Wolf*, Aylesbury, Ginn.

BLEACH, J. (1979) 'No turning back from awareness: mixed ability and English teaching', unpublished dissertation for MA in Education, University of London Institute of Education.

BLEACH, J. (1984) 'English', in CRAFT, A. and BARDELL, G. (Eds) *Curriculum Opportunities in a Multicultural Society*, London, Harper and Row.

BLEACH, J. and LEVINE, J. (1988) 'The potential of a language model for bilingual pupils' language development: match and mismatch?', in *Lessons in English Teaching*, papers presented at a NATE Conference, June 1988, Sheffield, National Association for the Teaching of English (NATE).

BLEACH, J. and RILEY, S. (Eds) (1984–1986) *Project Papers*, Nos 1–4, for ILEA Hackney and Islington Second Language Learners in Mainstream Classrooms Project; No. 1 September 1984; No. 2 November 1984; No. 3 March 1985; No. 4 January 1986 (Limited circulation), London.

BLEACH, J. and RILEY, S. (1985) 'Developing and extending the literacy of bilingual pupils through the secondary years', *English in Education*, **19**, 3, Autumn 1985, Sheffield National Association for the Teaching of English (NATE).

BORDIEU, P. (1977) 'Cultural reproduction and social reproduction', in KARABEL, J. and HALSEY, A. H. (Eds) *Power and Ideology in Education*, Oxford, Oxford University Press.

BOURNE, J. (1989) *Moving into the Mainstream: LEA Provision for Bilingual Pupils*, Windsor, NFER-Nelson.

BREINBERG, P. (1973) *My Brother Sean*, London, The Bodley Head.

BRITTON, J. (1970) *Language and Learning*, Harmondsworth, Penguin.

BRUMFIT, C., ELLIS, R. and LEVINE, J. (Eds) (1985) *English as a Second Language in the United Kingdom: Linguistic and Educational Contexts*, ELT Documents No. 121, London, Pergamon/British Council.

BRUNER, J. (1975) 'The ontogenesis of speech acts', *The Journal of Child Language*, 2.

BURGESS, A. (1972) *A Clockwork Orange*, Harmondsworth, Penguin.

BURGESS, A. and GORE, L. (1985) 'Developing bilinguals in a secondary school', *English in Education*, 19, 3, Autumn, Sheffield, National Association for the Teaching of English (NATE).

CARR, W. and KEMMIS, S. (1986) *Becoming Critical: Education, Knowledge and Action Research*, Lewes, Falmer Press.

CATTINI, F. *A Visit to my Aunt's House*, (limited circulation) London, Thomas Buxton Infant School.

CHATWIN, R. (1985) 'Can ESL teaching be racist?', in BRUMFIT, C., ELLIS, R. and LEVINE, J. (Eds) *English as a Second Langauge in the United Kingdom: Linguistic and Educational Contexts*, ELT Documents No. 121, Oxford, Pergamon.

COMMISSION FOR RACIAL EQUALITY (1986) *Teaching English as a Second Language: Report on the Formal Investigaiton in Calderdale LEA*, London, CRE.

CROLL, P. (1986) *Systematic Classroom Observation*, Lewes, Falmer Press.

CUMMINS, J. (1984) *Bilingualism and Special Education: Issues in Assessment and Pedagogy*, Clevedon, Multilingual Matters 6.

DAVIES, A. M. and STURMAN, E. (Eds) (1989) *Bilingual Learners in Secondary Schools*, London, ILEA Centre for Urban Educational Studies.

DEPARTMENT OF EDUCATION AND SCIENCE (1975) *A Language for Life* (The Bullock Report), London, HMSO, especially Chapter 20.

DEPARTMENT OF EDUCATION AND SCIENCE (1978) *Special Educational Needs* (Warnock Report), London, HMSO.

DEPARTMENT OF EDUCATION AND SCIENCE (1985) *Education for All* (Swann Report), London, HMSO.

DEPARTMENT OF EDUCATION AND SCIENCE (1988) *Report of the Committee of Enquiry into the Teaching of the English Language* (The Kingman Report), London, HMSO.

DEPARTMENT OF EDUCATION AND SCIENCE (1988) *National Curriculum Proposals for English for Ages 5 to 11* (The Cox Committee Report Part 1), London, HMSO.

DEPARTMENT OF EDUCATION AND SCIENCE (1989) *National Curriculum Proposals for English for Ages 5 to 16* (The Cox Committee Report, Part 2), London, HMSO.

DERRICK, J. (1977) *The Language Needs of Minority Group Children*, Windsor, National Foundation for Educational Research.

DULAY, H., BURT, M. and KRASHEN, S. (1982) *Language Two*, Oxford, Oxford University Press.

EDWARDS, C., MOORHOUSE, J. and WIDLAKE, S. (1988) 'Language or English?', in JONES, M. and WEST, A. (Eds) *Learning Me Your Language*, London, Mary Glasgow and Baker.

EDWARDS, D. and MERCER, N. (1987) *Common Knowledge: The Development of Understanding in the Classroom*, London, Methuen.

EDWARDS, V. (1983) *Language in Multicultural Classrooms*, London, Batsford.

ELBAJA, M. (1979) 'My life', in *Our Lives: Young People's Autobiographies*, London, ILEA English Centre.

ELLIS, R. (1985) *Classroom Second Language Development*, Oxford, Pergamon.

ELLIS, R. (1985) 'Policy and provision for ESL in schools', in BRUMFIT, C., ELLIS, R. and LEVINE, J. (Eds) *English as a Second Language in the United Kingdom: Linguistic and Educational Contexts*, ELT Documents No. 121, Oxford, Pergamon.

EMBLEN, V. (1988) 'Other mathematical puzzles: entering the discourse', in MEEK, M. and MILLS, C. (Eds) *Language and Literacy in the Primary School*, Lewes, Falmer Press.

FITZPATRICK, F. (1987) *The Open Door*, Clevedon, Multilingual Matters.

GORE, L. (1983) 'The recent move towards English as a Second Language Teaching in Mainstream English Classes; its origins and implications', unpublished dissertation for MA in Urban Education, King's College, University of London.

HALLIDAY, M. A. K. (1978) *Language as Social Semiotic*, London, Edward Arnold.

HAMMERSLEY, M. (Ed.) (1986) *Controversies in Classroom Research*, Milton Keynes, Open University Press.

HEATH, B. S. (1983) *Ways with Words*, Cambridge, Cambridge University Press.

HESTER, H. (1983) *Stories in the Multilingual Primary Classroom*, London, ILEA Learning Materials Service.

HESTER, H. (1985) *Learning from children learning'*, in BRUMFIT, C., ELLIS, R. and LEVINE, J. (Eds) *English as a Second Language in the United Kingdom: Linguistic and Educational Contexts*, ELT Documents No. 121, Oxford, Pergamon.

HINES, B. (1969) *Kes*, Harmondsworth, Penguin.

HINES, B. (1977) 'Speech Day', in MARLAND, M. (Ed.) *Pressures of Life: Four TV Plays*, London, Longman.

HICKMAN, J. and KIMBERLEY, K. (Eds) (1988) *Teachers, Language and Learning*, London, Routledge.

HITCHCOCK, G. and HUGHES, D. (1989) *Research and the Teacher: A Qualitative Introduction to School Based Research*, London, Routledge.

HOPKINS, D. (1985) *A Teacher's Guide to Action Research*, Milton Keynes, Croom Helm for the Open University.

HOULTON, D. (1986) *Cultural Diversity in Primary Classrooms*, London, Harper and Row.

HOULTON, D. and WILLEY, R. (1982) *Supporting Children's Bilingualism*, York, Longman for The Schools Council.

HUTCHINS, P. (1972) *Titch*, London, The Bodley Head.

ILEA ENGLISH CENTRE *School Under Seige*, London, ILEA English Centre.

ISER, W. (1974) *The Implied Reader*, Baltimore, Hopkins University Press.

JONES, C. and KIMBERLEY, K. (Eds) (1986) *Intercultural Education: Concept, Context, Curriculum Practice*, Strasbourg, Council of Europe.

JOSIPOVICI, G. (1976) *The Modern Novel: The Reader, the Writer and the Text*, London, Open Book Publishing.

KNOWLES, F. and THOMPSON, B. (1975) *Shirley Sharpeyes*, London, Longman.

LANGUAGE IN INNER CITY SCHOOLS (1985) *What the HMIs forgot: culture, bilingual students and the curriculum*, 18th Conference Report, Joint Department of English and Media Studies, University of London Institute of Education (limited circulation), London.

LEVINE, J. and MCLEOD, A. (1975) 'Children of families from overseas origin', in ROSEN, H. (Ed.) *Language and Literacy in our Schools*, London, University of London Institute of Education/National Foundation for Educational Research.

LEVINE, J. (1981) 'Developing pedagogies for multilingual classes', in *English in Education*, Sheffield, National Association for the Teaching of English (NATE).

LEVINE, J. (1982) 'Second language learning and mainstream curriculum: learning as we go', in collected papers of the *The Practice of Intercultural Education* conference, Nijenrode, Breukelen, Netherlands, March 1982 (limited circulation).

LEVINE, J. (1983) '"Going back" to the mainstream', *Issues in Race and Education*, **39**, Summer.

LEVINE, J. (1984) 'Miss, you liar', in MEEK, M. and MILLER, J. (Eds) *Changing English: Essays for Harold Rosen*, London, Heinemann/University of London Institute of Education.

LEVINE, J. (1985) 'A new professional mode', in BLEACH, J. and RILEY, S. (Eds) *Project Papers* No. 4, London, ILEA Second Language Learners in Mainstream Project.

LINGUISTIC MINORITIES PROJECT (1985) *The Other Languages of England*, London, Routledge and Kegan Paul.

LOMAX, P. (Ed.) (1989) The Management of Change, BERA Dialogues No. 1, Clevedon, Multilingual Matters.

MACKAY, D. and SCHAUB, P. (1972) *Crocodiles are Dangerous*, London, Longman.

MARLAND, M. (1987) *Multilingual Britain: The Educational Challenge*, London, Centre for Information on Language Teaching (CILT).

MARTIN, N. (1976) 'Encounters with "models"', *English in Education*, **10**, 1, Sheffield, National Association for the Teaching of English (NATE).

MILLER, J. (1983) *Many Voices*, London, Routledge and Kegan Paul.

MOY, B. and RALEIGH, M. (1981) 'Comprehension: Part III', *The English Magazine*, **6**, Spring, London, ILEA English Centre.

NATIONAL FOUNDATION FOR EDUCATIONAL RESEARCH (1973) *Tests in Proficiency in English* (Levels 1, 2, and 3 (nos 269/1, 269/2, 269/3) for Listening, Speaking, Reading and Writing), Windsor, NFER.

NICOLL, H. and PIENKOWSKI, J. (1972) *Meg and Mog*, London, Heinemann.

NICHOLLS, S. and HOADLEY-MAIDMENT, E. (Eds) (1988) *Current Issues in Teaching English as a Second Language to Adults*, London, Edward Arnold.

OLIPHANT, M. (1979) *Poems to Supplement Second Language Learning*, ILEA Netley Language Centre (limited circulation), London.

PARMLEY, W. and ROBERTS, P. (1988) 'Support for second language learning', in HICKMAN, J. and KIMBERLEY, K. (Eds) *Teachers, Language and Learning*, London, Routledge.

RAHMAN, R. *Jabin's Journey*, Thomas Buxton Infant School, (limited circulation), London.

RAMPTON, B. (1985) 'A critique of some educational attitudes of British Asian schoolchildren and their implications', in BRUMFIT, C., ELLIS, R. and LEVINE, J. (Eds) *English as a Second Language in the United Kingdom: Linguistic and Educational Cont.xts*, ELT Documents No. 121, Oxford, Pergamon.

RILEY, S. and BLEACH, J. (1985) 'Three moves in the Initiating of Mainstreaming at Secondary Level', in BRUMFIT, C., ELLIS, R. and LEVINE, J. (Eds) *English as a Second Language in the United Kingdom: Linguistic and Educational Contexts*, ELT Documents No. 121, Oxford, Pergamon.

ROBINSON, B. (1985) 'Bilingualism and mother tongue maintenance in Britain', in BRUMFIT, C., ELLIS, R. and LEVINE, J. (Eds) *English as a Second Language in the United Kingdom: Linguistic and Educational Contexts*, ELT Documents No. 121, Oxford, Pergamon.

ROSE, E. J. B. *et al.* (1969) *Colour and Citizenship*, Oxford University Press, for the Institute of Race Relations.

ROSEN, B. (1984) 'Storytime and beyond', in MEEK, M. and MILLER, J. (Eds) *Changing English: Essays for Harold Rosen*, London, Heinemann.

RUSHTON, B. (1982) 'Learning responsibility: an experiment in second language learning and teaching', unpublished dissertation for MA in Education, University of London Institute of Education.

SCHAUB, P. (1973) *A Fairy Story*, London, Longman.

SCHOOLS COUNCIL (1969; 2nd ed. 1978) *Scope, Stage 1*, London, Longman.

SCHOOLS COUNCIL (1972–74) *Scope, Stage 2: a Langauge Development Course* (Teachers' Book, Pupils' Books *Homes, Water* and *Travel*), London, Longman.

STENHOUSE, L. (1975) *An Introduction to Curriculum Research and Development*, London, Heinemann.

SUTTON, C. (1981) *Communicating in the Classroom*, London, Hodder and Stoughton.

THOMPSON, B. (1979) *My Dad*, London, Longman.

TOSI, A. (1984) *Immigration and Bilingual Education*, Oxford, Pergamon.

VYGOTSKY, L. S. (1962) *Thought and Language*, Cambridge, Mass., Massachusetts Institute of Technology (MIT).

VYGOTSKY, L. S. (1978) *Mind in Society*, Cambridge, Mass., Harvard University Press.

WALLACE, C. (1986) *Learning to Read in a Multicultural Society*, Oxford, Pergamon.

WELLS, G. (1981) *Learning through Interaction*, Cambridge, Cambridge University Press.

WELLS, G. and NICHOLLS, J. (Eds) (1985) *Language and Learning: an Interactional Perspective*, Lewes, Falmer Press.

WILES, S. (1981) 'Language issues in multicultural classrooms', in MERCER, N. (Ed.) *Language in School and Community*, London, Arnold.

WILES, S. (1985) 'Language and Learning in Multi-ethnic classrooms: strategies for supporting bilingual learners', in WELLS, G. and NICHOLLS, J. (Eds) *Language and Learning: an Interactional Perspective*, Lewes, Falmer Press.

WRIGHT, J. (1978) 'Bilingualism and schooling in multilingual Britain', *English Magazine*, 3, January.

Journals

The English Magazine published by ILEA English Centre carries regular articles relating to bilingual learners in Secondary Schools. Available from the English Centre (Magazine), Sutherland Street, London SW 1.

Issues in Race and Education is a specialist journal in this field. It is available from Issues Collectives, 75 Alkhan Road, London N16 6XE.

Bilingual Learners and the Mainstream Curriculum

Language Matters published by ILEA Centre for Language in Primary Education carries regular articles relating to bilingual learners in Primary Schools. Available from Centre for Language in Primary Education. The Teachers Centre, Webber Row, London SE 1.

Video Materials

BLEACH, J. and RILEY, S. *Learning in a Second Language in the Secondary Curriculum*, ILEA Television and Publishing Centre, Thackeray Road, London SW8 3TB (telephone: 071-622-9966). Videocassette VC MSS 1: Programme 1 'Bilingual students in mixed ability groups'; Programme 2 'Talking, reading and writing'. Videocassette VC MSS 2: Programme 3 'Changing schools to recognise bilingual pupils'; Programme 4: 'Teacher discussion — an antiracism approach in language and bilingualism in schools'.

Second Language Learners in Primary Classroom Project (SLIPP). Two videocassettes showing the work of the project are available. They are Programmes 2 and 3, 'Working together' and 'Supporting understanding', of a four programme series, *Language in the multiethnic primary classroom*, sponsored jointly by the DES, the Outer London Boroughs and ILEA. Programme 1 is a general programme, 'Linguistic diversity', Programme 4 focuses on dialect speakers of English, 'The way we speak'. Programmes 1 and 4 come on one cassette, programmes 2 and 3 come on a second cassette. Available from the Central Film Library, Government Building, Bromyard Avenue, London W3 5JB.

WALIA, S. and WALIA, Y. (1988) *Language is the Key*, Endboard Productions, Air Works, 111–119 Bishops Street, Birmingham B5 6JL (telephone: 021-622-1325). Filmed in schools in the Midlands and Wales, the programme tackles issues surrounding the teaching of 'English as a second language' and 'Bilingualism' from the standpoint of the use of language as a weapon of power and resistance. Part 1 gives examples of suppressions of cultures. Part 2 shows ways in which those cultures (currently dismissively termed 'minority') are fighting back. In both cases, language is seen as the key. The languages represented are Gujarati, Caribbean Creoles and Welsh. Children and teachers take part alongside Stuart Hall (Open University), Bikku Parekh (Centre for Racial Equality), Gwynn Williams (historian and author) and Benjamin Zephaniah (poet).